A SIGNET BOOK

TRUE CRIME STORIES BOOK V

Max Haines was born in Antigonish, Nova Scotia. *True Crime Stories, Book V*, is his twelfth book, all but one being devoted to non-fiction crime. His earlier work, *The Collected Works of Max Haines*, is considered one of the finest collections of non-fiction crime stories ever produced in Canada.

Crime Flashback is the apt title of Mr. Haines' newspaper column, which appears twice weekly in *The Toronto Sun*. The column is syndicated across Canada, appearing in newspapers from Newfoundland to British Columbia. *Crime Flashback* has been translated into French and Chinese.

A member of Crime Writers of Canada, Mr. Haines resides in Etobicoke, Ont., with his wife Marilyn.

TRUE CRIME STORIES
BOOK V

MAX HAINES

Ø

A SIGNET BOOK

NEW AMERICAN LIBRARY

Published in Canada by
Penguin Books Canada Limited, Toronto, Ontario

First published in Canada by the Toronto Sun Publishing
Corporation Limited, 1992

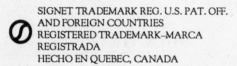

SIGNET TRADEMARK REG. U.S. PAT. OFF.
AND FOREIGN COUNTRIES
REGISTERED TRADEMARK–MARCA
REGISTRADA
HECHO EN QUEBEC, CANADA

Signet, Signet Classic, Mentor, Onyx, Plume, Meridian and
NAL Books are published in Canada by Penguin Books
Canada Limited,10 Alcorn Avenue, Toronto, Ontario,
Canada M4V 3B2

First printing November 1993

10 9 8 7 6 5 4 3 2 1

Printed in Canada

Canadian Cataloguing in Publication Data

Haines, Max
  True crime stories, book V

ISBN 0-451-17812-2

1. Murder. 2. Criminals. I. Title
HV6515.H368 1993   364.1'523   C93-093947-6

Foreword

Many of us dream of finding a niche we can truly call our own. Few have been as successful in finding one and developing it as well as Max Haines.

Through the years Max has brought us hundreds of well researched, well written tales of murder and mayhem, stories from the darker side of life. And he is Canada's only full time crime columnist.

In addition to his widely syndicated crime columns, Max also pens a lighter, weekly feature, *That's Life*, underlining his versatility as he looks, in his own way, at what goes on in and around the Haines household. Max always ranks high in *Sun* readership polls.

He serves the *Sun* and his readers well and this book, the latest in a series of collections, makes for entertaining, informative reading. I hope you enjoy it as much as I did.

Jim Tighe
Publisher
Toronto Sun

Contents

For
David and Elliot

MISSISSIPPI BURNING

The movie *Mississippi Burning* is a fictionalized version of events which took place during the turbulent summer of 1964, when scores of civil rights workers arrived in the state of Mississippi intent on having the black community register for the vote.

Opposing their efforts, local white officials did their utmost to instil fear into anyone who sympathized with the "Northern agitators."

On the night of June 21, 1964, a group of men, some of them officers of the law, committed an act which was to send shockwaves throughout the nation and the world. That was the night they murdered civil rights workers Mickey Schwerner, 24, James Chaney, 21, and Andrew Goodman, 20.

Mickey Schwerner didn't have to scour the back roads of Mississippi attempting to change the world. He didn't have to join the Congress of Racial Equality (CORE), and later the Council of Federated Organizations (COFO). He didn't have to live on $9.80 a week. Mickey Schwerner chose to do so, because he had the idea that the color of a person's skin shouldn't predicate their station in life.

After graduating from Cornell University and completing post-graduate studies at Columbia, Mickey set out to right certain wrongs. On January 19, 1964, he and his wife Rita arrived in Meridian, Miss., with the task of converting five empty rooms into a community centre. He also carried a list of young blacks who had indicated their desire to join the fight for freedom.

One of the names on the list was that of James Chaney.

It was hard work, but little by little, the young idealistic couple whipped the dilapidated rooms into an office, a library, and classrooms, where they taught subjects varying in content from children's stories to instructions on how to register to vote.

Mickey and Rita had difficulty finding a place to live. Appreciative blacks took them in for one or two nights, but they were always asked to leave. Pressure had been put on their hosts. Subtle and not so subtle threats proved to be a difficult obstacle.

Despite the problems, the efforts of the Schwerners resulted in some headway. Young blacks volunteered to join the movement. They passed out pamphlets and visited with black leaders. The white community took notice. They didn't like what they saw. "What was the Jew Commie with the beard agitating our blacks for anyway?"

James Chaney proved to be a valuable worker at what was now called the Meridian Community Centre. CORE even provided the centre with a blue station wagon.

Soon, James Chaney was devoting his full time to the movement. On several occasions, he and Mickey ventured into the neighboring town of Philadelphia, Miss., a 36-mile trip. Their mission was to feel out the black population, knowing full well that Philadelphia had the reputation of being a danger zone, vehemently opposed to integration of any kind. The town sheriff, Lawrence Rainey, had run for office on the promise that he'd "handle the niggers and the outsiders."

Chaney had been successful in talking the officials of Longdale's Mount Zion Methodist Church into letting Mickey Schwerner speak at a Sunday service. They even voted to approve the establishment of a freedom school in the church.

On June 16, Mickey, Rita and Chaney headed to Oxford,

2

Ohio, where hundreds of volunteers were in training to go to Mississippi later on that summer. They planned to pick one top-notch volunteer to help Chaney in the Longdale Freedom School.

That same night, four automobiles pulled up to Longdale's Mount Zion Methodist Church. Ten gallons of diesel fuel were poured inside. One of the men lit a match and the church burned to the ground. On Saturday, June 20, 1964, Mickey Schwerner, James Chaney and Andrew Goodman drove back to Meridian. Rita remained in Oxford. It is estimated that 200 students would travel to Mississippi that summer devoted to helping blacks register to vote.

There is evidence that by this time that Mickey was a marked man. Times were tense. Gov. Paul B. Johnson stated, "This action is repulsive to the American people. Turmoil, strife and bloodshed lie ahead." George Wallace declared, "It is ironical that this event occurs as we approach celebration of Independence Day. That day we won our freedom. On this day, we have largely lost it."

Next morning, Mickey was anxious to visit the burned out church in Longdale. He had heard that the mob who had torched the church had also beaten up the blacks who had been holding a meeting in the church that night.

By mid-afternoon, the three boys arrived at the burned out church. One of the men who had been beaten, mentioned ominously to Mickey that he heard members of the mob were looking for him. Unknown to Mickey, a plot was afoot to "kill the Jew with the beard."

As the three boys drove down the road, Dep. Sheriff Cecil Price, a member of the Ku Klux Klan and Sheriff Rainey's right hand man, stopped their blue station wagon. Price radioed Highway Patrolmen Poe and Wiggs. He told them he had taken three men into custody and required help in transporting them to jail.

By the time the two officers arrived at the scene, the three civil rights workers were changing a flat on their station wagon. Price told the two officers that he had arrested the boys for "speeding" and "suspicion of arson"

3

in the burning down of the Longdale Church.

The three boys were lodged in the Neshoba County Jail in Philadelphia. It was stifling hot. That day the temperature reached 101 degrees. What did Andy Goodman think of what was happening around him? It was his first day in Mississippi. But things were looking up. The three men were freed a little after 10 p.m.

Killers were waiting 10 miles outside Philadelphia. It was they who had given the signal for the three to be set free. Their leader was none other than Deputy Cecil Price. He was accompanied by other men intent on keeping Mississippi "free and pure."

Price intercepted the station wagon. Mickey, James and Andrew were placed in an official Neshoba County car and transported to unpaved Rock Cut Road. All three were shot to death and buried in an earthen dam under construction. One of the conspirators operated a bulldozer.

In minutes, Mickey Schwerner, James Chaney and Andrew Goodman ceased to exist. Their station wagon was burned with diesel fuel and deposited in Bogue Chitto swamp, several miles from the dam. The men then gathered at the courthouse square in Philadelphia, shook hands and congratulated each other on a job well done.

The three civil rights workers were immediately missed. FBI agents, headed by 37-year-old John Proctor, were dispatched to find them. They received little in the way of co-operation from Sheriff Rainey and his deputy, Cecil Price.

As the days passed and the search for the missing young men intensified, tempers grew short. There was even talk that the whole thing was a hoax. Locals said the missing trio was in Chicago drinking beer.

A week after the boys went missing, their burnt-out station wagon was removed from the swamp. It would take 44 days before the bodies were recovered from the dam. To this day, no one knows who informed on the conspirators. It was rumored at the time that the informer was paid $30,000 to reveal the location of the bodies.

Mickey Schwerner's parents wanted their son to be buried beside James Chaney in Mississippi. No white undertaker could be found who would accept the job. The body was cremated. Andrew Goodman was buried in Mount Judah Cemetery in Brooklyn.

Two months later, on August 16, a memorial service was held for all three victims, amidst the ashes of the Mount Zion Methodist Church at Longdale. The 11-year-old brother of James Chaney looked beyond the crowd at Sheriff Rainey and Deputy Price, who watched the service from a distance. The little boy made a speech. He closed by shouting, "We ain't scared no more of Sheriff Rainey!"

The Aftermath: Several of those involved were tried for conspiracy and denying the victims their civil rights by killing them.

Cecil Price received a six-year prison sentence for conspiracy. He was released after serving four years. He now is employed as a safety officer for a trucking firm.

Six others received sentences of three years to 10 years imprisonment. Many still reside in the Philadelphia/Meridian area.

Jimmy Jordan pleaded guilty and was sentenced to four years. It was Jordan who eventually revealed most of the details of the killings to the FBI.

John Proctor, the veteran FBI officer in charge of the case, is now retired. He operates a detective agency in Meridian and often bumps into the men he helped convict.

Sheriff Lawrence Rainey was acquitted of all charges. He is now employed as a security guard at McDonald's Security Guard Service. His employer, Mr. E.E. McDonald, is black.

Ben Chaney, the 11-year-old who shouted, "We ain't scared no more of Sheriff Rainey," has led a strange life since the murder of his older brother. Andrew Goodman's parents provided a scholarship for young Ben at a small private school in New York City.

The culture shock was too much. At age 17, Ben, with

5

two companions, was involved in a total of four murders in Florida and South Carolina. In each case, Ben did not kill anyone and could have walked away from his companions at any time. He received three life sentences and spent 13 years in prison before being paroled. He is now free and is attempting to set up an organization to assist blacks to register to vote in Meridian, Mississippi.

WHO KILLED WELDON?

It is commonly believed that the vast majority of murderers are apprehended. Such is not the case. Many remain unsolved forever, while others leave us with several possible scenarios and suspects.

Today, we are going to delve into the history of crime and focus our attention on a mystery which, although it had an unsatisfactory ending, will allow you to arrive at your own conclusions.

Weldon Atherstone was a 47-year-old English actor. He and his former wife, Monica Kelly, had two sons and two daughters before they separated some 10 years before our story unfolds. The two daughters never enter our tale, so we will dispense with them at the outset.

In 1910, Thomas, the elder son, was 21; William was 16. The boys were warehouse workers and lived on Wood St. in London, England. Their father lived alone at 14 Great Percy St. when he was in London. As an actor, he was often in productions which took him all over England.

For years, Weldon and acting teacher Elizabeth Earl had been lovers. Elizabeth lived at 17 Clifton Gardens, Prince of Wales Rd., Battersea in South West London. Weldon had lived with Elizabeth for years, but they had had an argument two months before the crucial night of July 16, 1910, and he had moved to his own lodgings on Great

Percy St.

Both of the Anderson boys (the name Atherstone was a stage name adopted by their father) were extremely fond of Elizabeth. They visited her often, accompanied by their father. After the dispute, they continued to visit Elizabeth alone. Later, they were to testify that she treated them like sons.

On the night of July 16, Thomas Anderson was having dinner with Elizabeth in her flat. Of the three flats in the building, it was the only one occupied. The ground floor flat had just been renovated and was for rent, while the occupants of the top flat were away for the weekend.

At 9:30 p.m., two shots rang out from the rear of 17 Clifton Gardens. Edward Noice, a chauffeur, was driving his car down Rosenau Rd. He saw a man climb over a wall and jump down to the sidewalk. There had been a recent rash of break-ins in the area. Noice, acting with admirable dispatch, went directly to a police station and returned with an officer.

The policeman tried to enter the ground floor flat and found the door closed. He didn't know it at the time, but the door was secured only by a piece of string tied to the inside catch. It could be opened by reaching through a mail box and releasing the catch.

The officer proceeded to the next flat, which was occupied by Elizabeth. She told him that she too had heard the shots and had run to a window. She had seen a man climb over a wall behind her flat. The officer realized that the intruder had to climb over a total of three walls in order to alight on the sidewalk of Rosenau Rd.

He went into the kitchen, where he encountered Thomas Anderson. Thomas said he had also heard the shots and, with Elizabeth, had seen the man climb over the wall.

The policeman, accompanied by Thomas, went down a back fire escape and came across a dying man underneath an iron staircase. The man, who had been shot twice in the head, was Weldon Atherstone. There were scratches about his hands and face. Strangely, the victim was wearing carpet slippers. His shoes were later found wrapped in paper on a shelf in the vacant flat.

Doctors were summoned, but despite their best efforts, Weldon died in less than an hour without regaining consciousness.

A search of the victim's clothing uncovered a homemade blackjack, several letters addressed to him, a watch and chain, his own personal cards, a pipe and tobacco, two keys, coins, an empty cigarette case and a box of matches.

While Thomas and Elizabeth had been quite calm concerning the events which had taken place in the back yard, once they were told the identity of the victim, both broke down and sobbed uncontrollably. Elizabeth required a doctor's attention.

Elizabeth told detectives that she and Weldon had been lovers for years. However, they had argued about two months before his death. He had accused her of entertaining another man in her flat, an accusation which she had denied. Weldon had left and secured lodgings for himself elsewhere. Later, he returned with the front door key. There was no key to the back door, as Elizabeth always left it unlocked.

She told the police that she had known Weldon's sons since they were small boys and was extremely attached to them. Thomas had been invited over for dinner and together they had heard the shots.

During the investigation, it was revealed that several people other than Thomas and Elizabeth had seen the man climb the walls right after the shots were heard. One woman walking in the streets that summer night thought the man was five feet six inches tall and wore a dark jacket. He was not carrying anything when she saw him, but the jacket appeared to be smeared with mud.

The chauffeur Noice thought the man used both hands to climb over the wall. He didn't notice anything in his hands. Noice swore that the fleeing man was not Thomas Anderson. Another man on the street that night said the killer appeared to be better dressed than a working man.

He also thought it strange that the fugitive made no noise as he ran. He believed he was wearing light shoes, as opposed to heavy workboots. Thomas and William Anderson swore that their father had no known enemies. They both appeared to have been genuinely fond of their father. He had reciprocated their affection. The entire community was canvassed. Weldon was well-liked and considered to be a competent actor.

Elizabeth told police that Weldon had become jealous some months earlier. His jealousy had gradually increased until it became an obsession. She had attempted to convince him that she didn't have a secret lover, but nothing could sway him from his unfounded suspicions.

Weldon Atherstone kept a diary. Its pages portrayed a man racked with jealousy until it almost drove him mad. It also revealed that he often spent nights in hiding around Elizabeth's flat, intent on intercepting her lover.

Footprints in the garden behind the house could not be matched to Weldon's shoes or to his son's. No gun was ever found. No known enemy was ever located. Yet, someone had shot Weldon Atherstone to death.

The set of circumstances surrounding the case lent themselves to mystery and conjecture. Why would a man enter an empty flat, take off his shoes and replace them with slippers, as Weldon must have done? Why would he carry a homemade blackjack with him if he was intent only on spying on his mistress' lover? In his diary, Weldon mentioned many men, whom he suspected of being Elizabeth's lover. Several were out of the country on acting assignments. All were checked out and cleared.

A coroner's jury returned a verdict of wilful murder by some person or persons unknown.

Now for theories. Criminologists have expressed great interest in the Atherstone murder because there are so many possibilities. Did Thomas' younger brother William kill their father? If Thomas and Elizabeth were lovers, did they talk William into committing murder? Fanciful, but just possible. However, one must think that if three people were planning a murder, they would not perform

10

the deed in their backyard. Besides, William was questioned soon after his father died. He had no scratches or marks on his person.

Did Elizabeth, tired of Weldon's jealousy, hire a killer? Maybe she found out that Weldon was hanging around the flat and, intent on having a younger lover, paid for Weldon's killing? Could be. Here again, in 1910, most hired killers would not have been as well-dressed as eyewitnesses reported.

There is the possibility that Elizabeth was lying and managed to hide the truth from investigators. Maybe Weldon actually did intercept Elizabeth's lover that night and got himself killed for his trouble. To accept this theory, you have to believe that Elizabeth's lover packed a gun, which is highly unlikely.

Here's my pet theory. Weldon shows up with his slippers wrapped in a parcel. He enters the bottom flat easily enough, puts on his slippers, wraps up his shoes and places them on a shelf. Crazed with jealousy, he plans to enter Elizabeth's flat by the back door, which he knows to be unlocked. He plans to silently approach the bedroom and catch Elizabeth in bed with her lover.

Just as he steps out, he is intercepted by an armed robber. Remember, there was a recent series of robberies in the area. The two men grapple, Weldon believing that he is struggling with Elizabeth's lover. The robber doesn't have time to think. A madman attacked him. He pulls out his gun, shoots Weldon and makes his way through two gardens and over three walls, leaving footprints in the mud. They are never matched to suspect's footprints, because the real killer never became a suspect.

Of course, my theory has drawbacks. Most robbers don't dress up to crawl through flats and run through muddy back gardens.

Give it a try. Maybe you can come up with an alternate case which takes into account all the known facts.

SCIENTIFIC SLEUTHING

Committing the perfect crime is becoming increasingly difficult. Advances in forensic science in the past 25 years have been such that the most insignificant pieces of evidence, when put under the scientist's scrutiny, can bring a criminal to justice.

The brisk morning of February 7, 1968 started off normally. Bernie and Claire Josephs had breakfast in their comfortable flat on Deepdene Court near Bromley, England.

The young couple had been married five months.

At a little after 9 a.m., Claire got a lift to work with a girlfriend. The friend worked as a telephone operator with Claire and picked her up every working day. The hours passed uneventfully. At 5:30 p.m., the same friend drove Claire to within a few minutes walk of her home. Claire arrived at her flat at 5:45 p.m., in time to answer a phone call from her mother.

The two women spoke for about 15 minutes. Claire was in normal good cheer and talked to her mother at length about her plans to bake a lemon soufflé. At the conclusion of the call, Claire Josephs put down the telephone. She had only moments to live.

Bernie Josephs left his place of employment at 6 p.m. He dropped into a nearby pub and had drinks with colleagues for about an hour. The group left the pub, but stopped to pick up six bottles of beer before continuing on their way. Bernie was dropped off at his flat a few minutes before 8 p.m.

As he walked up to the front door, Bernie found it strange that the flat was in darkness. Usually Claire had the lights on when he arrived home. Bernie switched on the lights. Somewhat mystified, he made his way through the flat. Everything was in perfect order until he approached the bedroom.

Claire lay dead on the bedroom floor. Bernie called his parents and Claire's parents. In his anguish, he didn't give police a passing thought. Claire's father was the first outsider at the scene. His call to police was recorded at 8:13 p.m.

Within five minutes, what had been the private home of two young people starting off together in life was transformed into a beehive of activity, with a medical examiner, detectives and a photographer scurrying about the small flat.

Detectives quickly established that Claire had begun to make her lemon soufflé. Her recipe book lay open on the kitchen counter. Ingredients, such as eggs, lemon and butter had been placed beside an electric mixer.

A cup of coffee was on a draining board. Maybe Claire was drinking it herself as she worked or maybe it was meant for her killer. A plate with the same pattern as the coffee cup held six shortbread biscuits. A packet of shortbread biscuits had been opened and was in plain view. Six biscuits had been removed from the packet and were obviously the six on the plate.

The police surmised that Claire's visitor may have been an acquaintance, but not a very close one. A close friend would probably have been offered the biscuits directly from the package. Certainly, the biscuits had been meant for a guest. Claire herself would have eaten them directly from the package.

The killer had carried away the murder weapon, believed to be a knife with a serrated blade, which Bernie said was missing from the flat. This tied in with post-mortem results indicating that Claire had been stabbed to death with a serrated-edged knife.

Fourteen wounds had been inflicted on Claire's throat and neck. She also had knife wounds on her arms and hands. From the position of the stab wounds and the condition of the apartment, it was felt that Claire knew her attacker and had invited him into the kitchen, where she had been attacked.

She struggled, but was dragged into the bedroom. Her assailant held his hand over her mouth from behind while he stabbed at her with his right hand. Claire's clothing was not disturbed, nor was she sexually interfered with in any way. The only thing left in the flat which didn't belong there was a bloody handkerchief.

Police routinely searched the Josephs' apartment. They uncovered the usual old letters, cards and invitations. Five days of following up the names found on this material, as well as interviewing all relatives and acquaintances, provided the authorities with a prime suspect.

Roger Payne, 26, had married a girlfriend of Claire's two years before the murder. Claire and Bernie had attended their wedding and had stayed in contact with the Paynes after their own marriage. In fact, the Paynes had visited the Josephs about a month before the murder.

Roger, a bank clerk, had a criminal history. At age 17, he had broken into a house and attempted to rape a young girl. He had received three years' probation for this offence. In 1965, he had forced himself upon a middle-aged woman after breaking into her flat. He had held one hand over her mouth before she broke free. In both cases, the women were not raped. Roger spent three months in prison for the latter attack.

When questioned, Roger had scratches on his hands and forehead. He told police that he had had a nasty disagreement with his wife. He was able to give police an account of all his activities on the day of the murder, right up until he arrived at his own home shortly after 9 p.m. Roger consented to give police a blood sample and the clothing he had worn on February 7, the day of the murder.

At this point in their investigation, police had a strong suspect, but no proof whatever to place the suspect in the victim's flat at the time of the murder.

Enter scientific sleuthing. The coffee cup found in the kitchen was tested for saliva. The saliva was Group A. Roger Payne was Group A, but so was 42% of the entire population of Britain.

Fibres found on Roger's overcoat, hat, scarf and suit were matched against those taken from Claire's cerise dress. They matched perfectly. A tiny piece of thread was extracted from underneath the dead girl's fingernail. It matched thread taken from Roger's scarf.

The bloody handkerchief was tested. The blood consisted of two different types; AB, MN, which was the same as Claire's and AM, which was the same as Roger's. Fibres taken from the handkerchief matched those from Claire's dress.

Scientific evidence was mounting. There was more. A single strand of hair found on Claire's clothing matched a hair taken from Roger's head. Even dog hair removed from Claire's dress matched the hair of a dog Roger owned.

Roger's car was examined. Inside the glove compartment, blood stains, identical to Claire's rare blood type, were discovered. Police surmised that Roger had thrown the bloody knife into the glove compartment after the murder.

The old wedding invitation no doubt was the initial piece of evidence which led police to Roger, but it was the scientific evidence which led to his arrest and conviction.

On May 8, 1968, Roger Payne was found guilty of murder and sentenced to life imprisonment.

SUICIDE PACT

Should you ever decide on a suicide pact, I suggest you insist that your partner be the first to go. If you ascribe to this common sense advice, your chances of survival are increased immeasurably.

Fred Cox had served with Britain's Royal Air Force during World War I. With peace came boredom. Fred attempted to break up the monotony of his clerical job by entering the holy state of matrimony. It didn't help. A few more boring years passed. Fred suggested to his wife that they emigrate to South Africa, where his father's brother was well established. Mrs. Cox didn't think much of the idea. In fact, she answered Fred's inquiry by stating succinctly, "I'm not going."

Fred arrived in Cape Town on June 7, 1922, to start a new life, minus his wife. He moved in with his uncle and had no difficulty obtaining a position as an accountant.

Unc had an 18-year-old daughter, Annie, who was a knockout. Initially, Fred and cousin Annie were just good friends. This platonic state gradually changed to dear friends, then to close friends. What the heck — faster than a bunny, those two cousins were intimate at every opportunity.

Unc didn't take kindly to the situation which was smouldering under his very roof. He knew Fred had a wife back home and that neither was anxious to obtain a divorce. Unc stuck his not inconsiderable nose into the potentially explosive situation. He told Annie that she was forbidden to see Fred and he told Fred to move. Fred moved bag and baggage to a room at 35 Warren St. in Cape Town.

Now domiciled in separate locales, the lovers commenced to write letters to each other. Both found they had a certain flair for letter writing and left us volumes which are so hot, they literally scorch with passion and lust. Six hundred of Annie's letters to Fred survive, while, by comparison, we have the miserly sum of 300 written by Fred to Annie. On occasion, Fred titillated with his own special brand of poetry.

> *"Love, when I touch your hand*
> *I know you understand.*
> *Just a tender touch*
> *So little, yet so much*
> *The speech of heart to heart*
> *That has no counterpart,*
> *Love, when I touch your hand,*
> *I know you understand."*

Fred was a devil with a sharp pencil. When they weren't writing letters, the lovers were making love. This happy state of affairs went on well into 1923, when Fred got into serious trouble.

Amorous Fred was spending more time in Annie's arms than at his accounting duties. As a result, he lost his job. While unemployed, he met a man at his rooming house who was interested in opening a retail business. The two men formed a business partnership. Of course, Fred didn't have a spare rand to invest in anything. He told his new associate that a wealthy relative in England had died and left him a small fortune.

Based on Fred's worthless word, his friend purchased stock for the new business. Fred advised his partner that funds had been transferred to his account at the Standard

17

Bank. On the strength of this fable, Fred extracted a quick loan of $60 from his gullible partner.

Next day, his partner went to the Standard Bank and found out that Fred didn't have an account there. In fact, they had never heard of him. Fred's partner ran all the way to the police station.

When Fred showed up that very night and heard of his partner's anxiety, he had a hard time stifling a laugh. He explained it was all a mistake. The funds had been transferred to the National Bank, not the Standard. To prove that his intent was honorable, he would accompany his partner to the bank the following day and personally hand over the money.

Fred's partner was doubtful. He told Fred that he had already been to the police and would be bringing along a detective to the bank. Fred doubled up with laughter. On the inside, he shuddered. The jig was up.

Bright and early next morning, the three men headed for the bank. Fred noted that they were a bit early. He excused himself as he had to meet his cousin Annie at the railway station. He told his companions that he would be back in plenty of time for the bank opening.

Fred dashed to the railway station. There was his Annie. It had all been planned. Rather than face the consequences of his swindle, they had agreed to a suicide pact. Even without the financial difficulties, Annie thought that dying in Fred's arms would be the ideal way to go. To alleviate anxiety, he would keep the method of death a secret from Annie. Fred was so very thoughtful.

The two lovers walked hand in hand to the Cape of Good Hope Savings Bank Building, where Annie was employed in the accounting office of Mr. A. K. Wolfe. Annie was a trusted private secretary and had the keys to the office. She usually opened up before Mr. Wolfe arrived for work.

On the landing of the second floor, Fred said good morning to painter John Ackerman. Mr. Ackerman saw the pair enter Wolfe's office. Then, all hell broke loose. Screams of "Murder, murder, murder!" came from behind the closed door of Wolfe's office. Ackerman and another man, Henry Thorpe, ran to the office and attempted to open the door. It was locked.

Inside, Fred stabbed the woman he loved over and over. When she tried to run, he stabbed at her back. When she fell to the floor, he pounced on her and stabbed again. So much for the romanticized notions Annie had about a suicide pact. Her screams stopped and pretty Annie Cox lay dead in a bloody heap on the floor. Fred opened the office door. Drenched in blood, he greeted Ackerman and Thorpe, "Yes, I did it and if I'd had time, I'd have finished off myself as well. I bought the knife five months ago." Then Fred excused himself to wash his hands.

A crowd gathered. Fred wasn't at all flustered as one might suspect. Instead, the curious were met by a man who was quite willing to explain his actions. He told various people that he had killed for love and with the full consent of his Annie. Now his only wish was to be dead. As he had not the time to do the job himself, he expressed the wish that he be hanged without delay.

On May 19, 1924, Fred stood trial for the murder of his cousin. His lawyers realized that an insanity plea was the only route open to save their client's life. Fred wouldn't hear of it. Besides, several doctors stated that Fred was sane and knew exactly what he was doing at all times.

It took the South African jury only 20 minutes to find Fred guilty of murder. The verdict didn't faze Fred. When asked if he had anything to say before sentence was passed, he spoke for the first time, advising the court that he had given his lawyer a statement which he would like to have read.

The statement was read in court. In it, Fred explained that he and Annie had agreed that if they were ever forced to separate, they would die together. They had overcome Annie's father's objections by seeing each other in secret, but could see no way that Fred could escape a jail sentence regarding his fraudulent business transactions. He also stated that Annie had sworn that if he was ever taken from her, she would kill herself. Since there was no way out, they had decided on a suicide pact.

Once alone in Wolfe's office, he had asked Annie, "Are you afraid to go, little wifey?" She answered, "No, my darling. Are you?" Fred replied, "No."

The only thing that went wrong was Fred's choice of murder weapon. He assumed that one quick thrust of the blade and Annie would slump into his arms. In reality, it had taken 20 wild swings of the knife to kill his true love. After the statement was read, there was some sympathy for Fred. It was obvious that after killing Annie he had lost his nerve and opened the office door. Fred was sentenced to death. At 6:30 a.m., on July 1, 1924, South Africa did not lose its nerve. Fred Cox was hanged for the murder of his cousin Annie.

BLACK MAGIC

As a general rule, it doesn't pay to become involved with witches. They're a spiteful lot and don't take rejection well. If you don't believe me, ask Eric Willmot. Then again, Eric won't answer; the witches killed him.

Thirty-six-year-old Eric eked out a precarious living selling pots and pans at country fairs in and around Dublin, Ireland. While pursuing this honorable profession one fine day in 1973, he wandered into a tent to have his fortune told by 43-year-old Phoebe Brady.

Eric took one look at Phoebe, with her startling good looks, shiny black hair and stunning figure and said, "That's for me." How was Eric to know that Phoebe was the High Priestess of a ragamuffin group of about 30 lost sheep who called themselves the Devil Worshippers?

Phoebe gazed into her crystal ball, smiled gently at Eric and advised him of an imminent love affair. Eric wouldn't have cared if High Priestess Phoebe worshipped the Blarney Stone. He had more earthy pursuits in mind. Before the week was out, the High Priestess and Eric were intimately worshipping each other.

Phoebe attempted to explain to Eric the responsibilities of her exalted position. She had inherited her lofty role from her mother, who had joined that great coven in the sky about a year earlier. Phoebe had married at the tender age of 16 and had given birth to a daughter, Verren, now 27. Hubby didn't take to the nude dancing by the light of the full moon and had skipped, never to be heard from again.

Marriage was meaningful to Phoebe. She thought she and Eric should tie the knot. It would be no great inconvenience. After all, as High Priestess she could perform the marriage herself. And that's exactly what she did.

Life with Phoebe was not a bed of shamrocks. When she wasn't dancing by the light of the moon, she expected sex on demand from Eric. Too much of a good thing can be tiresome. Like hubby number one, Eric skipped. However, he was not nearly as successful as Phoebe's first husband. She and her fellow Devil Worshippers caught up with Eric in Cork and gave him a sound thrashing. Eric would think twice or even three times before attempting to run out on the High Priestess again.

Every year or so, Eric tried to break away, but each time those Devil Worshippers caught up with him and beat him up. His most recent foiled escape, in mid-1979, resulted in a broken arm and three cracked ribs. No question about, life wasn't easy for Eric. Things got worse.

On December 23, 1979, Thomas Gilligan was chugging along in his old truck outside Cork. He was in a chipper mood, looking forward to spending Christmas with his family when he absently scanned a barren field beside the road. He thought he saw a shoe sticking out of the ground. Thomas stopped to investigate. He attempted to pick up the shoe, but found that it wouldn't budge. With good reason, too. It was attached to the foot and the rest of the body of Eric Willmot.

Thomas summoned police. Dublin detectives noted scuff marks around the shallow grave. It appeared as if a group of people had danced around the body, which had been buried about six inches under the earth. Another six inches and the shoe would have been covered. Quite possibly, the body would never have been found.

An autopsy indicated that Eric had been dead for a very short time. He might very well have been killed the night before, a fact which took on an eerie significance. December 22 was the winter solstice, the shortest day of the year, an important factor in the witch business.

The body had been tied hand and foot. Eric's skull was fractured and his rib cage was smashed, so that several ribs had penetrated vital organs.

In a routine manner, police questioned Phoebe. They learned of her devil worship activities and her followers' habit of beating up the deceased. Phoebe explained that Eric had to be taught a lesson from time to time, but swore by all that's devilish that she had nothing to do with her husband's death. Daughter Verren also swore that she had not harmed her stepfather.

There was nothing of a material nature connecting Phoebe and her daughter to Eric's murder. Police proceeded to reconstruct Eric's last hours. They learned that in the months before his demise, he had told several acquaintances that he was saving money little by little in order to purchase a ticket to Toronto, Canada. A few days before his death, he confided that once he sold the wedding ring Phoebe had given him, he would have enough money to leave the High Priestess forever.

Detectives were able to trace the activities of Phoebe, Verren and most of the Devil Worshippers gang. They had all been elsewhere, at least up to 10 o'clock on the night of the murder. It was verified that they were performing a special dance in honor of the winter solstice. Despite their alibi, authorities were positive that Phoebe and her daughter were involved in the murder in some way. They felt that the two women would have had a hard time overpowering Eric and lugging him to the gravesite, but believed they could have hired someone to do the dirty work. But who?

Michael Harmsworth, that's who. Mike's name surfaced when teams of detectives questioned everyone in the bar where Eric spent the last night of his life. Mike, who had a lengthy police record, including robbery and assault,

23

had left the bar shortly after Eric left at 10 p.m. Taken into custody and questioned, Mike maintained that he knew absolutely nothing about the murder of Eric Willmot, nor was he acquainted with Phoebe and her daughter.

Police were at an impasse. They felt sure they had their killer, but couldn't prove it. They decided to gamble. They would charge Mike with murder and hope that the shock would crack him. The sham worked. Once he was officially charged with murder, his entire demeanor changed. Mike swore that Eric was alive when he last saw him.

He went on to state that he had met Phoebe while having his fortune told. During the course of the sitting, he had revealed to Phoebe that he was broke. Phoebe let him know that she would pay £800 for a rather delicate job. He was to render a man named Eric Willmot helpless and deliver him to her in a field outside the city. Mike swore that Phoebe said it was all a practical joke. He would receive £400 upon acceptance of his assignment and £400 when the job was completed. He took the job.

Mike, who had been provided with Eric's photo, followed the doomed man from the bar. He sneaked up behind Eric and, with his two fists clenched together, struck him on the back of the neck. Eric fell to the ground. Mike, a big, strong man, carried Eric through the streets and out onto the country road. Those who saw him thought he was carrying a drunk.

At the appointed spot in the field, Mike delivered his unconscious cargo to Phoebe and Verren. Both ladies were attired in their official Devil Worshipper's robes. There, on the windswept moor, the ladies passed over the balance of £400 owing to Mike. He noted the iron bars they had in their possession and took off.

The High Priestess and her daughter were taken into custody and were informed that Mike had told all. Initially, Phoebe called Mike a barefaced liar. As the questioning intensified, she took on a regal air, stating that Eric had not been murdered at all. He had been executed. As High Priestess, she was authorized to carry out such legal executions. Eric had been tried in absentia by the Devil Worshippers for attempting to desert her and flee to Toronto. She was merely carrying out the sect's orders. She and Verren had even performed a ritual dance around the grave, so that Eric would go directly to hell.

The Irish jury, although well-versed in tales of leprechauns and such, simply didn't take kindly to Phoebe, Verren or Mike Harmsworth. On July 25, 1980, all three were found guilty of murder and sentenced to life imprisonment.

HIS RAGE
FINALLY
ERUPTS

On February 10, 1964, Cameron Kerley was born on the Sioux Valley Reserve, about 150 miles west of Winnipeg, Manitoba. His name was Cameron Hapas then.

There were five children in the Hapas family. From the very beginning, they never had a great deal of good fortune. When Cameron was eight years old, his father got into a dispute with a man who was making improper advances to Cameron's sister. The man hit Cameron's father over the head with a large rock. Arthur Hapas died in hospital the next day.

Cameron's mother drank heavily after her husband's death. That same year, the Children's Aid Society took the Hapas children and lodged them in an institution. Two years later, Cameron's mother was found frozen to death on a Brandon street.

During the 1960s and '70s, several agencies in the U.S. specialized in placing underprivileged Canadian children in American homes. Some of these children had physical deformities. Others were older and had been passed over for years. Still others were children belonging to minority groups, such as blacks and Indians. Cameron fell into this latter group. Some referred to them as "give-away kids."

It is difficult to fault the motives of the Lutheran Social Service organization. The Kansas-based group was receiving scores of requests from American families for adoptable children. Across the border in Manitoba, there seemed to be an unlimited supply. What better way to relieve an overtaxed situation and, at the same time, provide good homes for native children in the U.S.?

It mattered little to all concerned that the U.S. agencies did little to insure that the children's new parents were loving, responsible individuals. Even less concern was expressed regarding the children's culture shock. Besides, the agencies received $4,000 for each child placed in a home.

There was some cursory screening. The Lutheran Social Service advertised on TV in Wichita for suitable parents. They called their effort a "minority adoption program." Manitoba officials left the screening of prospective parents to the Wichita organization.

In 1974, Dick Kerley, a plant manager for a construction supply company, applied to adopt a child. He was well-known to the agency, having adopted a Sioux youngster, Robert, from South Dakota a year earlier. Dick was a bachelor, who appeared to be genuinely interested in the welfare of underprivileged youngsters and often attended meetings where individuals who had already adopted children encouraged others to do so.

When Dick expressed an interest in adopting another Indian child, everyone thought it was a great idea. No one asked Cameron Hapas what he thought. In 1975, he was picked up by his new father, Dick Kerley. It was the first time the two had laid eyes on each other. Cameron was 11 years old.

According to Cameron, the abuse started as soon as he moved in with his adoptive father. He was told to go to bed, take off his pyjamas, and fondle the older man. Later, he was made to pose in the nude. If Cameron refused to take part in his father's sexual activity, he was threatened with beatings.

Pleasant, good-humored Dick Kerley was not the man he appeared to be on the surface. From the outside, the attractive house looked normal enough. Inside, it was a

27

filthy mess. Newspapers, food and dirty dishes were everywhere. Dick kept a large supply of gay magazines and photographs of men posing in the nude.

Both Robert and Cameron continually ran away from home. Once, Cameron was caught heading north because he had heard that that was the way to Canada. Somehow, Cameron managed to complete Grade 9, but dropped out of school the following year.

In subsequent years, Cameron ran afoul of the law, mostly as a result of his heavy drinking. In 1981 and 1982, he was arrested for burglary. For a while, he moved in with a 23-year-old woman, who had a young son. Cameron liked the arrangement. For a short time, he worked at the only job he ever held, but the heavy drinking continued. The girlfriend gathered up her little boy and moved out.

On Labor Day weekend, 1983, Cameron sat under a tree in Sim Park, directly across the street from his father's home. He and his friends were drinking. One by one, the friends left. Cameron stayed on, drinking. Inside, 19-year-old Cameron Kerley raged. His rage was deep, unforgiving, and directed at his tumultuous life in general and his abusive father in particular.

Cameron crossed the street, broke a window and crawled into the Kerley home. He found a baseball bat in a closet and proceeded to his father's bedroom. Cameron swung the bat at Dick Kerley's head and killed him as he slept. He then managed to roll the bloody body into a blanket and lugged it into the basement. After disposing of the body, Cameron took off in Dick's truck. He was picked up a short time later and charged with drunk driving.

When Dick didn't report for work after the Labor Day weekend, his body was discovered in the basement. Cameron was charged with burglary and first-degree murder.

Today, Monte Vines is with the same law firm in Wichita as he was on the day in 1983 when he became Cameron Kerley's court-appointed lawyer. It was he who discovered the sordid circumstances of Cameron's life in the pleasant-looking house in Wichita. Initially, Cameron kept the details to himself. Vines felt that despite Cameron's history, he did not have a viable legal defence. After all, he had killed a sleeping man. However, Vines was successful in plea bargaining the charges down to second-degree murder and Cameron was allowed to plead guilty to this charge.

In hindsight, everyone involved agrees that Cameron Hapas should not have been adopted by Dick Kerley. Monte Vines explains why the adoption of native Canadian children had become a popular practice at that time, "U.S. Congress had just passed a law affording Indian tribes the right of refusal when it came to whites adopting Indian children in the U.S. As a result, the supply of adoptable children dried up. Agencies looked to Canada, where no such restrictions applied."

In 1983, the government of Manitoba placed a permanent ban on the adoption of native children to the U.S. It was too late for Cameron Kerley. On January 5, 1984, when sentencing Cameron, Judge Robert Helsel stated, "I don't think the fact his father was a homosexual gives him the right to murder him."

Cameron was sentenced to 18 years to life. Four months later, when the sentence was reviewed, it was reduced to 15 years to life. Eventually, Cameron applied for transfer to a Canadian prison. In June 1985, he was flown to Winnipeg and on to Stony Mountain Penitentiary. He has since been transferred to a minimum security institution.

SPANISH FLY
DEATHS

You are forgiven if you have never heard of the drug cantharidies. Under the name Spanish Fly, it has gained worldwide notoriety. What young, virile male hasn't heard of Spanish Fly, a substance which is supposed to enhance sexual desire in a female to such an extent that she actually craves sexual intercourse? Very few are aware that cantharidies is a deadly poison.

Arthur Kendrick Ford had served in the Far East with the British Army. Aboard ship, on his way home, there was much lighthearted conversation among the men. Many had been away from home for years. They talked of the copious amounts of liquor they would consume and the long-legged ladies they would entice between the sheets. One of the men explained that if all else failed, he would use Spanish Fly back in England. That little trick would bring the women flocking into his arms. Art Ford listened, but didn't give the good-natured Army jargon another thought until much later.

Art returned to his position as office manager of a wholesale drug firm, where he oversaw a staff of 22 women and four men. The years passed rapidly. Art was typical of many men whose stint in the service was over. He adapted to civilian life. In due course, he met a pleasant young woman and fell in love. He and Marjorie married. In 1954, when our bizarre story begins, the Fords were the proud parents of two young children.

In April 1954, Art had a customer inquiry concerning cantharidies. Art's mind raced back to the shipboard conversation. He remembered well the rumored qualities of the drug. What better way to have one of the office girls throw herself at his feet than to give her Spanish Fly? Pretty Betty Grant, 27, had been the object of Art's attention for some time. Unfortunately, his little office ploys to get her to like him had failed miserably. She simply rejected his every advance.

Art had a chat with the company's senior chemist, Richard Lushington. On the morning of April 26, he asked Lushington if the firm stocked cantharidies. Art said a neighbor was breeding rabbits and had heard that the drug might help. Lushington confirmed that a bottle of the drug was in stock, adding that it was a powerful poison. Art replied, "Oh, well, if that's the case I don't want it."

Later that day Art, by his own admission, took some cantharidies out of the bottle. With the aid of a pair of scissors, he inserted a quantity of the deadly poison into a chocolate commonly called coconut ice. The candy has a white and pink centre and is covered with chocolate. Art had no trouble inserting and concealing the poison in the candy which he had purchased from a local sweetshop.

At around 2:30 in the afternoon, Art walked through the office carrying a bag of candy. He stuck his fingers into the bag and extracted a coconut ice. He gave it to Betty Grant. Other pieces were offered to other women. Some declined. June Malins hadn't been offered a piece of candy, but was seen eating a coconut ice, which had probably been given to her by one of the other women.

An hour later, June felt ill. Betty Grant assisted her colleague to the company's sick room. Twenty minutes later, Betty also complained of feeling ill. At 4 p.m., Art developed a severe headache. As the afternoon wore on, the condition of the three sick employees worsened. They were taken to London's University College Hospital. Next day, the two women died. Art's condition improved.

Autopsies performed on the two dead women revealed that both had died as a result of poisoning by cantharidies. Detectives informed Art of the deaths and received an unusual response. "Oh, dear God, what an awful thing I've done! Why didn't someone tell me? I've been a fool. Let me tell you the whole story."

From his sickbed, Art related the story of how he had heard of Spanish Fly years earlier and how his memory was jarred by the customer's inquiry. He decided to try some Spanish Fly on Betty Grant, and admitted that he had inserted the drug into a chocolate meant for her. He claimed that the drug must have adhered to June Malins' chocolate accidentally.

Art stated, "I gave one of the pieces to Miss Grant. We were very fond of each other. She kept putting me off and I made up my mind to give her cantharidies in the coconut ice to stimulate her desire for me. I cannot say how Miss Malins got the other piece, except that it was an accident. I am deeply sorry I gave Betty Grant the drug. I now realize that I caused the death of these girls by doing this crazy thing at the expense of losing my dear wife and children."

It was too late for self-recriminations. Two women had died in agony because of Ford's foolish and reckless action.

In due course, Art stood trial for manslaughter in London's famed Old Bailey. Defence attorneys stated that there was no doubt in anyone's mind that Art Ford had not intended to kill the two women.

Yet he had been warned by his company's senior chemist that the drug was a "Number One poison." Crown attorneys emphasized that at that point a reasonable man should have cancelled any harebrained schemes to gain a girl's affection through drug stimulation.

Marjorie Ford stood by her husband throughout his well-publicized trial and forgave his infatuation with Betty Grant. Arthur Ford was found guilty of manslaughter and was sentenced to five years imprisonment.

THE RALLO
MURDERS

To all outward appearances, the Rallos were a loving, close-knit family. Their home at 16 Lantana Court in Hamilton was typical of a young family seeking the good life.

Jon Rallo, 33, the head of the family, had done pretty well for himself, working his way up in the municipal government to a responsible position as office manager in the engineering department. Attractive Sandra Rallo was four years younger than her husband. The Rallos had two children — Jason, 7, and Stephanie, 5.

Neighbors on Lantana Court liked the Rallos. They often socialized. So did Sandra's parents. Like grandparents everywhere, Doug and Margaret Pollington doted on their grandchildren and looked forward to the children's periodic visits to their home in nearby Cambridge.

Nothing is perfect. There were rumors that all was not smooth in the Rallo marriage. Jon had accused Sandra of having an affair with another man. She, in turn, had her suspicions about her husband's fidelity. They had gone through a rough period, but it was over. By 1976, their marriage appeared to be stable. Appearances can be deceiving.

On the night of Monday, August 16, a friend called at the Rallo home, saw the entire family and left at 11 p.m.

From that moment, no one other than their killer was to lay eyes on Sandra, Jason and Stephanie Rallo.

Jon didn't show up for work the next morning or the next. In fact, the first anyone was to hear of the fate of his family occurred when he called on his father-in-law, Doug Pollington, at 11:30 a.m. on Wednesday. Mr. Pollington was shocked at Jon's appearance. He was wearing old clothes, needed a shave and acted in a nervous manner.

Jon explained that Sandra had left him for another man. She had taken the children with her. He went on to say that it all happened while he was asleep in the basement. When he woke up Tuesday morning, his entire family was gone. In their place was an unsigned, typewritten note.

Doug Pollington was astounded as he read, "I'm writing this letter to say goodbye and ask you to try and understand what I am doing, Jon. I've met someone who I love very much. He's a rich lawyer from out West who I met while working last year. He can give us everything we would ever want."

Jon later told his mother-in-law that Sandra had left everything behind except her wallet. The Pollingtons were skeptical. The note, the abruptness of Sandra's decision to walk out of their lives, was not typical of their daughter. They consented to Jon's request to contact a lawyer rather than the police.

While they were telling their story to Hamilton lawyer Dennis Roy, another drama was being enacted on the shores of Jordan Harbor, not far from St. Catharines. Shawn Labonde, 14, and his brother were fishing when they came upon a duffel bag in the water. The boys opened the bag and then opened a green garbage bag they found inside. There, before their terrified eyes, was the nude body of a little girl. Unaware of the gruesome find, Doug Pollington informed Hamilton police that his daughter and her children were missing. Next day, the little girl in the garbage bag was identified as Stephanie Rallo.

Sgt. Gary King of the Hamilton Police, together with William Towstiak of Toronto Forensic Sciences Centre, searched the Rallos' west-end Hamilton home. Towstiak, a veteran of 21 years of scientific sleuthing, found an abundance of incriminating evidence in the Rallo home. Blocking a doorway to a bedroom was a mattress stained with minute drops of blood. The broadloom which had covered the master bedroom floor had been torn up and was nowhere to be found.

Towstiak also found seven small drops of blood on the deep maroon drapes in the bedroom. Later, he would testify they were "consistent with blood splashed, with being thrown with some force." The blood proved to be the same type as that of Sandra Rallo.

More blood was found on the walls leading to the basement. Traces of blood were found in water trapped in a floor drain. In a bedroom closet, the forensic detective discovered Jon Rallo's bloodstained slippers.

Rallo was taken into custody and charged with first-degree murder. Meanwhile, police actively searched for the bodies of the two missing members of his family. On August 26, an OPP officer, scanning the Welland Canal from a helicopter, spotted a parcel floating in the water. It proved to be Sandra's body, wrapped in garbage bags. Medical examination of her body indicated that Sandra had been beaten and strangled. Little Stephanie had been smothered to death.

Jon Rallo stood trial for the murder of his wife and two children. Prosecution attorneys presented a formidable case. They were able to trace the garbage bags used to dispose of the bodies back to the manufacturer and prove that they came from an open package of bags found in the Rallo home. A guard at a local garbage dump identified Rallo as the man who had disposed of several bags of garbage on August 18. Broadloom removed from the Rallo home had been recovered from the dump.

Rallo took the witness stand in his own defence. He admitted that he had had an affair with a colleague at City Hall, but steadfastly claimed that his wife had taken the children and left him for another man. He stated he had no idea how his wife and daughter ended up in garbage bags. He dismissed the condition of his home with a shrug, saying he had become so despondent when he read his wife's letter that he had dismantled the bed. The carpet had been ripped up because the dog had recently soiled it. The bloodstains? Sandra had had a nosebleed.

No one believed Jon Rallo. He was found guilty of three counts of first-degree murder and sentenced to three terms of life imprisonment with no possibility of parole for 25 years.

Before being sentenced, Rallo addressed the court, "What has kept my head above water these past 16 months is the fact I know I did not do it; but more importantly, Sandra knows I did not do it, Stephanie knows I didn't do it and Jason, wherever he is, knows I didn't."

The search for Jason's body appeared to be over when skeletal remains of a young boy found near Barrie were erroneously identified as Jason. Some time after the body was buried, it was discovered that the dead boy was Jaime Shearer, a youngster from Alberta who had disappeared a year earlier. The boy's mother was questioned by OPP officers. She insisted her son was staying with friends in Toronto. Before she could be questioned a second time, she committed suicide. Jason Rallo's body has never been found.

Almost 13 years have passed since Sandra Rallo and her two children were murdered in their comfortable Lantana Court home in Hamilton. Jon Rallo has been in prison for all of those years. He is presently in a medium security facility and will be eligible to apply for a judicial review after serving 15 years.

HER
LIVING HELL

Kay Hupfeldt took one look at handsome Francesco Sandiford and fell hard. Dr. Sandiford was the most exciting man Kay had ever met.

Years earlier, in 1958, Kay had married her childhood sweetheart. The marriage lasted long enough for Kay to give birth to a son, Charles. But that was all behind her now.

On July 17, 1963, Kay met Dr. Francesco Sandiford, a dashing Italian in every sense of the word. He was polite, charming and, above all, obviously enthralled with Kay. With dark eyes flashing, the handsome doctor made Kay feel like a queen.

Dr. Sandiford had received his medical degree in Italy, but felt there were more opportunities in the U.S. He had been accepted as an intern at Baltimore's University of Maryland Hospital. The 35-year-old medic dated Kay with a vengeance. For her part, Kay felt totally dominated by her aggressive boyfriend. She liked it.

In old world fashion, Frank asked Kay's father, Dr. Hubert Hupfeldt, for her hand in marriage. Consent was not required, but was granted without question.

When Frank's internship was completed, he was accepted as a fellow in general surgery at the Texas Medical Centre in Houston, one of the most prestigious medical institutions in the U.S. His salary was the not too princely sum of $5,000 per annum.

With his career in place, Frank felt it was time he and Kay married. With strangers as witnesses, they were wed in a courtroom. A week later, the bride's parents held a lavish reception for the happy couple at the Baltimore Country Club. Shortly after the reception, the Hupfeldts left Baltimore for a few days, leaving the newlyweds to start off their honeymoon in their lovely home.

Frank and Kay, alone in the house, had a romantic dinner by candlelight. After dinner, Frank, for no apparent reason, punched Kay in the face. Then he hit her in the stomach. As she sank to the floor, he kicked her again and again. Finally, she passed out. When she regained consciousness, charming Frank was bathing her face. He explained that every wife needs a good beating to impress upon her who is the ultimate authority in the marriage.

Kay's face was a mess, but Frank had a ready explanation for her parents and friends. Some idiot had rearended them. Kay's head had smashed into the dashboard of the car. A few days in bed and she would be her old self again. Everyone sympathized.

Once Kay recovered from her accident, the newlyweds took off for the Virgin Islands. Frank was enthusiastic. After settling in, he hired a Sailfish. Over the smooth Caribbean, they zoomed into the Atlantic. Once they hit open water, it was a bit of a bumpy ride, but Kay felt exhilarated as she leaned forward, wind blowing through her hair. This was more like it, she thought.

Without warning, charming Frank shoved Kay from behind. Into the rough sea she tumbled. Kay surfaced and couldn't believe her eyes. The Sailfish was moving further away. Frank was making no attempt to pick her up. Eventually, he disappeared behind a spit of land which protected a cove and beach.

Kay, a strong swimmer, didn't panic. She treaded water, bucked the waves, floated on her back. It was tough going, but she made it to the cove with its welcome calmer waters. She fully expected to find Frank, but the Sailfish was nowhere to be seen. Now nearing exhaustion, Kay was forced to swim some considerable distance to the beach, where she collapsed on the sand.

She located charming Frank downing a cool one in the bar. He smiled, but offered no excuse or explanation for his actions. Kay, too exhausted to argue, felt that once again she must have passed some test that her brilliant husband had thought up. The rest of the honeymoon was uneventful.

The Sandifords settled into a one-bedroom apartment in Houston. In the following year, Frank worked incessantly at the hospital. Kay took up tennis. At the conclusion of his fellowship, Frank was accepted in residency at the Texas Heart Institute. Kay's father gave the Sandifords the gift of a small but comfortable home. Now working with some of the finest cardiac surgeons in the world, Frank's salary escalated rapidly.

Years passed. Occasionally, Frank would strike Kay for no reason. His outbreaks left no bruises or scars on Kay's body. Sometimes, he punished her by not conversing with her for days. At other times, he would berate her for her manners, her walk and her conversation. Kay could do nothing right. Privately, Frank called her his American peasant.

By 1974, Dr. Frank Sandiford was a successful heart surgeon. Within a few years, he was earning in excess of $400,000 annually. Frank decided a man of his reputation and standing in the community required a more prestigious residence. He purchased a home on Del Monte Dr. in Houston's exclusive River Oaks district, one of the most expensive residential areas in the entire U.S.

With all the trappings of wealth and the outward signs of affection they displayed towards each other, the Sandifords were thought to be the ideal couple. Kay's son Charles attended school in Connecticut, and so did not witness the beatings his mother received at the hands of charming Frank.

Alone, with only servants in the big rambling house,

Frank perfected a method of torture which left no visible bruises or scars. He would raise one of Kay's arms and twist his clenched fist into her ribs. Outside the luxurious home, the Sandifords' three cars shone in the Texas sun. Lush flower beds accentuated the rolling lawns, which were manicured twice a week. Inside, Kay Sandiford was experiencing a living hell.

As the years passed, various honors were heaped upon Dr. Sandiford. One he cherished most was a private audience with the Pope. For that occasion, Kay had to learn Italian, how to eat as the Romans did and, in general, take lessons in an attempt to be transformed into an Italian lady of substance. Rarely did a month pass that Kay did not receive a beating at the hands of her husband.

Gradually, Kay began to avoid Frank at every opportunity. She took baths which lasted for hours. When she was in her husband's company, she agreed with his every word. To disagree meant a beating.

Toward the end of January 1980, Frank grew more abusive than ever. He constantly berated Kay, ridiculing her in front of friends. At home, he beat her. As if casting out an old shoe, he shouted at her one day, "I want a divorce, I want a divorce." He gave her three days to vacate the house.

On Tuesday, January 29, 1980, Kay Sandiford had overstayed her three days. Her husband had ordered her to pay all the bills and gather up all the receipts pertaining to income tax. When Frank arrived home that day, Kay, as instructed, went upstairs to show her husband his receipts. Frank, clutching a tennis racket, approached the stairs. He growled, ``I'm going to get you."

Kay dashed into the bedroom, grabbed Frank's .357 Colt Python and returned to the head of the stairs. She pulled the trigger five times. Four bullets found their mark. The well-ventilated Frank would never strike her again. He was very dead.

Kay called a friend and a lawyer. In minutes, police

were at the scene and took her into custody.

On January 15, 1981, Kay stood trial for the murder of her husband. Her counsel didn't deny that Kay had killed Frank. They claimed that she was driven to the act by an abusive husband and had acted in self-defence.

Prosecution attorneys pointed out that Kay could have walked away at any time over the years, but obviously had chosen not to do so. Kay testified that it was possible to fear and love a man at the same time.

Kay Sandiford was found guilty of voluntary manslaughter, a verdict which could bring a sentence of up to 20 years imprisonment. Kay was sentenced to 10 years probation and a fine of $10,000. She walked out of court a free woman. Three years later, her probation officer was successful in having her released from the remaining years of her probation sentence.

THE GREAT ESCAPE

Wallace Floody wasn't as fast on his feet as he used to be, when he left Toronto for Kirkland Lake to play softball and basketball in the Dirty Thirties. I interviewed him as he lay in bed

"There were no jobs in Toronto in those days. Because I was lucky enough to be an athlete, I was given a job in the mines," Floody told me.

One of his softball teammates in those days was Bill Durnan, who went on to win six consecutive Vezina trophies as goaltender of the Montreal Canadiens. Wallace Floody went on to become chief tunnel digger in a prisoner of war camp in Nazi Germany.

Wally joined the Air Force at the outbreak of the war and soon became a pilot officer. At age 25, he found himself stationed at Biggin Hill, England, with No. 1 Canadian Fighter Squadron.

On October 27, 1941, Wally's Mosquito was shot down over St. Omer, France. He parachuted out of his burning plane and landed on the hard cobblestones of the village's main street. It wasn't a graceful landing, but things immediately took a turn for the better. An elderly French woman ran to Wally's assistance. Without saying a word, she poured a generous portion of cognac into a glass. Wally managed to gulp it down and to have a second glass before two German soldiers dragged him off to the local army headquarters.

In the months and years which followed, Wally spent time in several P.O.W. camps. "I didn't like barbed wire right from the beginning," he told me. "There were only three ways to get out of prison — through the wire, over the wire or under the wire. I favored under the wire."

Tunnels seemed to pop up wherever six-foot, four-inch, 210-pound Wally Floody was transferred. But it is the granddaddy of all tunnels at Stalag Luft III, located at Sagan, northeast of Berlin in what is now Poland, for which Wally Floody and his fellow P.O.W.s will forever be remembered.

The airmen built three tunnels, aptly named Tom, Dick and Harry. They reasoned that the Germans would not discover all three. When a new compound was built, Tom was accidentally uncovered. Eventually, Dick was used for storage. Harry became the focus of 600 desperate Allied air force officers.

Wally was quick to point out that The Great Escape, as it came to be known both in the book and the movie which later immortalized their feat, was a highly organized operation. Many of the men had only the information which was necessary to enable them to complete their assigned tasks. Entire departments were formed to do nothing but forge documents. Wally says that some of these documents were amazing and would pass the closest inspection. Other men were assigned to make civilian clothing out of the most basic scraps of material.

Harry was a year in the making. It was quite an accomplishment. Harry started under a stove through a trap door and went straight down for 30 feet. It had to be that deep to avoid German detector microphones. At the base of the 30-foot shaft was a workshop where sand was unloaded from trolleys before being dragged to the surface. Off the workshop was a homemade air pump, which moved air into the tunnel through vents made of Klim milk cans. The tunnel, equipped with electric lights and trolley rails, ran for 350 feet to a wooded area beyond the barbed wire. It measured two feet in height by two feet in width and was shored by wooden boards and bed slats.

Sand, laboriously dragged up the 30-foot shaft, was placed in pockets and specially sewn-in sacks inside the airmen's pant legs. It was taken outside and trampled in gardens. At one point, the Germans had the prisoners build a theatre. More earth from the tunnel was deposited under the theatre.

Two weeks before the date set for The Great Escape, Wally Floody was transferred to another camp five miles away. He was devastated at the time, but realizes that the move probably saved his life. There were 19 other men transferred with Wally, two of whom had tunnelling experience. Wally feels the Germans may have suspected them, but he will never know for sure.

The plan was for 200 men to escape. They would leave in two waves of 100 each. Each group of 100 had 30 men who were fully equipped with money, forged documents, railway tickets and acceptable clothing. They also spoke German or some other European language which coincided with their credentials. The next 70, who were chosen according to their contribution to the project, were on their own.

On March 24, 1944, the men slowly made their way down the shaft and into the tunnel. The other end was broken open and the airmen crawled through to freedom. Hour after hour, singly, lying flat on their stomachs, they rode the interminable 350 feet to the other end.

Suddenly, there was the wail of an air raid siren. All the lights went out, including those in the tunnel. Wally recalls, "Some of those men had never been in the tunnel or any tunnel in their lives. You can imagine their claustrophobic feeling, being 30 feet down in a two-foot wide tunnel in pitch darkness." As the seventy-sixth man bolted out of the tunnel, a German guard caught sight of him and raised the alarm.

Wally explained, "We knew that a few fighter pilots wouldn't change the course of the war. We wanted to disrupt and harass the German war machine and we accomplished that."

Every train in Germany that morning was stopped and searched. The radio barked out details of The Great Escape every 15 minutes. Rounding up escaped prisoners of war involved the Gestapo, Army, SS and Luftwaffe. More than 60,000 men were employed in recapturing the escapees. When Adolph Hitler was given the news of the escape in his hideaway in Berchtesgaden, he strongly suggested that every recaptured prisoner be shot. Aides convinced him that it would be more prudent to shoot only 50. The official reason for the murders was to be that the prisoners, once recaptured, had attempted to escape while being returned to camp.

Within three weeks, 73 escapees were apprehended. Among the 50 Allied airmen murdered were six Canadians — F.O. Henry Birkland, 26, Calgary; F.O. Gordon A. Kidder, 29, St.Catharines; F.O. George W. Wiley, 22, Windsor; Flt. Lt. Patrick Langford, 24, Field, B.C.; Flt. Lt. George McGill, 25, Toronto; and Flt. Lt. James Wenhem, 26, Winnipeg. Of the 76 men who crawled out of Harry, only three — two Norwegians and a Dutchman — made it back to England. At the conclusion of the war, a British military court stood in judgment of 18 German personnel accused of murdering the Allied prisoners. Thirteen were hanged.

Since those days, when life revolved around a hole in the ground called Harry in faraway Germany, Wally Floody, sometimes called the Tunnel King, is from time to time reminded of his past. In 1946, he was made a member of the Order of the British Empire.In 1962, he was flown to Germany as technical advisor for the movie, *The Great Escape*.

For years, Wally Floody lived in retirement in the fashionable Toronto area of Rosedale with his wife, Betty. On the walls of his home hung paintings and photographs of the The Great Escape, and of a time long ago when a tunnel named Harry held hope for 600 desperate Allied airmen.

On September 25, 1989, Clark Wallace Floody died after a lengthy illness.

DEATH ON
A LONELY
ENGLISH ROAD

Evelyn Foster led an idyllic life in the tiny village of Otterburn, England. Her family owned the main business in the village, a large garage and bus line. All the members of the Foster family took an active interest in the business.

The Fosters were a close-knit, loving group, consisting of Evelyn's father, Joseph, the founder of the business; his wife, Margaret; and their grown children — Gordon, in his early thirties; Dorothy, 22; and Margaret, 20. Evelyn was 29 on that dreadfully cold day of January 6, 1931, when the family's fortunes changed forever.

At 6:30 p.m., Gordon Foster dispatched bus driver Cecil Johnstone to take passengers on the 30-mile run to Newcastle. Three other passengers were left at the garage awaiting a car to transport them in the opposite direction to Rochester. Gordon crossed the street to his family's home. There he found Evelyn dressing warmly as she prepared to drive the three passengers the short distance to Rochester in her 1928 Hudson Super Six.

Evelyn picked up her passengers, James Amos, William Glendenning and Mrs. Esther Murray, who sat in the front seat with Evelyn. After a run of about five miles, the two men were dropped off. Mrs. Murray lived a few miles beyond the village. Evelyn drove her home and parked for a while, to let Mrs. Murray finish relating a choice bit of village gossip.

While they were parked, a car whizzed by, heading toward Otterburn. Later, Mrs. Murray remembered the vehicle, but for the life of her couldn't describe the car or its occupants.

Evelyn drove back to her home in Otterburn, arriving at 7 p.m. She told her parents that, after dropping off Mrs. Murray, she had picked up a man and had driven him back to the village. Mrs. Foster idly inquired how she had met her new fare. Evelyn explained that she had been hailed by some people beside a car at Elishaw. A man had come over to her vehicle and told her that he was travelling from Edinburgh to Newcastle, but had missed his bus. The people in the car had given him a lift as far as Elishaw.

In fact, they had all just finished having tea, but as they were now veering off in another direction, he required a lift into Otterburn to catch the bus.

Evelyn informed him that the bus for Newcastle had already left, but she would give him a lift into Otterburn and on into Ponteland, a distance of some 24 miles, for the sum of around two pounds. Once in Ponteland, he could catch the bus for Newcastle. Evelyn went on to explain that she had to check the rate at the family garage to be sure of the correct amount.

The stranger told Evelyn that he would attempt to get a lift for free down at the Percy Arms, but if he wasn't successful, he would hire her for the trip. Evelyn thought his chances were very slim. She went home to check the correct fare to Ponteland. Her father told her that she had quoted too high a figure; the price was somewhat less that two pounds.

Evelyn's sister Dorothy suggested that she take along George Phillipson for company. George was an old beau of Evelyn's. She nodded in agreement to her sister. At 7:15 p.m., Evelyn bid goodbye to her family.

Remember Cecil Johnstone, who had earlier driven the bus to Newcastle? Now, together with conductor Tommy

47

Rutherford, he was heading back to his home base in Otterburn. They dropped off passengers along the way until the bus was empty. As they drove along, Johnstone spotted what he thought was a campfire a short distance off the road. He stopped the bus and he and Rutherford got out to investigate. As they drew closer, they realized that what they had seen was a car with the interior ablaze. The licence number was visible TN8135 — Evelyn Foster's Hudson.

The driver's door and the rear door on the same side were open. The vehicle appeared to be empty. The men heard a low moan. About 10 yards from the Hudson, they found Evelyn Foster. Naked from the waist down, she was horribly burned over most of her body. Evelyn was pathetically clawing and sucking on ice.

Johnstone, who knew Evelyn well, took off his overcoat and placed it gently over the badly burned woman. He bent over her and said, "It's me, Evelyn, Cecil Johnstone." Despite her condition, Evelyn was conscious and said, "Oh, that awful man."

"What man?" Johnstone asked.

"He has gone in a motorcar," replied Evelyn.

Johnstone and Rutherford gently lifted Evelyn from the cold ground and drove her home in their bus.

Back in Otterburn, we can only imagine the shock experienced by the Foster family when the men carried Evelyn into the house.

"What has happened?" Gordon Foster asked his sister.

"It's that man," she replied.

"What, the one you took to Ponteland?"

"Yes, he has burned me and the car."

Gordon, beside himself at his sister's condition, pressed on. "What did the man look like, Evie?"

"He is about your build, maybe a little taller and not quite as stout. He had a bowler hat on. He was dark and wore a dark coat."

Evelyn's father called a doctor and the local constable. A mechanic at the garage, Thomas Vasey, had the opportunity to ask Evelyn, "Who has done this?" She replied, "He threw something over me and set me on fire in the car."

After Evelyn had been placed in bed, her mother had a chance to speak to her. "What has happened?" she asked. "He hit me and burned me. I don't know who the man was," Evelyn answered.

Two doctors arrived at the Foster residence. After ministering to Evelyn until midnight, they informed the family that, other than easing her pain somewhat, there was little they could do. Evelyn would most certainly die.

Andrew Fergusson, the village constable, ill-equipped to handle anything more serious than a Saturday night scuffle at the village pub, arrived at the Foster home. He phoned the closest police station at Bellingham and was told that Sgt. Robert Shanks was on his way.

With the arrival of Shanks, it was decided to question Evelyn once more regarding her attacker. She repeated her earlier statements, adding that the man attacked her about 18 miles into the trip. He took hold of the steering wheel and insisted that he drive. Then, he struck her with his fists about the head. "He struck me twice and knocked me into the back of the car. He did not appear to be drunk."

Evelyn's mother asked, "Did he interfere with you?"

"Yes, mother. Oh, mother, I couldn't help it. I fought for my life."

Evelyn went on to say that her attacker threw something over her and then the interior of the car was on fire. She crawled out of the car and lay on the ground. She heard a car pull up and then drive away.

In the wee hours of the morning of January 7, Evelyn Foster died.

Police examining the burnt-out vehicle found an empty Shell gasoline can beside the car. They also examined the engine and confirmed that the fire had not originated in that area but rather in the interior of the vehicle. That's about all the inexperienced local police established. No fingerprints were taken and the area around the Hudson was soon contaminated by curious villagers. Scotland

Yard was not called in to assist the local police.

It was quickly established that George Phillipson, the old beau who Evelyn was supposed to take with her that fateful night, was elsewhere at the time of the crime. He had not been picked up by Evelyn and was innocent of all guilty knowledge.

Tea room employees in Elishaw were questioned. It was the quiet season. They would certainly remember strangers, but had no recollection of such strangers on the night of January 6.

The car Mrs. Murray recalled seeing while parked with Evelyn that night was seen by no others. A great manhunt was instituted for the man in the bowler hat. While scores of men in bowler hats were detained, all managed to clear themselves.

An autopsy was performed. The results were startling. Dr. Stuart McDonald stated that, despite the fact that the body was terribly burned, he was able to establish that Evelyn had died a virgin. He further stated that he found no bruising about the deceased's head.

Most students of this old crime believe that the doctor's testing methods concerning the virginity of the victim may have been faulty, considering the extent of the burns to the body. The extreme burning may also have accounted for the lack of discernible bruising about the head. They further point out that when Mrs. Foster asked her dying daughter if she had been interfered with, Evelyn may not have interpreted the question to mean rape.

An official inquest ruled that Evelyn Foster was murdered by a person or persons unknown. Why this innocent girl met such a horrible death on a lonely English road has never been explained, nor has her killer ever been apprehended.

CANNIBAL GARY HEIDNIK

This is the story of Gary Heidnik, a bright and evil man, whose violent crimes are among the most hideous ever inflicted by one human being upon another.

Heidnik was born in Cleveland, Ohio in 1943. His parents separated when he was still a youngster. Despite this disruption in his life, Gary appears to have been a well-adjusted boy. He was a boy scout, played baseball and had an urge to attend West Point.

In 1961, at age 18, he dropped out of Cleveland's East High School and joined the army. A year later, he was serving as an orderly in West Germany when he took ill for the first time. He complained of seeing things moving about. Army doctors thought he was suffering from schizophrenia and, a short time later, had him shipped back to the U.S., where he received an honorable discharge and a 10% disability pension.

Gary settled in Philadelphia and graduated as a licensed practical nurse. In the years which followed, he was in and out of mental hospitals on a regular basis. In all, he spent time in 21 different institutions. Eventually, his army pension was raised to 100% disability which, together with social security benefits, gave him an income of some $2,000 a month.

In 1971, Gary found religion. More specifically, he

started his own, appointing himself Bishop of the United Church of the Ministers of God. He had the organization incorporated and actually gathered together a few followers for prayer meetings.

Four years of revolving mental institutions followed. It was in 1975 that Gary decided to try his luck at the stocks and bonds game. Using his church's name, he opened an account with Merrill, Lynch, Pierce, Fenner and Smith, placing $1,500 on deposit. The investment firm knew him as Bishop Heidnik, an astute investor who ran his initial capital of $1,500 up to $545,000 within a few years.

Over the years, between stays in mental institutions, Gary Heidnik led an active love life. Strangely, he preferred marginally retarded women as lovers and lived with several of them. From time to time, because of his own mental health problems, his intelligence quotient was tested. He had an IQ of 130, which is considered superior. In 1986, Gary had an interest income in his church's name, a 100% disability pension from the army, as well as Social Security benefits. He drove a new Cadillac Coupe de Ville and had a 1971 Rolls-Royce parked in his garage. Despite his penchant for top of the line cars, he lived in a dilapidated, filthy house at 3520 North Marshall St. in the slums of Philadelphia.

Around 1986, Gary Heidnik had a dream which turned into an obsession. He wanted to manufacture babies. What better way than to capture prostitutes and father his own family?

Josefina Rivera was patrolling her turf at the corner of Third and Gerard when a flashy new Caddy pulled up at the curb. A deal was struck — $20 for a good time. Josefina hopped inside. Gary drove home to the house at 3520 North Marshall St.

Up into the bedroom went the prostitute and the madman. They stripped and had sex. Immediately after, Gary placed both his hands around Josefina's neck and squeezed. Just as she was about to lose consciousness, he released his grip. Placing her hands behind her back, he handcuffed the helpless girl. Then he led his captive down the stairs into the dank, smelly cellar. Naked except for a flimsy shirt, Josefina shivered from the cold.

Gary led her to a five-inch thick pipe which ran across the top of the room. Using a clamp and chains, he secured her to the pipe and left. Josefina surveyed her surroundings. The cellar was lit by a lone bulb. An electric freezer stood at the far wall. The concrete floor of the cellar was cold. It was dark and foreboding.

When Gary returned with a sandwich, Josefina refused the kind offer. Gary didn't seem to mind. He busied himself extracting earth from a small hole in the concrete floor. In the days to follow, he extracted enough earth from under the concrete that a person could crawl down into the hole.

Gary explained to Josefina that he was now 43 years old and desperately wanted a large number of children. He planned to capture 10 women and get them all pregnant in the cellar. The children would live in the cellar as well. Gary's eyes lit up. "We'll be one big, happy family." Josefina shivered.

To initiate Josefina into the lifestyle she could expect in the cellar, Gary had her perform both oral and conventional sex. He then left her to her own thoughts. Josefina screamed. Gary returned and as punishment forced her down into the hole he had dug under the concrete floor. It was just big enough for him to place a board over the opening. Gary brought a radio down into the cellar and turned the volume up. Josefina could scream to her heart's content. No one could hear her.

Two days later, Gary brought another girl to his cellar. Sandy Lindsay had known Gary for about four years. This mildly-retarded woman had had sex with Gary before, but didn't comprehend what was happening to her. When she was chained nude to the pipe, she cried uncontrollably.

The two girls were given water and crackers. They ate while Gary enlarged his underground pit. Both girls were then forced to take part in Gary's particular brand of sexual gratification.

It was well-known that Sandy was acquainted with

Gary. When she didn't show up at her usual haunts, her sister, Teresa, called at 3520 North Marshall St. Gary didn't answer the door.

Down in the cellar, the two girls, existing on oatmeal crackers and bread, huddled together for warmth. Sometimes they were beaten, sometimes given treats, such as chicken. Daily, there was sexual activity.

November gave way to December. Just before Christmas, Gary picked up 19-year-old Lisa Thomas. She was introduced to the two scrawny, dirty girls in the cellar before being forced to perform sexually for her master.

Deborah Dudley was the fourth girl to be incarcerated in Gary's cellar. She, too, was initiated into the routine of sex and beatings. Sometimes, Gary had the girls beat each other with a board. If the wielder of the board didn't act with enough vigor, she herself would be beaten. Another punishment, instituted on a whim, was feeding the girls dog food if they misbehaved. If they refused to eat it, they were beaten. Eventually, each girl succumbed to the threats and ate the dog food.

On January 18, 1987, prostitute Jacqueline Askins, 18, joined Gary's harem, making a total of five prostitutes in the cellar. To celebrate the addition of his latest acquisition, Gary treated all five women to Chinese food.

Having endured months of deprivation, by early February Sandy Lindsay's health deteriorated. The more listless she became, the more beatings she suffered. Finally, living in dampness and without proper food, Sandy Lindsay died.

Sandy's death posed a problem for Gary. She was the only one of his captives who could be traced to him. In Gary's warped mind, the body had to be destroyed. He carried Sandy's body upstairs and dissected it with a chain saw.

Some body parts were placed in plastic bags and put in an upstairs refrigerator, while others were mixed with dog food in a food processor and fed to the remaining captives. Body parts which could not be processed were cooked, which caused a nauseating odor. Neighbors complained to police. An officer showed up at Gary's door, but was placated when Gary told him he had simply overcooked a roast. Satisfied, the officer went away.

On March 18, Gary forced Josefina to assist him in a new type of torture. Lisa, Jacqueline and Deborah were squeezed into the hole in the floor, while Josefina was told to fill the pit with water. Gary bared one end of an electric wire and placed it against the girls' chains. The resulting shock didn't torture Deborah; it killed her. Next day, Gary placed Deborah's body in his freezer, where it was to remain for four days.

On March 22, Gary, with Josefina's help, drove Deborah's body to an isolated spot in New Jersey, where it was dumped into a grove of trees. Next day, Gary picked up slave number six, Agnes Adams. She was unceremoniously initiated into the now well-established cellar routine.

Josefina Rivera realized that sooner or later she would become a murder victim of the strange man who controlled her every move. She decided to attempt to make a deal. She slowly talked Gary into letting her visit her family. Josefina had been in the cellar for four months and had gained a measure of Gary's confidence. He made a deal. If she didn't return, he would kill the remaining three girls.

In addition, he had her sign a letter confessing that she had been jointly responsible for the deaths of the two girls. If she informed on him, he would produce the letter. That night, Gary released Josefina with the strict understanding that she would meet him at a gas station at midnight. Once out of the Caddy, the terrified girl ran the four blocks to her boyfriend's apartment. After she hysterically convinced him that her horror story was true, the police were called. They, too, had to be convinced that the tale of kidnapping, rape, cannibalism and murder was authentic. Finally, they paid a visit to the cellar of horrors at 3520 North Marshall St.

Gary Heidnik was taken into custody, tried, convicted and sentenced to death. He is presently on Death Row at the Western Pennsylvania Correctional Institute in Pittsburgh.

FRENZY
OF FAITH

The hard-working folks, who farm the rich soil of southeast Pennsylvania, are steeped in superstition, passed down from generation to generation. To this day, you can see the faded hex symbols on the barns, placed there to ward off evil spirits and ensure abundant crops. Conversely, individuals have been known to put evil hexes on enemies to bring them bad luck or ill health.

Aurelius Angelino and Benjamino Evangelista, natives of Naples, Italy, emigrated to Pennsylvania and settled near York. Both men worked on the same railroad section gang and soon became obsessed with cults and hexes. They married and raised families.

Their paths abruptly parted when, in 1919, Angelino killed his two children during a fanatical religious ceremony. Confined to a mental institution, he escaped on three different occasions. His last escape, in 1923, was successful. Aurelius Angelino has not been seen since.

We can only assume that Benjamino, while living near York, was steeped in religious fanaticism and that he missed his dear old insane friend. In 1921, Benny, as he now called himself, took his family and kooky religious beliefs and moved to Detroit.

During the following years Benny, who was a building and repair contractor by profession, practised his own very special brand of religion. He called his outfit the Great Union Federation of America, which sounds more like a wheat board than a religion.

When he wasn't conducting services for his small group of fanatic followers, Benny busied himself writing *The Oldest History of the World Discovered by Occult Science* in Detroit, Michigan. As a sideline, he cured anyone who came to him with cash. It was in this medical area that Benny struck gold. On a good day, he cured about 50 people at $10 a pop.

Occasionally, someone would die, which in the healing business is considered an occupational hazard. In certain circles, friends and relatives of the victim have been known to kill the healer. However, Benny managed to dodge the bullet until July 3, 1929.

That was the day Vincent Elias called on Benny at his office/temple/home at 3587 St.Aubin Ave. Elias, a landlord, was calling on Benny concerning a repair job. No one answered his knock, so he gingerly opened the unlocked front door and made his way to Benny's office. He opened the office door and stepped inside. Elias was never to forget the sight which greeted him.

Benny was seated on a chair behind his desk. There was little doubt in Elias' mind that he was deader than a mackerel. You see, Benny's head was on the floor beside his body. Poor Elias didn't stay in the office long. In fact, he got out of there as fast as his feet could propel him and notified police.

Patrolmen Costage and Lawrence were dispatched to check out Elias' incoherent story. Once in Benny's office, they knew they weren't on any wild goose chase. There was Benny and his head, as well as a cheap reproduction of the Last Supper and an oversized crucifix hanging on the wall. On the floor were three photographs of a child in a coffin.

Bloody footprints led officers upstairs to the master bedroom. Mrs. Evangelista's body lay on the bed. She had almost been decapitated and one arm had been deeply cut at the shoulder, indicating that the killer had attempted to amputate her arm. Lying in the crook of her intact arm lay the body of her 18-month-old-son, Mario. He, too, had been mutilated.

Now realizing that they had entered a house of horrors, the two officers proceeded to a room directly across the hall. On twin beds lay the bodies of daughters Margaret, 6, and Jean, 4. Angelina, 8, lay on the floor. Her arm bore the same hideous mutilations as that of her mother.

While Benny's body had been fully clothed, the five bodies of his family were clad in nightclothes. One set of bloody footprints led from body to body, but these prints proved to be untraceable. A lone bloody thumbprint was found on the latch of the front door. It was never identified. No weapon was found at the scene of the Evangelista massacre.

I would be less than candid if I failed to point out that Benny was well known to the local police as a religious fanatic. He often conducted religious parades in which he gesticulated wildly and held up traffic. A few weeks before his untimely demise, Benny had requested permission from the city to hold an exhibition in his home.

Permission was denied, but after the six bodies were found, artifacts discovered in the house led police to believe that Benny had held his exhibition anyway. There was an altar in the basement. Hanging from the ceiling were papier-mâché figures of human beings, hideously malformed, trimmed with wigs and human hair. The figures moved at the slightest touch. In the basement window a sign proclaimed, Great Celestial Planet Exhibition.

Police were able to locate the craftsman who had made the figures. He had been paid $100 for his work, but knew nothing more. Benny had been the designer of the macabre display. An attempt was made to locate Benny's religious followers, but no one would admit to having belonged to his religious order. Police were successful in finding a few individuals who had called on Benny to cure assorted ailments. All proved to be superstitious souls who were innocent of any wrongdoing.

The weird photographs of the child in the coffin caused police all sorts of trouble. One theory which was thoroughly investigated was that the youngster's family had consulted Benny to cure their child. When things went wrong, they may have sought revenge. However, the boy in the coffin was never identified and this tangent of the investigation led nowhere.

Anyone who murdered and butchered six people had to be spattered with blood. Yet neighbors, who were sitting out that evening, as well as pedestrians who could be placed on the streets around the time of the murder, had seen no such person.

The murder of an entire family caused a sensation in Detroit. More than 3,000 mourners attended the funeral. It was revealed by the Evangelistas' parish priest that while Benny preached his own brand of religion, he secretly remained a regular communicant of the Roman Catholic Church, worshipping at St. Francesco's with his family.

Of course, police found out about Benny's old friend Angelino, who 10 years earlier had killed his two children in a religious frenzy. Try as they might, police could come up with nothing to link the two crimes. Was it a mere coincidence that two friends could have their families wiped out 10 years apart in crimes with religious connotations? We know who killed the Angelino children, but the Evangelista slaughter remains a mystery to this day.

THE
STEINBERG
AFFAIR

Certain crimes have held cities and nations in a state of siege. Who can forget Peter Sutcliffe, England's Yorkshire Ripper, who murdered prostitutes year after year, or Los Angeles' Hillside Stranglers Buono and Bianchi, whose torture killings held the City of Angels in a vice-like grip of fear?

Mass murderers and serial killers, by their ferocity and number of victims, boggle the imagination. It is a much rarer phenomenon when the death of one individual shocks an entire country.

The abuse and death of six-year-old Lisa Steinberg was such a case. Her fate riveted the nation's attention on the lifestyle of Joel Steinberg, Hedda Nussbaum, and 16-month-old Mitchell Steinberg.

Joel Steinberg had a privileged youth. The only son of a New York attorney, he was brought up in a garden apartment in Yonkers. Always a good student, Joel won a scholarship to Fordham University. After receiving a degree in political science, he pursued a law degree at New York University.

Law school proved to be Joel's first setback. He had trouble in his second year and was forced to drop out. With nothing better to do, he enlisted in the air force and served in Vietnam as an intelligence officer.

Back on civvie street in 1968, Joel again entered New York University to obtain his law degree. This time, he was successful, graduating in 1970.

Joel lived in an apartment on West 10th St. and was one of the thousands of smart young professionals sipping red wine in the Village each evening. He even bought a Great Dane to complete what some would call the "in" picture.

Joel's law practice consisted of dope peddlers and assorted hoods. He also specialized in illegal adoptions. While his ability as a lawyer has always been suspect, there is no question that he prospered. By the mid seventies he was a millionaire. His fees were astronomical. He often charged drug kingpins $200,000 for their defence. Adoptions brought $10,000 to $25,000 each.

To Joel Steinberg's way of thinking, he had everything — everything except a wife and children. But that would soon be remedied.

Hedda Nussbaum was born on August 8, 1942 in New York City. Her Polish immigrant parents were strict disciplinarians. Hedda grew up to be a shy, introverted girl with a deep sense of worthlessness. Despite this drawback, she was a bright student, who sailed through George Washington High School and later obtained a degree in English from Hunter College.

Hedda accepted a position as a Grade 3 teacher in Manhattan, but left the profession to take a job as editor of juvenile books at a division of Random House. She was well-liked by superiors and fellow employees. When she moved to her new position, she was a five-foot, five inch, 130-pound, attractive young woman.

Socially, Hedda didn't mix much with other members of Random House, nor did she have outside interests. Shy Hedda kept to herself.

Then she met Joel Steinberg.

Hedda had been coerced into attending a house party on Long Island. It was here she met bombastic, confident Joel. She was immediately overwhelmed by the attention he showered on her. No one had ever treated her in quite the same manner. His conversation was far different from that of the other young men she knew. Joel was on a first name basis with Mafia kingpins, notorious men whose exploits could be read in the newspapers each day. He was bright, articulate, and even of the same religious faith. Truly, Hedda figured God had smiled down upon her. At Random House she talked of little else but her Joel.

There was one thing. Joel insisted that Hedda improve herself. Psychiatric consultations might help. Then, there was her hair. At Joel's insistence, she changed hairstyles. Joel thought that, at 130 pounds, Hedda was a bit heavy. She went on a diet. By 1975, Joel and Hedda were talking marriage. In January 1976, she moved into Joel's apartment, number 3W at 14 West 10th St.

Once ensconced in the apartment, it seemed as if nothing Hedda did pleased Joel. One day, in a temper tantrum, he let her know that it was he who had improved her appearance, he who had brought her out of her shell. For two years, Hedda endured what amounted to psychological abuse. Then, in the winter of 1978, for the first time, Joel punched Hedda in the face. The force of the blow affected Hedda's eyesight. It was necessary for her to see a doctor. When she showed up at Random House with a black eye, she told co-workers she had been mugged.

A couple of weeks later, Hedda again showed up with bruises around her eyes. This time she told friends she had walked into a door. There followed a long string of inventive excuses for bruises to her body. She wasn't fooling anyone. Her colleagues knew she was abused. Summer and winter, Hedda wore sunglasses. Neighbors grew accustomed to her screams.

To ease her pain, Hedda tried cocaine. It wasn't hard to come by. After all, the drug was the stock in trade of Joel's clients. By 1980, Joel too was addicted to the drug. The pair often got high together. In fact, Joel became a freebase freak. When he was high, he punched out Hedda.

During the day, Hedda dragged her dissipated body down to Random House, where she immersed herself in her work. At night, she returned to her apartment and the living hell which she chose to endure.

In the winter of 1981, Hedda received such a heavy pounding from Joel that her spleen was ruptured. She crawled out of the apartment and hailed a cab to St. Vincent's Hospital, where her spleen was removed. Joel claimed he saved her life.

When a young unwed Catholic girl, Michele Launders, became pregnant, she was referred to an obstetrician who could take care of a discreet adoption. He knew a lawyer who would see the baby was placed with good parents. The lawyer was Joel Steinberg.

When the baby was born, all documents at the hospital were falsified, with the newborn's address given as c/o Joel Steinberg. Initially, Joel had no intention of keeping the baby. He had a couple who were willing to pay $50,000, no questions asked. When the prospective parents reneged on the deal, Joel presented Hedda with a brand new baby. She was an overnight mother. The child was never legally adopted.

Lisa, as the baby was called, was placed in a cradle in the living room. Hedda tried day care, but it didn't work out. Most days, she took baby Lisa to work at Random House, but finally her superiors told her it was too disruptive. More often than not, Hedda missed work. When she stayed away for two weeks without explanation, she was fired.

At 41 years of age, grey-haired Hedda Nussbaum looked 60. The beatings didn't stop. To vent his insane anger, Joel choked Hedda, burned her legs and stomped on her knees. She developed a permanent limp.

In 1986, when Lisa was five, Joel brought home another baby, Mitchell. To those who knew her, Lisa was a happy, pleasant child. In public, her father doted on her. Inside apartment 3W, Hedda, Lisa and Mitchell lived in squalor. The baby lay in urine soaked clothing all day. Bits of food lay scattered about the house. Joel had accumulated over

$1 million, but was constantly hounded by the superintendent for back rent.

In 1987, Lisa's condition deteriorated. She attended school in dirty clothing. A year earlier, she had been a punctual, attentive pupil. She now either came late or missed school altogether. Lisa wore long-sleeved shirts and heavy socks. She had to. Her arms were covered with bruises. Joel Steinberg was abusing Lisa as well as Hedda.

On November 2, 1987, Hedda Nussbaum called police. Her daughter, Lisa, had stopped breathing. Hedda opened the door to apartment 3W and let the police inside. The officers reeled at the stench of urine. It was cold. The wind whistled through a missing window. Rotting food lay around the apartment. Walls were blood spattered. Mitchell, 16 months old, played on the floor, tied to a playpen with a piece of rope. He sucked on a milk bottle filled with curdled milk.

Lisa, weighing only 43 pounds, was black and blue with bruises. She lay in Joel's arms, perfectly still. Paramedics detected a pulse and rushed her to St. Vincent's Hospital. Three days later, she died of her injuries.

Both Joel and Hedda were arrested and charged with the murder of their daughter. Charges against Hedda Nussbaum were dropped when it was ascertained that she was "so physically and mentally incapacitated on the night of the murder that she was not criminally responsible for Lisa's death."

Joel Steinberg was convicted of second degree manslaughter. He was sentenced to the maximum term of eight to 25 years in jail.

THEY SHOWED
NO MERCY

David Hollis, 15, thought Terry Losicco, 16, was one tough dude. The other boys at the Lincoln Hall School for Boys thought so too. Terry could handle his fists, was street smart and mean. No one in the institution messed with Terry Losicco.

Dave was a more timid boy. He needed someone with a reputation who would take his side in disputes. Terry was that someone.

The Lincoln Hall School for Boys is located in Westchester County, New York, about 55 miles from New York City. It is home to boys who are little more than truants, as well as those who are confirmed juvenile delinquents.

Dave's mother had gone through three divorces by the time her son was 14. He didn't know a father. To him, they were just men who lived with his mother for a while. Left alone during the day while his mother worked, he pilfered from stores.

Finally, Dave, who sprouted to a lean six feet, proved to be too much to handle. He was turned over to juvenile authorities, who shipped him off to Lincoln, where strict discipline and fresh country air were supposed to convert him into a law-abiding citizen.

Terry was one of a family of 13 children born into abject

poverty in New York City. One by one, the children were taken away from their parents by social workers and placed in agencies. Terry was shunted from foster home to foster home until, at the age of 10, he was adopted by business executive Anthony Losicco.

Terry's personality was set. He robbed, lied and cheated as naturally as he breathed. Often, he would disappear for weeks at a time. At age 13, he lived on the streets for a full year. It was while living alone that he graduated from pilfering to robbing homes. At the ripe old age of 15, he was hustled off to Lincoln, ostensibly to be turned into a useful member of society.

A year after he established himself as a tough dude at Lincoln, Terry erroneously learned from another boy, Gary Bouknight, that a house about a mile down the road was chock-full of gold chains, watches and cold, hard cash. In a few weeks, Terry was to be transferred to a halfway house in the city. It was only fitting that he start his new life with a stake.

On occasion, Gary chopped wood and did odd jobs for the folks who lived in the comfortable home down the road. He brought back stories to Terry. It seemed easy. The people in the house were so vulnerable — an old lady and her crippled husband. Terry knew he just had to rob that house. He looked over his companions for an accomplice, someone he could trust. He talked to several boys outlining his plan to rob the house during the night. Some agreed. Others turned him down. No one squealed to officials at the school.

Eleanor Prouty lived with her invalid husband, Normand, in the big house on Route 139, just across from Plum Brook Rd. At age 48, she had started working at the Reader's Digest, the most widely read magazine in the world, as editor of those bits of wit which appear at the end of most Digest articles. The job title sounds impressive, but in reality Eleanor was one of 12 staff members sifting through the three million entries sent each year to the magazine in quest of monetary rewards for jokes and anecdotes.

Eleanor had been forced to obtain employment when her husband developed multiple sclerosis and was confined to a wheelchair. She advanced rapidly in what till then had been a man's world. At age 63 she was at the top of the heap — Senior Editor. Two years of fulfilling her career dream ended all too quickly with compulsory retirement at age 65.

Terry woke up in the middle of the night. It was May 24, 1980. He jostled the boy who had promised to help him rob the house down the road. The boy, half-asleep, begged off. Terry then tried Dave Hollis, who quickly agreed to help his friend. The two boys dressed quietly, crawled out of their cottage and jogged the mile to the Prouty home. They tried all the doors, but found them locked. So were the windows. All except one. The boys removed a screen, opened the window and crawled in.

Terry carried a piece of firewood. They could hear snoring from upstairs. Dave was surprised. After all, Terry had assured him there would be no one at home.

The two boys made their way upstairs to a second-storey bedroom, where they observed an elderly man and woman sleeping in a double bed. Without a word, Terry brought the piece of firewood down on the man's head. Eleanor awoke with a start and screamed. The form lurking over her said, "I don't want to hurt you. I just want the money. My mother's in the hospital. We need the money."

Eleanor replied, "Come downstairs and I'll give you some money."

Eleanor arose from bed, extracted $10 from her husband's wallet and gave it to Dave Hollis. Terry led the terrified woman downstairs while Dave ransacked the bedroom. He found an additional $10 in a purse, as well as a gold wristwatch. Then he joined his companion.

The frightened woman realized she was in mortal danger. These boys would not be satisfied with a few dollars. Eleanor decided to make a break for it. She pulled herself from Terry's grip and ran to a light switch, turning it on and off as she screamed desperately for assistance.

Maybe, just maybe, some passing motorist would notice. No one did. Eleanor raced to the dining room and, after turning on more lights, picked up a cut glass vase and threw it at Terry. She missed.

Terry caught up to Eleanor, who at 65 was no match for the trim 170-pound youth. He threw Eleanor to the floor and hit her over and over with the stick of firewood. Then he kicked her.

Dave Hollis entered the room and was ordered by Terry to turn out the lights. He did as he was told. Terry then told him to search the rec. room for money. Dave ransacked the room for nonexistent riches. There was some thought of stealing one of the cars parked in the driveway. Terry even had the car keys in his hands, but Dave pointed out that a car parked near Lincoln would be a sure giveaway. Terry dropped the keys on the driveway. Just as they had run the mile to the Prouty home, they now jogged back to Lincoln. The boys arrived at the institution at about 4 a.m. and sneaked inside. They had been gone around two hours.

Next morning, Eleanor Prouty's badly beaten body was found on the floor of her home. Normand, his face horribly smashed, survived the attack, but thereafter could only speak with great difficulty.

The hunt was on for the intruders who had ended a life and disfigured a man already confined to a wheelchair. Next day, at his cottage at Lincoln, Terry bragged about the killing to his friends. Dave told some of his buddies how Terry had attacked the old couple with a stick of firewood. They were impressed.

A week passed. In a few days Terry would be transferred to a group home in the Bronx. Members of Lincoln's staff took him to McDonald's for hamburgers to celebrate the occasion. The great day arrived. Terry was moved to Camillus House in the city.

After spending a month there, Terry and another boy ran away. They spent their nights robbing houses in Queens and their days getting high on drugs in a park. Terry had a plan. He would accumulate money and dope.

Then he would stow away on a ship and get out of the country.

Meanwhile, unknown to Terry, the investigation into the murder of Eleanor Prouty had taken an unexpected turn. Gary Bouknight, the boy who had chopped wood and run errands for Eleanor, had called police with the startling revelation, "I know who killed the lady." Gary told police that Terry had boasted to him exactly how the murder had taken place. The same night he was told of the murder, Gary had written everything down in his diary. He turned the diary over to police and even gave them a photograph of the killer.

Dave Hollis was picked up without incident at Lincoln. He readily confessed. The other boys who were privy to guilty knowledge before and after the murder also told the police what they knew as soon as they were asked. Terry Losicco was traced to a friend's home in New York City. He had just changed clothes and was about to make his way to the docks to catch that boat which would take him far away from his troubles. He too confessed.

I have often described the trials of notorious murderers as being covered by the press of the world. Such cannot be said of the Losicco/Hollis trial. It was attended by few spectators. Only local reporters covered the proceedings.

Terry was found guilty of murder in the second degree and sentenced to not less that 25 years imprisonment. In addition, he was found guilty of assaulting Normand Prouty. For this crime, he was sentenced to not less that two and a half years imprisonment. In all, Terry was sentenced to a minimum of 27 1/2 years behind bars.

David Hollis was also found guilty of murder. He was sentenced to 20 years to life, with no possibility of parole until 20 years has been served.

Both boys entered prison at age 17. They are presently still serving their prison sentences.

WILLIE'S WIVES

William Bennison was a fine Irish lad who loved the ladies. He was religious, too.

We have to go back over 150 years to delve into Willie's private life, which abruptly became public when he broke the law. Willie was married to one Mary Mullen, but left Mary high and dry shortly after the honeymoon to seek his fortune in Edinburgh, Scotland.

Now, Willie was not one to be concerned with details. Without benefit of divorce, he married Jean Hamilton in December 1839. We will never know if it was conscience or not, but whatever the reason Willie returned to Ireland, fetched Mary and brought her back to Scotland. Things worked out swell for a while. Willie serviced both wives without either being the wiser.

Willie, who had acquired the Scottish propensity for thrift, obviously did not believe in expensive funerals. When Mary died, she was quietly buried in an unmarked grave in Airdrie. Later, Willie was suspected of hastening Mary's departure, but as there is no proof that he was responsible for this one, we won't dwell on it.

With the conventional singular wife, Willie settled into married life in Edinburgh. He obtained gainful employment at Shotts' Iron Co. and moved on up to a dismal tenement, a move made imperative by the birth of a daughter, Helen.

Let's describe Willie's abode. In total, Willie, Jean and Helen occupied two rooms and a closet on the ground floor. Underneath his flat, in the basement, lived Elizabeth Wilkie. Alexander Milne and his dog lived across the hall from Willie's menage. Soon after occupying the flat, Willie took in a roomer, Mrs. Moffat, which added considerably to the density of the flat.

For reasons known only to himself, Willie took to religion with a vengeance. He joined the local Wesleyan church and became a downright enthusiastic member of Rev. John Hays' flock. Willie was forever signing hymns and imploring the wretched heathen to see the light.

It was while being saturated with the true word at a prayer meeting that Willie met a young lass named Margaret Robertson. Middle-aged Willie looked at rosy-cheeked Margaret and discovered that the true word was not nearly as interesting as Margaret's physical attributes. Margaret was stacked.

Soon, naive, admiring Margaret was strolling home from prayer meetings with Willie. It wasn't long before they dispensed with the prayer meetings altogether and just strolled and whatever. You can imagine how tongues wagged. Religious Willie, in his own way, was a pillar of his neighborhood. Here he was, seen in public, big as life, with a girl young enough to be his daughter. Wife Jean was at home scrubbing the floor.

As if on cue, Jean took ill. Willie, never the soul of discretion, joined a funeral society, which isn't quite as suspicious as it first appears. Around the middle of the 19th century, poorer members of the community regularly joined funeral societies as the only way to assure themselves of a dignified funeral. Still, Willie's timing left a lot to be desired.

In February 1850, Willie dropped into William MacDonald's Apothecary and purchased arsenic from the pharmacist's wife. Mrs. MacDonald knew Willie and asked him why he wanted the poison. Willie replied that his wife had complained of rats. She had asked him to pick up the poison. Mrs. MacDonald accepted this explanation, as it was the most common reason given at the time for the purchase of poisons.

Unfortunately for Willie, his conversation with Mrs. MacDonald was the very first time anyone had ever mentioned rats in or around his flat. Neighbors later swore there were no rats in the building.

Just to make things pay, Willie joined a second funeral society. That's called chutzpah.

On Friday, April 12, Willie spent the evening with his wife, which was a bit unusual. Normally, he went out on the pretext of exercising, which may have been true enough in a way. He saw Margaret almost every night. That evening, according to Willie, his wife felt poorly and asked him for a bowl of porridge, which, at the time, was the equivalent of chicken soup.

Willie cooked and served the porridge to Jean. By Saturday morning, she was continually vomiting. Willie sought the advice of neighbors, Mr. and Mrs. Porteous. They suggested he call a doctor. Willie demurred, mumbling something about the unnecessary expense. That entire weekend, good neighbors dropped into Willie's digs. All agreed that Jean was gravely ill. By Sunday morning, someone suggested Helen Glass, Jean's sister, be notified. This was done and Helen tended to her sister from Sunday on.

One of the neighbors helped clean up the flat. In so doing, she noticed an old pot of porridge. She fed it to a neighbor's dog. The dog died the next day. When the canine met its untimely death, there were those who looked at Willie and, for the first time, suspected foul play.

As everyone knows, the murder business is not an exact science. Later, when an autopsy was performed on the dog, no arsenic was found. Perhaps the inconsiderate mutt had simply died at a most inopportune time.

Jean grew weaker. Finally, on Sunday, a Dr. Gillespie was summoned to her bedside. He prescribed a mustard poultice and a tablespoon of wine every half hour. Down at the chapel, Rev. Hays offered up prayers for the stricken member of his congregation.

On Monday at noon, Jean died. Willie said, 'Thank God, she has gone to glory.' Other than that colorful exclamation, Willie didn't mourn much. He was more concerned with a hasty funeral. Jean was buried that Wednesday.

Between the time Jean breathed her last and her funeral on Wednesday, Willie spent every free moment with Margaret Robertson. One has to wonder at Willie's bravado or, if you will, stupidity. The deceased's sister, Helen Glass, was furious. She insisted to one and all that something was drastically wrong. By the time of the funeral, Helen's suspicions had spread throughout the community. Willie was heartbroken to learn that he was suspected of hastening his wife's demise.

Helen succeeded in having Jean's body exhumed and a post-mortem performed. Willie was beside himself. That's when he acted out of desperation.

Willie called on MacDonald's Apothecary. He spoke to Mr. MacDonald, who knew nothing of his purchase of arsenic. Willie explained his position and asked MacDonald to deny that he had every purchased arsenic at his shop. MacDonald refused to co-operate. Willie shouted at the startled pharmacist, "They may find it, but I declare to God that I am innocent."

On Saturday, five days after her death, Jean's body was exhumed. Willie, tears in his eye's, identified the corpse. "It's my dear Jean," he said. Dear Jean was found to be chock-full of arsenic.

Willie was arrested and charged with his wife's murder. Neighbors swore that there were no rats in his residence. The connection between the accused and Margaret Robertson was aired. Willie's affinity for funeral societies was placed in evidence. The MacDonalds told their tale of the purchase of arsenic and the unsuccessful bid to fabricate an alibi.

Willie didn't have a chance. Protesting his innocence, he was found guilty after the jury deliberated only 20 minutes.

Willie continued to profess innocence while he awaited his date with death. However, as his execution date grew near, he confessed in detail, hoping against hope that if he told all, he might be spared. It didn't work. The home secretary rejected his appeal.

On August 26, 1850, Willie Bennison was hanged for the murder of his wife Jean.

KILLER
CHARLIE
MANSON

Can over 20 years have passed since that night of horror? That night when the rage within Charlie Manson's soul was unleashed inside the home of director Roman Polanski and his pregnant wife, movie actress Sharon Tate.

The time was ripe. It was the '60s. LSD guru Timothy Leary's turn-on, tune-in, drop-out chant excited a generation.

Acid. Peace. Love. Sex. Dope. Communes.

When small time thief and pseudo folk singer Charlie Manson was paroled from Terminal Island in San Pedro, Cal. in 1967, no one was aware that the 5-foot-2 misfit with the magnetic personality would commit crimes so horrible they are remembered over 20 years later.

There was Charlie, 32, free at last, after serving almost seven years in prison. It was the era of love and peace, peace and love; homeless girls wandering the country in search of a meaning to life. LSD helped. It was an era custom-made for Charlie Manson, his guitar and charismatic personality.

Gravitating to San Francisco, Charlie's inner circle of sub-culture followers grew in number. Mary Brunner, Lynette (Squeaky) Fromme and Patricia Krenwinkel became known as Charlie's girls. They slept, travelled, stole and begged together. They purchased an old bus and scoured the countryside. They were like family.

New recruits joined the Manson family. Susan Atkins, a 19-year-old hellion, came aboard. Robert Beausoleil, a 20-year-old actor, who sometimes lived with Gary Hinman, became a Manson follower. Diane Lake, 14, who was later renamed Snake because of her distinctive movements during intercourse, joined the family in their nomadic existence. Tex Watson was an avid Manson disciple. Later, Tex would prove to be a valuable and loyal member of the family.

Growth in the family was not derived solely from outsiders. Some of the girls became pregnant. Susan Atkins had a child. Mary Brunner gave birth to Charlie's baby.

In 1968, Charlie and his followers made their headquarters at the Spahn movie ranch, a dilapidated group of buildings near Los Angeles. The sect had evolved from love and peace to Satanism, hate and revenge. Charlie would send out groups of his followers to change the world, make it a better place in which to live.

In July 1969, Gary Hinman had a falling out with Charlie. Although Gary had always allowed members of Charlie's family to crash at his house, he was never a committed member of the sect. When Gary, who reputedly had money hidden in his house, steadfastly refused to devote himself to Charlie and his children, he signed his own death warrant.

Robert Beausoleil and a couple of the girls paid Hinman a visit. Gary wouldn't give them the time of day. Charlie showed up and, in a fit of rage, stabbed Hinman in the head with a sword, almost severing his ear. Then he left. Beausoleil and the girls bound Hinman with rope. When they phoned Charlie for instructions, they were told to kill their captive.

Hinman was stabbed twice in the chest and died on his living room floor from loss of blood. Charlie's girls wrote "Political Piggy" on the wall in Hinman's blood, after which they returned to the Spahn ranch and sang songs. Within two weeks, police had matched a fingerprint in Hinman's home to Robert Beausoleil. He was picked up and charged with murder.

On the night of August 8 and early morning of August 9, 1969, Charlie's followers went on a mission. They were well-equipped. Inside their vehicle they had placed a pair of bolt cutters and a quantity of nylon rope. Linda Kasabian, Susan Atkins and Patricia Krenwinkel jumped in. Tex Watson drove. Charlie instructed: "Leave a sign. You girls know what to do. Something witchy." On the way, Tex told the girls they were going to kill everyone in a house once owned by Doris Day's son, Terry Melcher.

Tex drove up to 10050 Cielo Drive, then leased by director Roman Polanski. Polanski was on a roll. His movies in the '60s included Repulsion and The Fearless Vampire Killers, as well as the runaway hit, Rosemary's Baby. On this night, he was in Europe.

His wife, actress Sharon Tate, 8 1/2 months pregnant, was at home entertaining friends: coffee heiress Abigail Folger, hairstylist Jay Sebring and Voityck Frykowski.

It was Steve Parent's misfortune to have picked that particular night to visit the Polanskis' caretaker, Bill Garretson, in a separate dwelling on the estate. Steve was in his car, just about to pull away, when he spotted Tex Watson.

According to later testimony, Steve said: "Hey, what are you doing here?" Tex thrust his .22-calibre revolver into the open driver's window. As Steve said: "Please don't hurt me," Tex pulled the trigger five times. He probably thought he had killed the caretaker. Inside his house, Bill Garretson heard nothing. He would not hear a sound the rest of the night.

Once inside Polanski's house, Tex accosted Frykowski. He shouted: "I'm the devil. I'm here to do the devil's business." The girls were instructed to secure Frykowski with nylon rope. Abigail Folger was found reading in bed in her room. Sharon Tate was lying in bed in another room. Jay Sebring, fully clothed, sat on the bed talking to

Sharon. All the occupants of the house were gathered together in the living room.

It was killing time. Jay Sebring was shot by Tex for suggesting that the gang should allow Sharon to sit down. After all, she was pregnant. While Sebring lay on the floor, unconscious, Tex kicked him in the head.

Abigail and Sharon were tied around the neck with nylon cord. One end of the cord was tossed over a beam. Susan Atkins pulled the rope taut. Abigail and Sharon had to stand straight up or strangle. Tex announced that they were all about to die. He ordered Susan to kill. She complied, stabbing Voityck Frykowski repeatedly. When Frykowski continued to struggle, Tex clubbed the wounded man with his gun and shot him. Frykowski made it outside before being killed on the lawn. Later, 51 separate stab wounds were found on his body.

Sharon and Abigail frantically struggled to free themselves. Abigail was successful. She ran to the back door. Patricia Krenwinkel stabbed at her wildly, but Abigail warded off the blows, her hands and arms now horribly cut. Tex spotted the melee. He ran over and cut Abigail's throat and abdomen.

Outside the house, Linda Kasabian stood watch. She observed Steve Parent's body in his vehicle. She saw Frykowski stagger out, screaming for help. It certainly was an action-filled night. Linda wondered how much money would be taken from such a nice home. Inside, the killing continued. Sharon Tate, unattended for a few moments, freed herself. She started toward her front door, but was seen by Patricia Krenwinkel. Patricia solicitously assisted Sharon to a chair. Then Susan Atkins held her, while Tex Watson stabbed her to death. The three members of Charlie's family took turns stabbing the body.

It was quiet. Tex decorated the bodies with nylon rope. Susan wrote the word "PIG" in blood on the door. Only 30 minutes had elapsed. It was so very quiet. Everyone was dead. Sharon's black kitten meowed forlornly amidst the silent bodies.

Charlie would be delighted. As they drove, the family

members changed out of their bloody clothing. Blood soaked garments and knives were tossed out of the car. Tex's revolver was thrown into a ravine.

Back at the Spahn ranch, the children of evil reported to Satan. He was pleased. They were tired. Everyone slept well.

Next morning, the scene of death was discovered. Horror swept Los Angeles. America — and ultimately the entire world — was made aware of the ritual-type massacre that had taken place in exclusive Benedict Canyon.

Charlie and his children were ecstatic at the publicity his crime was receiving. It had been a commendable job, but messy. That very night they would do it all again, but Satan himself would lead the way.

Linda Kasabian drove the '59 Ford to the home of grocery chain store owner Leno LaBianca, 44, at 3301 Waverly Dr. His wife, Rosemary, 38, was in bed when Charlie Manson appeared in the living room waving a sword at her husband. Charlie tied the LaBiancas standing up back to back.

Charlie walked out of the house. His family, waiting in the car, was ready for action. It was killing time again. Tex Watson, Leslie Van Houten and Patricia Krenwinkel were given their instructions. After the job was completed, they were to hitch-hike back to the ranch. Linda Kasabian and Charlie sped off.

The killing squad did their work efficiently. They led Rosemary into the bedroom, where they stabbed her to death. Leno was killed in the living room. Neither victim panicked until the very end. Tex carved the word WAR on Leno LaBianca's chest. Using the dead man's blood, they wrote DEATH TO PIGS on the walls. On the refrigerator door, Patricia wrote HELTER SKELTER. The killing squad then bathed and raided the fridge. Killing was hard work, but it was worth it. The LaBiancas' house was quiet. The family left.

Rosemary's children by a previous marriage called on the house of death and the second night of horror was made known to the world. The ritualistic aspects of the two killing sprees linked them forever. They became known as the Tate-LaBianca murders.

As the days turned into weeks without the killers being apprehended, famous movie actors such as Warren Beatty, Peter Sellers and Yul Brynner established a reward of $25,000 for the apprehension and conviction of the killers.

Weeks turned into months. The family kept busy. They stole gasoline and robbed indiscriminately. One man, Shorty Shea, 40, somehow found out details of the Tate-LaBianca killings. Charlie's clan, led by Steve Grogan, tortured, killed and buried Shorty in the desert.

By the end of September, members of the Manson family were being rounded up for minor crimes. Many were in and out of jail on various charges. Fingerprints recovered at murder scenes were checked against suspects. Snitches were placed in cells. A myriad of evidence pointed to the family as perpetrators of the Tate-LaBianca murders. Finally, the family's leader was taken into custody.

The world was shocked. These suspects were young girls from middle class American families. They likened their leader to Jesus Christ and displayed no remorse for what they had done. Tex Watson was a high school track star from Texas. Leslie Van Houten had been a small town high school princess. Yet these same young people had stabbed a pregnant woman and stuck a fork in the stomach of a man they had just killed.

Somewhere in the deep recesses of his mind, Charlie Manson believed that the blacks of the world would rise against the whites. He would be the catalyst, the trigger that would change the world. Instead, his madness was directly responsible for nine known deaths.

The Manson Family received various prison sentences for their part in the summer of horror. Their leader was sentenced to death on eight counts of first degree murder, but his sentence was commuted to life imprisonment during the short time when the state of California abolished capital punishment. Charlie Manson is still in prison.

Flower power is gone and the hippies with it.

But the children of the '60s will remember that terrifying summer night when evil triumphed over peace and love.

SUNDAY MORNING SLASHER

Good riddance to bad rubbish. Coral Eugene Watts had left their state and Michigan authorities breathed a sigh of relief.

The 28-year-old mechanic was lean, mean and street smart. Watts had been in and out of trouble all his adult life. Despite early escapades, he had managed to get through high school and enter Western Michigan University. It was during his freshman year that the body of Gloria Steele was found in Kalamazoo. She had been viciously attacked and stabbed 33 times. However, she had not been raped or sexually assaulted in any way.

Watts was a prime suspect as the result of an unprovoked attack on a girl, which had taken place only five days before the Steele slaying. The 22-year-old student, who had been choked into unconsciousness, identified Watts as her attacker.

Coral Watts knew all the angles. He voluntarily had himself committed to a mental institution, hired a good lawyer and refused to respond to police questioning concerning the murder of Gloria Steele.

In December 1975, Watts was found guilty of choking the co-ed and was sentenced to a year in jail. When he was released, authorities, who couldn't prove he was the slayer of Gloria Steele, realized they were releasing a mad dog killer. Yet there was little they could do other than keep him under cursory surveillance.

No one knew it at the time, but Coral Watts had developed a deep hatred for women — all women. The product of an abusive mother, Watts wasn't interested in sex. He never molested or raped his victims. In fact, there is some evidence that he carried away some personal object from his victims and later destroyed that object as a further symbol of his revenge.

Watts moved on to Detroit. On Halloween night, 1979, Mrs. Jeanne Clyne was stabbed to death in Detroit's exclusive Grosse Pointe area. Mrs. Clyne was walking home after keeping an appointment with her doctor. Watts was suspected of the slaying as he was seen jogging in the area around the time of the murder. However, there was no concrete evidence that he was the killer.

A few months later, a series of crimes, committed by an unknown assailant, erupted in Ann Arbor. The press dubbed the perpetrator the Sunday Morning Slasher. In April 1980, Shirley Small, 18, a University of Michigan student, was stabbed to death. Two months later, Glenda Richmond, 20, also a student, was killed in the same way. In August, the killer took a holiday but in September, Rebecca Huff was stabbed to death. All three women had been attacked between 3 and 5 a.m., giving rise to the name attached to the series of killings. They had not been raped or robbed of valuables. Coral Watts was living in Ann Arbor that summer and fall and was strongly suspected of committing the murders. Occasionally, he was picked up on minor traffic infractions, but was released each time.

Watts was well-aware that he was being kept under surveillance, but was clever enough never to commit a serious crime while being tailed. When he lost his mechanic job in Detroit, he decided to move to Houston. Michigan authorities informed Houston that a strongly suspected psychopathic serial killer was headed their way. For a while Houston police kept a strict watch on Watts' activities, but tight surveillance can't last forever. As soon as they relaxed their surveillance, a rash of murders similar to those committed by the Sunday Morning Slasher took place in Houston and surrounding cities. The attacker generally struck on Sundays.

Mrs. Edith Anna Ledet was a fourth-year medical student at the University of Texas' medical school in Galveston. She was stabbed to death on March 27, 1981 as she jogged near the university campus.

Elizabeth Montgomery, 25, was walking her dog when she was stabbed in the chest. She stumbled to her nearby apartment before dying. Two hours later, Susan Marie Wolfe, 21, was opening the door of her apartment when she was fatally stabbed six times in the chest.

On January 4, 1982, Phyllis Tamm, 27, was found hanging from a tree near the Rice University campus. When Margaret Fossi failed to return home, police were called. They pried open the trunk of the missing woman's car and discovered her body stuffed inside. She had been manually strangled and had died of asphyxia.

The string of killings continued. On Sunday, February 7, 21-year-old Elena Semander, a University of Houston student, was found strangled to death in a garbage bin. In March, 14-year-old Emily La Qua was reported missing from the town of Brookshire, located about 40 miles north of Houston.

The following month, Carrie Jefferson, 34, disappeared. On the same day that Carrie disappeared, Suzanne Searles, 25, left a party and vanished. The contents of her purse were found on the floor and seat of her car. At 6 a.m. of April 16, Yolanda Degrasie was stabbed six times. She died on the sidewalk near her home.

In the path of destruction left by the killer, only one concrete piece of evidence was left behind. A bloody sweatshirt was found near Mrs. Ledet's body. Since the killer didn't rape his victims, there were no hairs to compare, no sperm to analyze. Despite the best attempts of the police to apprehend the killer, their big break in the case did not come from investigative efforts.

On May 23, a police car was dispatched to an apartment shared by two young women, Lori Lister and Melinda Aquilar. As the car pulled up to the apartment building, officers observed a man racing down the front stairs. They gave chase. When the desperate man raced down a blind alley, he was taken into custody. The man was Coral Watts.

Back at the apartment building, police discovered neighbors attempting to revive Lori Lister. The 25-year-old girl had been found in a half-filled bathtub. She told of being choked into unconsciousness in her parking lot. Her assailant left her there, took her key and walked into her apartment, where Melinda was asleep. The terrified woman was choked and bound with a coat hanger and belt. The man went out to the parking lot, dragged Lori inside and continued to beat her. He then dropped her into the tub and half-filled it with water.

Meanwhile, Melinda had run outside, stumbled over a railing and ran screaming for her life. It was her screams which alerted a neighbor to call police. Unbelievably, that same Sunday morning, another woman had been strangled to death and placed in her bathtub.

Watts was put under a psychiatric microscope. He was found to have a total abhorrence of women, believing them to be evil, hateful creatures who deserved punishment. Despite the certainty that Watts was a serial killer, the only proof police had was evidence concerning the attacks on Lori Lister and Melinda Aquilar.

Once again, displaying the cunning of a cornered animal, Watts had his lawyers plea-bargain. He would plead guilty to the attacks on the latest two women and accept a 60-year prison sentence in return for a guarantee that he would not be prosecuted for any of the murders. In addition, Watts would lead detectives to gravesites of the girls whose bodies had never been found.

Authorities were in a quandary. It was possible that they would not obtain a murder conviction against Watts if they prosecuted him for any of the murders. Even if they did get a conviction, there was no reason to believe he would receive the death penalty. Then there were the relatives of the missing girls to consider. They wanted to know the fates of their loved ones.

A deal was struck. Watts' attorneys agreed to a 60-year sentence. In return, Watts confessed to the murders briefly outlined here.

In addition, Watts admitted to the attempted murder of another girl, a cocktail waitress. An innocent man was serving a life sentence for this crime, which was reopened. As a result, the man in prison was exonerated and released.

In relating his recital of death, Watts also cleared up a case which had been regarded as an accidental death. Linda Tilley was believed to have tripped over a garden hose on September 5, 1981 and to have fallen into her swimming pool. Watts told how he had attacked the woman. When they both fell into the pool, he held her face under water until she drowned.

Watts led authorities to the bodies of Suzanne Searles, Carrie Jefferson and Emily La Qua.

So hated was Coral Watts that when he appeared in a Houston courtroom, trained dogs had to be used to sniff out bombs which police suspected might have been planted in the courtroom. Spectators were searched before gaining admittance to hear Watts being sentenced.

Coral Watts will be eligible for parole on September 3, 2002, after he has served 20 years in prison.

MUNCHAUSEN'S SYNDROME

There was nothing unusual about Priscilla and Steve Phillips. They met in university and married after Steve completed his stint in Vietnam. By 1974, they had two young sons, Eric and Jason. Steve had a good position with the Department of Vocational Rehabilitation in Oakland. When Priscilla had a hysterectomy, they decided to adopt a little girl.

At the time, there was a great deal of publicity concerning the children of American servicemen and deserted Vietnamese women. It appeared to the Phillips that their chances of adopting one of these children would be far greater than of adopting an American child. They applied through several agencies and were delighted when they were informed that a six-month-old Korean infant girl was available to them.

Little dark-eyed Tia was an immediate hit with the Phillips family. She was christened Tia Michelle Phillips. Tia received a medical examination as part of the adoption procedure. Other than a severe rash, she was a healthy, normal infant.

Almost from the time Priscilla Phillips had her new daughter at home, medical complications developed. There was an irritating ear infection which cleared up, but always came back. A urinary tract infection proved to be more serious, as were the child's persistent bouts of diarrhea.

Priscilla brought Tia to the clinic at San Raphael's Kaiser Hospital. Dr. Evelyn Callas assured Priscilla that there didn't appear to be anything seriously wrong with Tia. They would keep her for a few days for testing. The doctor also informed Priscilla that it was a general policy of the hospital to have mothers take as much interest as possible in their child's care while the patient was confined to the institution. Mothers often helped out by giving infants their bottles and that sort of thing. Priscilla was pleased being allowed to pitch in.

Tia never did improve. For four straight months she stayed in hospital. Priscilla got to know the staff well. They had difficulty recalling a more loving parent than Priscilla Phillips.

Tia continued to have diarrhea, so that dehydration was a threat which constantly had to be combated. When she wasn't suffering from diarrhea, Tia vomited, had cramps and often developed a fever. She became lethargic and stared into space for long periods of time.

Various theories were put forward as to what was causing the child's illness. Irritation of the intestinal lining was considered. In order for the infection to heal, Tia was fed intravenously. On April 1, 1975, she was transferred to the Kaiser facility in San Francisco, where she could receive better care. Priscilla rode with her daughter in the ambulance. Once there, Tia improved to the point that Priscilla requested she be returned to San Raphael. Her request was granted.

At San Raphael, Tia's diarrhea returned. Her weight dropped until she was an emaciated 13 pounds. Tests were continually being conducted to find the cause of Tia's illness, but nothing seemed to get to the root of her problem.

Central venous hyperalimentation was attempted — a catheter was inserted surgically into a vein leading directly to the heart. During the night, Priscilla, who often slept beside her daughter, excitedly reported that the child had pulled the tube out. The catheter was replaced.

Tia was transferred to San Francisco for a second time. She improved dramatically. Slowly, she took on weight until she reached an all time high of 17 1/2 lbs. Doctors now had her on solids, such as banana and rice cereal. On July 28, Tia was released from the hospital after spending five long months in institutions. The Phillips' long ordeal appeared to be over. Their little girl, who had been through so much, was on the mend. They would have her home forever.

Priscilla took Tia back for her first post hospital checkup. The little girl was now 15 months old and attempting to walk. While her illness had never been diagnosed, everyone was extremely pleased at her improvement.

Without warning, it happened. Priscilla rushed Tia to hospital. She was suffering from diarrhea and vomiting. She had lost two pounds overnight, was lethargic and stared straight ahead. Tia was in shock. Every conceivable test and emergency procedure was used to save her. The most puzzling of all test results was an excessively high sodium level.

For no apparent reason, the child rallied. Experts across the country were consulted. More tests were conducted, more theories explored. Little Tia underwent exploratory surgery in search of a tumor. Nothing was found. She recovered from surgery and the Phillips were thankful for that.

By now, Priscilla was well-known around the hospital and was on a first-name basis with doctors and nurses. They told her that Tia might never be really well. Eventually, Tia was released from hospital.

Three weeks passed without incident. Tia's progress was so encouraging there was talk that she might grow out of her delicate condition. However, such was not to be the case.

In the middle of the night, Tia had an attack of diarrhea and vomiting. Priscilla rushed her to hospital, where doctors frantically worked over her. It was no use. The little girl's heart stopped beating.

Shortly after Tia's funeral, the Phillips decided to adopt another child. A year later, Priscilla and Steve became the proud parents of their second adopted Korean child. Mindy Phillips was sickly right from the beginning. At 13 months, she was diagnosed as having congenital cytomegalovirus and intermittent cyanosis. Since her first birthday, she had been hospitalized several times with chronic diarrhea. Various treatments were attempted, but nothing seemed to help.

Because her sister Tia's case had been so unusual and because many of the same doctors and nurses had tended Tia, all felt very close to Mindy and her mother, Priscilla. It was common knowledge that Tia and Mindy were not natural sisters. This was deemed important because it ruled out the hereditary factor.

Doctors took pains to explain to Priscilla exactly which procedures they were following to find the root cause of Mindy's condition. Priscilla insisted on being informed of every detail. As with Tia, she was totally involved with Mindy's illness.

The doctors were puzzled. What was causing the diarrhea? No matter what they put into Mindy and no matter what method they used, the state of her gastrointestinal tract did not reflect her diet. Could an evasive parasite which did not show upon tests be the culprit? It was worth a try. More tests. More remedies. As before, nothing helped.

Throughout the child's ordeal, Priscilla was constantly at her side. She helped hold the child and stroked her straight black hair. She slept beside her baby. The hospital staff's hearts went out to the mother who so obviously loved her adopted daughter.

The first break in the cause of the vomiting and continual diarrhea occurred when a doctor ordered a stool sodium list. The doctor knew the child's intake had been 14 milliequivalents of sodium, which should have equalled the test results of the stool. Mindy's stool sodium level had reached an incredible 251 milliequivalents.

The doctor did all the necessary checks. There were no defective products given to the child. The only non staff member with access to her had been her mother. The shadow of little Tia's death now loomed large. Why had no one thought of the mother before? But why should anyone think of Priscilla, worn to a frazzle because of her sick children? Doctors seek cures; they don't play detective with patients. Their aim is to make sick patients well.

The doctor's suspicions were related to the head of pediatrics, Dr. Evelyn Callas. She had recently read about Munchausen's Syndrome, a hideous malady which manifests itself in individuals seeking to be the centre of attention. They arrive at emergency wards complaining of excruciating pains, complete with fictional medical histories. They long to be hospitalized. Some have studied the symptoms of serious illnesses and, as a result, undergo unnecessary operations. Many hospitals in the U.S. keep names and photos of these people in the emergency room so that they may be spotted before taking up valuable time and hospital space.

Could Priscilla Phillips be suffering from Munchausen's Syndrome by proxy? Could she be seeking attention for herself by introducing salt into her daughter's diet? It seemed the only answer. All tests indicated that Mindy was receiving large quantities of sodium from an external source.

Dr. Callas met with the Phillips. They were told that Priscilla would be allowed to see Mindy under supervised conditions for only five minutes per hour. The child was watched constantly and given nourishment by staff only. The improvement in her condition was dramatic. As soon as Priscilla was cut off from Mindy, the child's condition improved rapidly. Dr. Callas called in the police. Mindy recovered and was placed in a foster home until the investigation into Tia's death was concluded.

After a thorough investigation, Priscilla Phillips was charged with the murder of Tia Phillips and the attempted murder of Mindy Phillips.

On March 19, 1979, Priscilla stood trial for murder and attempted murder in Marin County Superior Court. After a two-month trial, the jury deliberated for two days. They found Priscilla guilty of murder in the second degree in the death of Tia and guilty of endangering the life of Mindy. She was sentenced to five years to life for murder and two years imprisonment for endangering life, the sentences to run concurrently.

Priscilla was released on bail, appealed and lost. She was returned to prison to serve out her sentence.

THE KILLER
WROTE
LETTERS

Strange as it may sound, many murderers have an uncontrollable urge to stay close to the investigation into their crimes. Some have been known to phone and even write the police.

Before the turn of the century, Jack the Ripper wrote taunting letters to the authorities, advising them that he would strike again. In more recent times, Richard Loeb became totally fascinated with detectives who were searching for clues into the murder of Bobby Franks in Chicago's infamous "compulsion" case. Loeb turned out to be one of the youngster's killers.

Today we will look at the tragic death of a young English girl, Sarah Gibson, and her murderer's urge to correspond with the police.

Sarah was born into the horse racing set. Her father, Col. John Gibson, was a famous trainer and breeder of race horses. One of her brothers was an accomplished rider. The family lived in the village of Lambourn in Berkshire, England. They led the good life, but Sarah wanted something different. Horses and the pleasant social life of the village didn't satisfy her.

At 19, Sarah told her mother and father that she wanted a career in the hotel business and planned on achieving success without their influence. Sarah left the genteel life of Lambourn to strike out on her own in London. Her first job was that of a domestic at the Norfolk Hotel in the West End.

A few months later, Sarah was successful in obtaining employment with the Royal Automobile Club as assistant housekeeper. This was a giant step forward in Sarah's dogged determination to carve out a career for herself.

The Royal Automobile Club had a staff of 250 employees, of which 15 lived on the premises. Sarah was one of the huge club's live-in employees. The prestigious club had a 200 seat restaurant, 15,000 paid members and maintained 80 bedrooms for male guests only.

In 1971, the Gibson family moved from Lambourn to a beautiful restored farmhouse near Cheltenham. Sarah spent many weekends with her family. She was happy in her work and enjoyed living in London.

On Sunday, July 2, 1972, Sarah had the day off. It was one of those weekends she chose to stay in the city. That evening, Sarah had dinner in the staff dining room. A little after 7:30 p.m., she was seen strolling over to the Fun City Bingo Hall, located about 300 yards from the club. Two hours later, she was seen leaving the bingo hall, but no one saw her return to her room.

Next morning, a housemaid looked in on Room 519 on the fifth floor and found Sarah's nude body on her bed. Her hands and feet were tied. A pink nightgown was knotted around her neck and a handkerchief had been stuffed in her mouth. She had been raped.

Detectives didn't take long to ascertain that Sarah didn't have a steady boyfriend. She had been a hard-working, happy young woman who enjoyed the sights of London. Her movements were traced up until she left the bingo hall, but there the trail abruptly stopped. Because nothing seemed to be disturbed in the room, it was felt that Sarah might have known her killer and had been attacked without warning.

When a list of Sarah's possessions was compiled, it was learned that several pieces of jewelry were missing. Gold earrings, a travelling clock, a silver locket, a gold charm bracelet and mother-of-pearl cigarette lighter had been taken from the room. On July 7, the bracelet and lighter were sold to a Soho jeweller.

Scotland Yard detective, Chief Superintendent James Neville believed that robbery might have been the motive with rape and murder an afterthought. On the other hand, he knew it was quite possible that a cunning killer could have taken the jewelry from the room to throw the police off the trail.

Of the 80 bedrooms available to males at the club, only 17 had been occupied on the night of the murder. It was decided to check the fingerprints of not only the occupants of these 17, but those of everyone who had stayed at the Royal Automobile Club since Sarah joined the staff. Their prints would be checked against prints found in Sarah's room.

On July 9, Superintendent Neville received a surprise in the mail. It was an unsigned letter from the killer. It read: "I thought you might like some help in the case as it seems you are approaching it from the wrong angle. I did not like the idea of Sarah's departure but it couldn't be helped, but what can be done is to stop it happening again. I found a strange sense of power in depriving a body of life, though Sarah was a mistake.

"On the night Sarah died I felt no sense of remorse or guilt so hurry up and catch me. I won't give myself up for incarceration because that would destroy me as I have a great longing for life."

Had this letter not been written, it is doubtful if the killer of Sarah Gibson would ever have been identified. Fingerprints on the letter were checked with prints on file with Scotland Yard. The prints matched those of 25-year-old David Charles Richard Frooms, a ne'er-do-well who had served several terms in prison for theft, robbery and indecently assaulting a 13-year-old girl.

Frooms was located and taken into custody. He was asked to write a few words on paper. Handwriting experts compared these words to the handwriting on the letter sent to Superintendent Neville. There was no doubt about it — both had been written by Frooms.

When confronted by this overwhelming evidence, Frooms blurted out, "I am glad you have got me. I killed her, strangled her with something she was wearing."

When asked if he had had sexual intercourse with his victim, he replied, "She was dead then."

In December 1972, Frooms was tried for murder in London's famed Old Bailey. He pleaded not guilty, claiming he had no recollection of the killing itself, although he remembered climbing through an open window and making his way up to the fifth floor looking for something to steal. He saw a bedroom door ajar and walked quietly into the room. Sarah was asleep on the bed. He took whatever appeared to be valuable.

When Sarah stirred, he stuffed something in her mouth and tied her hands and feet with her underclothing. He claimed to remember having his hands around her throat, but nothing more. He further claimed that he had no recollection of intending or wanting to kill the girl. In addition, he had no memory of having written the incriminating letter to police.

Despite his lawyer's insinuation of diminished responsibility, it took the English jury only half an hour to bring in a guilty verdict. David Frooms was sentenced to life imprisonment.

GUYS
AND DOLLS

The good citizens of Venice were shocked out of their gondolas when, on December 2, 1982, they observed a trunk floating in with the tide. The trunk was lugged to a flight of stairs and pulled out of the water. The curious were rewarded by the sight of sheets of blue plastic, two large dolls and the body of a woman dressed only in baby doll pajamas.

I would like to report that police responded by quickly driving to the scene, but this is Venice. They made it as fast as they could by police launch. Several packages of nails had been placed inside the trunk to weigh it down. They had obviously not been heavy enough.

The medical examiner stated that the woman had been strangled. Detectives theorized that the killer was not domiciled in the city. Every citizen of Venice knew that anything thrown in the lagoon would wash in and out with the tide for days. From the condition of the body, it was ascertained that it had been placed in the water on the same day it was recovered from the canal.

The nails were of a common variety sold all over Italy and proved to be untraceable. The two dolls posed a puzzle; never before had anyone heard of packing dolls with a corpse. They were expensive dolls in mint condition. The blue plastic, which had been used to wrap the body, was traced to the small resort town of Vipiteno, located about 125 miles north of Venice.

Detectives checked with Vipiteno police to see if any woman matching the description of the body in the trunk had been reported missing. Sure enough, Emma Giraldo had vanished on December 1. Emma was a 36-year-old waitress, who lived in a room above the Alta Post Tavern, where she was employed. When she didn't show up for her shift, the tavern owner entered her room, found all her clothing intact and her room undisturbed. Since it wasn't like Emma to miss work, he immediately reported her absence to police. Fingerprints taken from the corpse matched those of Emma Giraldo.

A thorough examination of the body revealed that Emma had been strangled with something soft, possibly a towel or scarf. She had been hit over the head and had been unconscious when she was strangled. There were no marks on her fingernails or hands, indicating that she had not had an opportunity to defend herself.

That's where matters stood. Police knew a great deal about Emma Giraldo, except where she had been killed. Had the murder taken place in Vipiteno or Venice?

Emma's last known movements were traced. She had completed her shift at the tavern at 7 p.m. on November 30 and had not been seen since. Vipiteno is a small town of 5,000 inhabitants, located high in the Alps. Surely, any unusual activity would have been noticed by someone. Since the town was ill-equipped to handle a murder case, Venice detectives were dispatched to the resort area to continue their investigation.

More was learned about the dead woman. Emma was the daughter of a successful businessman. Her parents had opposed her choice of a husband, causing a deep rift between her and her parents. Emma's marriage hadn't lasted. Since her marriage break-up six years previously, she had been a hard-working, conscientious waitress at the Alta Post, where she had been treated like a member of the tavern owner's family.

Emma had loved dolls and had longed to live in Venice. The two dolls found in the trunk were her favorites from a small collection she kept in her room. She had often expressed her desire to live and die in beautiful Venice. Emma was so well-liked by the tavern owner and the tavern's patrons that they collected the necessary funds to bury her in Venice. In death, Emma received one of her lifelong wishes.

Venetian police located several witnesses who recalled seeing a man pulling a large wooden cart through the streets. The cart had held a trunk. Lugging his load was no easy task, as the streets of Venice are joined by bridges, most of which are reached by flights of stairs. The man had been conspicuous in his attempts to move the cart up the stairs. Two or three citizens had assisted him and remembered the incident well.

Police figured the murderer may have carted the body out to the last landing in the island, believing that the trunk would be carried out to sea. Following their hunch, they searched the area around the last landing. Using grappling hooks, police recovered a roughly-made wooden cart. The cart didn't reveal any important clues other than to fortify the police theory that the trunk had been carted through the streets of Venice. The murderer most probably dumped the trunk at the furthest point in the island and did the same thing with the cart. No one would have been the wiser had the trunk sunk.

Emma's former husband, Luciano Muti, was strongly suspected once police found out that he was a part-time pimp with a long criminal record of petty crimes. He could have struck Emma over the head in her room and strangled her while she was unconscious. If he had waited until the wee hours of the morning, he could have transported the body to Venice in Emma's Renault without being seen.

The theory was great, except Muti proved without a doubt that he had been elsewhere at the crucial hours when the murder and the disposal of the body had taken place.

Dogged police work uncovered Emma's secret lover — a 45-year-old pizza maker, Roberto Festinese. Roberto confessed as soon as police appeared on the scene. He proved to be an unhappily married man with two children, who lived in the nearby town of Wiesen. He had been secretly meeting Emma in her room above the tavern for the past four years.

Roberto claimed that he had joined Emma on the night of her death. She had been drinking and had uncharacteristically attacked him, scratching at his eyes. Instinctively, he had picked up a heavy glass ashtray and had thrown it at her. The ashtray had struck Emma, knocking her unconscious. Terrified, Roberto had taken a scarf and strangled her. Knowing of her love of dolls, he had placed two of her favorites in the trunk. Sentimental Roberto decided that Emma's beloved Venice should be her last resting place.

It was a great story. Police even believed the part about the dolls and transportation of the body to Venice. Roberto couldn't explain the homemade cart, constructed in advance, or the trunk so conveniently available for use at a moment's notice; nor could he explain why he had purchased sheets of blue plastic two days before the murder.

On May 4, 1984, Roberto Festinese was found guilty of murder and sentenced to 15 years imprisonment.

THE DENTIST LIED

It is difficult to apprehend a murderer when no crime is known to have been committed.

Grace Hunt hailed from a well-known California family. When she met and married Patrick Grogan in 1909, her happiness seemed assured. After all, Pat Grogan had made a fortune in the olive trade and was a bona fide millionaire. Grace and Pat had one son, Charles.

As the years drifted by, Grace and her husband agreed to disagree. When Charles was 10, she and Patrick were divorced. The divorce was a civilized affair. Grace was given custody of Charles and a cool half million dollars to soothe any hurts and to keep the wolf from the door.

There were wolves of a far different kind at Grace's door. She was an attractive young woman with oodles of cash, just waiting for the right swain to come a-calling.

Two years later, when Patrick died, leaving the balance of his estate to his son, with Grace sole administratrix, she became an extremely attractive catch indeed. After Patrick had been duly planted, Grace became a regular in Los Angeles' social circles. Many a young stud with one eye on Grace's figure and the other on the figures in her bank book courted the widow with a vengeance. One such suitor emerged with the prize.

Dr. Thomas Young was a newly turned out dentist who had decided to establish his practice among the socially prominent of Los Angeles. He homed in on Grace like the lead hound pursuing the fox. Initially, Grace rejected the dentist, but eventually his persistence paid off.

In the winter of 1923, Grace became Mrs. Thomas Young. For two years, Dr. Young's practice flourished, as did his marriage to Grace. The attractive couple were seen in the best restaurants and were asked to the most prestigious parties. The Youngs were definitely leading the good life in Lotus Land.

And then it happened. On February 22, 1925, Dr. Young contacted Los Angeles police, informing them that his wife Grace had disappeared. The dentist told his story.

Twenty-four hours earlier, he and Grace had left their Beverley Glen cottage for dinner in Venice. They had a few drinks, enjoyed dinner and were about to leave the restaurant when they happened to bump into a woman he knew. It was nothing more than a chance meeting, but afterwards Grace flew into a jealous rage. According to Young, this was not an isolated incident. Grace was insanely jealous. Embarrassed, he hustled his wife out to their car.

While driving back to Los Angeles, Grace was beside herself with rage. During the trip, she took a swing at her husband and broke his glasses. Eventually, she quieted down and even apologized for causing a scene. The Youngs made up and decided to drop into Los Angeles' Hotel Biltmore to dance and have a few drinks.

Grace excused herself in the lobby of the hotel and made her way to the powder room. As far as her husband knew, no one had seen her since that moment. Dr. Young added that Grace was carrying $150,000 in negotiable securities and all her jewelry. In total, Grace was lugging around a quarter of a million dollars on her person. Young's statement begged the question — why would a woman carry a fortune in her purse? Dr. Young told police he thought his wife may have been afraid that their cottage in Beverley Glen was susceptible to being burglarized.

The unusual disappearance made front page headlines. It's not often that a socially prominent woman disappears carrying a fortune in her purse.

A few weeks after the disappearance, Grace's friends began to receive letters, apparently in Grace's handwriting. The letters were postmarked from towns and cities within 500 miles of Los Angeles. In these letters, Grace informed friends that she was tired of the incessant arguments with her husband. She planned to get away from it all for a while in Europe.

It all seemed so perfect, except for one thing. Anyone who knew Grace realized that she would write or contact her son, Charles, if she were leaving her home for any prolonged period of time. Grace's father, Earl R. Hunt, was not satisfied with the way the investigation was being conducted. He hired the famed Burns Detective Agency to find out what had happened to his daughter. Dr. Young hired another detective agency to locate his wife. In all, there were now three different organizations searching for Grace Young.

Months passed. The investigation wound down. Dr. Young and Charles spent a lot of time together at their cottage. Gradually, Young started to live a normal life again. He even threw a few parties for friends.

Early that summer, the Burns Detective Agency came up with the disconcerting information that Dr. Young's secretary had been seen wearing one of Grace's rings. When questioned, the secretary said Young had showed up at work one day with the ring. She had worn it for a day or so and had returned it to him. For the first time, it was discovered that Dr. Young had lied. He had told police that his wife had taken all her jewelry with her. The Burns boys shared their information with the authorities.

A meeting was held. It was decided that the various organizations conducting inquiries into Grace Young's disappearance share their information. It seems everyone had found out something which incriminated Dr. Young.

Since his mother's disappearance, Charles Grogan had changed his will, which had previously left everything to his mother. His new will made his stepfather sole beneficiary.

Witnesses were located who swore Grace had been carrying a tiny purse on the night she disappeared. It could not possibly have held all her jewelry as well as negotiable securities. The Burns Agency had unearthed the hitherto unknown fact that Young had been married twice before.

Police were successful in obtaining a search warrant to go over the Beverley Glen cottage during Young's absence. They found a three-carat diamond ring.

Dr. Young was questioned. When he was shown the ring, he was as cool as a cucumber, claiming that Grace often placed various pieces of her jewelry in the side pockets of their automobile. He had found the ring in the car and had placed it with his personal papers in the cottage. Dr. Young apologized for not informing police that he had found the ring.

Everyone concerned was now sure that Young was lying, but they had absolutely no proof that he had committed any crime. In fact, they had no positive proof that any crime had been committed at all.

On June 14, 1925, Young was brought to police headquarters for another round of questioning. Worn to a frazzle by the constant harassment, he broke down and revealed what had happened to Grace. He blurted out that she had accidentally struck her head and had fallen into a cistern at their cottage.

Police rushed out to the cottage. In the cistern, under a thin layer of concrete, they uncovered the body of Grace Young. A piece of rubber tubing was in her mouth. Dr. Young changed his story. He now told police that after an argument in the hotel, he had taken his wife to his office, where he had given her enough Scotch to render her unconscious. He then drove to the cottage and put her to bed. He administered a gas called sommonoform (used by dentists during that era) through a rubber tube until

Grace was dead. Then he threw her body into the cistern.

The very next day, he had Charles mix the cement which was to cover Grace's body. Young told police, "I had covered the body with newspapers and I thought it would be a great joke on the boy to have him unknowingly cover his mother's body with cement."

Dr. Young went on to state that he had killed Grace to get rid of her and obtain her fortune. He revealed that he was planning to kill his stepson Charles and place him in the cistern as well.

Dr. Young's murder trial was in its tenth day when he was found dead in his cell. He had managed to strangle himself with a piece of wire.

UNSOLVED MURDER

Unfortunately, not all murder cases are concluded in a satisfactory manner. Yes, people do get away with murder.

More than a hundred years ago, in a suburb of London, England, murder most foul was committed. No one was brought to trial; no one was convicted and no one was punished, although almost everyone involved had a pretty good idea who had perpetrated the crime.

Two youngsters, George Bacon, 10, and Alfred Overall, 9, were strolling from Lower Sydenham to Penge through some fields when they reached a pond near the Penge cricket field. The boys spotted the body of an adult male, partially submerged in the water. Alfred ran home and informed members of his family of the gruesome discovery.

Soon, three local constables were at the pond. The scene they encountered was a strange one, indeed. The man was in about two feet of water with his head underwater, stuck fast in the muck of the pond's bank. It took all the strength of the three constables to extract the man from his second to last resting place.

Dr. Dean Longrigg examined the body. He revealed that the man's jaw and nose had been broken. The victim had a severe wound on the right side of his head and a deep jagged cut above the left eye. One of the locals identified the dead man as Bill Saunders.

Bill, 34, was well-known in the area, having worked as a laborer for years at the Crystal Palace Gas Co. in Sydenham. A couple of years before the tragedy, he had married Mrs. Sarah Inman. Sarah, who was a matronly 45 years of age, had lost her husband via natural causes sometime before she had gone to the altar with Bill. She brought quite a retinue to the marriage. Let's see now, Sarah had six children by hubby number one, and a balanced family they were — three girls and three boys. The oldest, a girl, was 20.

The day of Bill's death had been disruptive in more ways than one. It had been moving day for the Saunders family, who had moved a few streets to a new home at 4 Hillmore Grove in Lower Sydenham. The relocation was considered a step up for the entire clan.

The gentleman who had identified Bill, one Thomas Fitzgerald, called on Mrs. Saunders to break the sad news. When he said, "I have bad news to tell you," Sarah replied, "What is it? Has he drowned himself?" Everyone would forever consider Sarah's remarks as a bad choice of words.

Police investigated the murder. They had a chat with the twice-widowed Sarah. She responded to their inquiries by informing them that Bill had been on good terms with all six of his stepchildren, four of whom lived at home with them. Besides Sarah's offspring, the Saunders had a lodger, James Dempsey, who was engaged to marry Sarah's eldest daughter. So much for historical family matters.

Police got down to tracing Bill's last known movements. Sarah told them that the family had moved that Saturday. At 9 in the evening, she had given her husband a few shillings as a sort of reward. Bill had worked hard all day and deserved to down a few ales with his friends at the local pub. Sarah swore that was the last time she had seen her Bill alive. She also volunteered that neither Dempsey or any of her four children had left the house after 5 p.m. Sarah's eldest son, Alfred, 19, and Dempsey corroborated Sarah's statement.

Detectives interrogated neighbors. The Saunders' immediate neighbor, John Quittenden, told them that Bill had spent the evening with him. The two friends had consumed a few beers before Bill left around 9 p.m. Quittenden said that during the course of the evening Bill had told him that his home life was terrible.

Another neighbor, 17-year-old Ann Winn, told police that she had seen Bill Saunders at about 10:30 on the night he was killed. He had been with two men. She was "quite sure" one of the men was James Dempsey. Ann even recalled seeing Dempsey alone only a few minutes later, close to where she had seen him with Bill Saunders.

Well, folks, the officers had come across an obvious discrepancy regarding time. They dropped in on Sarah and her brood once again. Dempsey now said that he had not stepped out of the house after 6 p.m., an hour later than he had previously stated. As the police left the house, Dempsey ran after them. He now remembered that he had been out around 8 p.m., but no later than that.

On Tuesday, three days after Bill's body was taken from the muddy pond, an inquest was held into his death at the Park Tavern Public House. Ann Winn was to be the chief witness. She had placed James Dempsey with the victim at a time when the man claimed to have been at home.

Sarah, the first witness called, told her story. She had begun to worry about Bill at one in the morning. He had never stayed out all night before. Believing that he may have lingered at Quittenden's, she sent one of her younger children next door. He was told that his stepfather had left hours earlier.

When Sarah was asked why she had insisted that no one had left the house after 5 p.m., when Dempsey now admitted that he was out much later, she could only say that she had forgotten. She apologized and stated that she had been confused.

Mr. Quittenden testified that Bill had left his house at about 9 p.m. While having a few beers, Bill had told his friend that he was leading a life of misery with Sarah and was thinking of leaving her.

James Dempsey now stated that he had last seen Bill about 9 p.m., when Bill must have left Quittenden's home. Under intense questioning, he admitted that he had lied earlier as to the hour he himself had left the house. He testified that he had gone for a drop of whiskey at about 10 p.m., but had not seen Bill Saunders.

The investigation's star witness, Ann Winn, then gave her testimony. She knew both James Dempsey and Bill Saunders well. After returning from an errand with her sister, she left to meet her boyfriend at Kent House Road. While waiting for her friend, she saw Bill Saunders with a man in a light-colored suit. It was a little after 10 p.m. She heard Bill Saunders say, "That's a bloody lie." She did not see the face of the man with Saunders. She went home and returned to Kent House Road 10 minutes later.

This time, she distinctly saw James Dempsey in a light-colored suit. When questioned further, Ann wouldn't swear that Dempsey was the man whom she had seen with Saunders. It had been exactly 10:45 p.m. when she saw Dempsey alone.

Most people listening to the testimony that day felt certain that James Dempsey had gotten into a dispute with Bill Saunders shortly after 10 p.m. and had killed him between 10 p.m. and 10:45 p.m.

On the second day of the inquest, Alfred Inman testified that he and Dempsey had heard of Ann Winn's first statement to police. They had gone to the girl's house and had asked her if it was true that she could swear she had seen Dempsey with Saunders on the night he was killed. Alfred swore that they hadn't threatened the girl. She had admitted of her own free will that she wasn't sure whether or not the man in the light suit she had seen with Bill Saunders was Dempsey.

And there the inquest into the death of Bill Saunders ended. The inquest jury returned a verdict of "Wilful murder by some person or persons unknown." No one was ever charged with the crime. Had a young girl been coerced into changing her testimony? One is inclined to believe that James Dempsey did indeed get away with murder.

THE HONEYMOON'S OVER

Everyone in La Crosse, Wisconsin thought that the widow Hattie Hales was the luckiest lady in the entire state. Hattie's husband, who had passed away some years earlier, had been employed with the Northwestern Railroad as a conductor. Just imagine, matronly Hattie coming off the shelf at the mature age of 53.

It was in the summer of 1926, at a church social, that Hattie made the acquaintance of William Coffee. Willie was three years younger than Hattie. He talked a lot about his property in Madison and his comfortable home in Detroit. Buxom Hattie thought she had died and gone to heaven. It was rough living on her late husband's tiny railroad pension and the small wages she garnered from her position as a buyer for a local department store. Besides, Willie was a handsome specimen, in a roguish sort of way.

All that summer, the pair of mature lovers were inseparable. On September 15, they slipped away to Minnesota in Willie's car and tied the knot. The happy couple spent their honeymoon touring. Occasionally, they dropped into a church to cleanse their souls and whatever.

Hattie insisted that they spend a few weeks with her

mother in Rockford, Ill. While in Rockford, it was only natural that Willie made the acquaintance of other members of Hattie's family. A sister, Annette Holdridge, didn't cotton to Willie. She just couldn't fathom the idea that wealthy, worldly Willie would scoop up her sister. On the other hand, such things did happen. Annette decided to keep her feelings to herself.

The newlyweds continued on their idyllic honeymoon. Annette received a letter signed by Hattie, postmarked Dubuque. However, after leaving Dubuque, Hattie obviously tired of writing. From then on, all the letter writing was done by Willie and signed B and H. Annette was a bit annoyed at not receiving correspondence directly from her sister. She dropped Hattie a line, urging her to write a letter herself.

Hattie obviously ignored the request. Further letters were received from B and H describing what a wonderful time they were having, attending plays and seeing the sights. From Chicago, Willie wrote that he and Hattie would be attending a banquet that very night in his honor. Other friends and relatives received similar letters.

Shortly after the Chicago banquet, Annette received a letter from B and H. The letter was generally one of good cheer, but Willie slipped in an ominous paragraph about Hattie meeting a Mr. St. Clair. Evidently, Mr. St. Clair had spent an uncommon amount of time in Hattie's company at the banquet. Subsequent letters often mentioned Mr. St. Clair, who seemed to pop up every so often like a bad penny.

Annette received a typewritten letter directly from her sister. Hattie explained that Willie had purchased a typewriter for her so that she could personally write more often. The letter was signed in what was unmistakably Hattie's signature. Annette was puzzled. Her sister couldn't type.

Surprisingly, after Hattie's chubby little fingers got accustomed to dancing over the keyboard of her typewriter, she sent out a veritable barrage of missives. One was to the Elroy Service Oil Co., transferring a $500 stock certificate to her dear husband William. Other letters to friends never failed to mention Mr. St. Clair, who now seemed to be with Hattie on a regular basis.

Hattie's mother was devastated by a letter received from her son-in-law on November 3. Willie revealed that Hattie had left him. She had run away with that rascal, Mr. St. Clair. It had been messy. Willie and Hattie had tried their hand at camping near Asheville, N.C. One fine day, Willie returned to their tent to find Hattie and Mr. St. Clair doing what comes naturally.

Willie related that he had been so shocked, he fainted. When he came to, all he could find was a note from Hattie saying she was leaving with St. Clair. As an afterthought, Willie mentioned that Hattie had left the signed-off Elroy stock certificate with him. He figured it was kind of a goodwill gesture.

Annette was told about the letter. It was too much. Hattie simply wasn't the type. She compared signatures of the various letters written by her sister. When placed up to the sunlight, they proved to be identical. Annette believed that the signatures had been made with a rubber stamp.

Sister Annette informed the Elroy Oil Co. of the signed-off stock and was told that a shareholders' meeting was to be held on January 20, 1927. Willie showed up, was taken into custody and charged with forgery.

While behind bars, Willie was asked the question which was on everyone's mind — where was his wife, Hattie? That was a tough one. According to Willie, his dear wife was somewhere with the elusive Mr. St. Clair. As for the rubber stamp, it was true Hattie had used one to sign letters and documents. Willie pointed out there was no law against that.

There matters stood until someone decided to check out William Coffee's background. The trail led to Madison, where, surprise of surprises, police discovered another Mrs. Coffee. She had been married to Willie for 23 long years and knew nothing about his extra-marital activities. The real Mrs. Coffee readily consented to having her house searched. Police found the rubber stamp Willie had used to sign Hattie's letters.

Mrs. Coffee informed police that Willie had rented a car, which was stored at the Madison Nash Co. garage under William Coffee's name. Inside the trunk was a suitcase containing women's clothing and jewelry. Tearfully, Annette identified the contents of the suitcase as belonging to her sister.

Willie's job as a piano salesman allowed him to be away from home for long periods of time, allowing him to lead a double life. Now, the heat was definitely on. In jail, he was questioned intensely. At the ungodly hour of 5 a.m. on January 24, 1927, he confessed. According to Willie, Hattie had accused him of running around with other women. They argued that night in the tent in Dubuque. He hit her over the head with a baseball bat and was shocked when the blow killed her. He panicked and threw the body into a nearby river. After Hattie's death, he had the rubber stamp made up and created the fictional Mr. St. Clair.

No one believed the pat story. Willie was charged with bigamy and the questioning continued. Two days later, he gave a revised version of Hattie's demise. He revealed that after killing her with the baseball bat, he dissected Hattie's body and buried her assorted parts in nearby woods.

Willie led police to the woods where the foul deed had been done. Portion by portion of Hattie was removed from shallow graves. When Hattie's head was found, it didn't take a pathologist to see that several wounds had been inflicted on the victim. So much for Willie's declaration that one blow from a baseball bat had caused Hattie's death.

Why had Willie gone through a bigamous marriage and committed murder? It had all been for the few thousand dollars Hattie's husband had left her. Try as he might, Willie simply couldn't think of a way to get his hands on Hattie's funds without killing her.

Willie was examined by a psychiatrist and adjudged to

be sane. On February 4, 1927, he pleaded guilty to murder and was sentenced to life imprisonment at hard labor with no possibility of parole.

William Coffee remained in Wisconsin State Prison for 35 years, four months and seven days. He died in prison of pneumonia in 1962 at age 85. Willie had outlived all his relatives. He is buried in grave number 276 in the prison cemetery.

HE HEARD
VOICES

He beat the old cans with a stick and made music. The chunky blonde eight-year-old loved to hide away in the room he shared with his older brother and play with his homemade set of drums. Marie and John Gordon encouraged their son. They had no idea that Jim would become what many would consider to be the finest drummer of his era.

By the time Jim was 12, his dad had purchased a real set of drums. Jim even had his own room in which to practise.

Life was sweet. This was middle-class America. Dad was an accountant, Mum a nurse. The house in Los Angeles' San Fernando Valley was big and comfortable. Jim's only brother John was protective and supportive. The Gordon brothers had paper routes, mowed lawns and had spending money in their jeans.

Always, for Jim, there were the drums. In high school he played with the Burbank Symphony. He played in a band in the Tournament of Roses parade. One summer, he toured Europe. Together with friends, he formed a group of his own called Frankie Knight and the Jesters. They played in tiny clubs around Los Angeles, commanding the princely sum of $10 a gig. Jimmy wasn't in it for the coin. He loved to play.

In high school, he sprouted to an imposing six feet, three inches. With his crop of curly blonde hair, he cut quite a figure surrounded by the instruments he loved.

It was decision time — go to university or become a struggling musician. Despite being offered a music scholarship at UCLA, Jim passed up university. He took sound studio jobs when he could get them. In the jungle of Los Angeles' studios, Jim honed his talent. His big break came when he was heard playing with the Jesters and was recommended to the Everly Brothers. Once they heard Jim, they insisted he join them on a tour of England that summer of 1963. Jim accepted. The tour was so successful, it was repeated the following summer.

When Jim returned to Los Angeles, the established drummers felt confident in passing along their overflow work at the studios to him. It didn't take long. Once you heard Jim Gordon on the skins, you knew you were hearing the best. Work poured in. Sometimes Jim did as many as three recording sessions a day. Some weeks he worked seven days. Jim worked with the very best — Glen Campbell, Bobby Darin and Canadian Gordon Lightfoot.

The Gordon family was proud. Their Jim was making his mark, as they always knew he would.

Later, psychiatrists were to state that, even then, with the world his oyster, Jim was hearing the voices. They weren't persuasive; they didn't command. And always there were the drums, which could drive the voices away.

In 1964, Jim married Jill, a dancer he had known for years. These were the good times. Both caught on with the TV rock program, Shindig. Cars and a home near Jim's parents quickly followed. Over the good years Jim worked with the giants of his profession, such as John Lennon, Bob Dylan and George Harrison. He toured England with Delaney and Bonnie Bramlett. Somewhere along the line, he and Jill divorced.

The tour was a huge success. Upon its conclusion, Jim joined Joe Cocker's Mad Dogs and Englishmen Tour across the U.S. Together with 41 other musicians, wives, girlfriends, and assorted hangers-on, the madcap tour was an artistic success and a doper's dream. Jim took to the lifestyle like a duck takes to water. Cocaine, acid, speed, mescaline, heroin and rivers of booze were at arm's reach from city to city.

The lifestyle had its effect on Jim Gordon. The voices came back, more persuasive now; they told him to be suspicious of everyone and everything. There was no returning. The voices were in command. Once Jim struck his best friend for no apparent reason. He apologized.

After the Cocker tour, George Harrison asked Jim to join him in London for his first solo album. When the album was completed, Jim, together with a friend, formed his own group, Derek and the Dominoes. The group toured in 1972 and then broke up.

Throughout the '70s, Jim worked with several groups, but now the word was out. He was a druggie. Not that that was unusual in the rock music business, but it was common knowledge that Jim couldn't control his habit.

Even at this low point in his career, Jim's talent was recognized. He obtained studio work with Frank Zappa, Johnny Rivers and others. Jim switched from drugs only to alcohol and drugs. He drank with a vengeance, often consuming a 40-ouncer a day for days at a time.

Jim underwent a personality change. We now know the voices had taken over completely. One minute he was happy, the next, morose. Paranoid, he refused to talk to anyone for long periods of time. In 1973, Jim's father died, after which he went into a prolonged state of depression.

A hazy brief marriage of six months' duration ended when Jim's unreasonable paranoid behavior was constantly directed toward his wife. Around 1977, Jim had difficulty playing his beloved drums. He became a detriment at recording sessions. Producers shunned the man they had once sought. Jim retreated within himself.

He had only the voices now and, for some unfathomable reason, they turned him against his mother.

Jim phoned his mother often, begging her to stop tormenting him. Mrs. Gordon had no idea what her son was referring to, but she did realize something was drastically wrong. She suggested he seek help.

Jim listened to his mother. He admitted himself into the Van Nuys Psychiatric Hospital. His mother visited. Mother and son embraced. The voices stopped. Jim went home on weekend visits. Two months later, he was discharged from hospital, but the voices started again. His mother's voice continued to torment him, wouldn't leave him alone. For six years, Jim was in and out of hospital a total of 15 times. Once, he attempted suicide. Mammoth drinking bouts were sandwiched between hospital visits.

By 1980, Jim no longer played the drums. Money wasn't a problem. Shrewd investments initiated by his late father, coupled with royalties, kept him relatively well supplied with cash. He went for long periods of time in dirty clothing without bathing or shaving. At other times he showed up meticulously groomed in a freshly pressed suit. All the while, he alternated between hating and loving his mother and her voice, which he now heard daily.

The hated voice became the dominating factor of Jim's life. On June 3, 1983, the voice told him what he must do — he had to kill his mother. Following the voice's instructions, he placed a hammer and a knife in his briefcase and drove to his mother's apartment around 11:30 p.m. Marie Gordon, 72, answered her son's knock. She screamed as the hammer was held over her head. In all, Jim swung four times. He then stabbed his mother in the chest, leaving the knife protruding from her body.

Next morning, when police contacted Jim to inform him of his mother's murder, they found him sobbing uncontrollably on the living room floor of his own apartment. He confessed immediately, explaining, "She wanted me to kill her."

Jim stood trial for murder in Los Angeles. Although judged to be an acute paranoid schizophrenic by five psychiatrists testifying for the defence, he was deemed to be legally sane. Jim was found guilty of second-degree murder and sentenced to 16 years to life imprisonment. Initially, he was confined to the California Men's Colony in San Luis Obispo. He has since been transferred to the Atascadero State Hospital, an institution which houses the correctional facility's mentally ill inmates.

There, on Ward 22, the best drummer of the '60s and '70s, now number C89262, wanders in and out of reality. Jay Osmond, of the Osmond Brothers, has sent him sticks and a practise pad. Sometimes, Jim Gordon practises in his room.

FANTASIES TURN TO CANNIBALISM

It isn't every day that a quiet, intelligent Japanese boy murders, rapes and eats selected portions of a Dutch girl in Paris.

Renee Hartewelt had received her Bachelor's degree from the University of Leyden, majoring in French literature. In the spring of 1981, the 25-year-old student was continuing her studies at Université Censier in Paris. In addition to her native tongue, the attractive Dutch girl spoke both German and French. She lived in an apartment at 59 rue Bonaparte on the Left Bank.

Issei Sagawa, who weighed in at 88 pounds and stood one inch under five feet, sat beside Renee at one of the lectures both attended at the university. Issei was the son of a wealthy Japanese industrialist. He had obtained his bachelor and masters degrees from the University of Osaka.

At Université Censier, he was pursuing his doctorate on the Japanese influence on French literature. Like Renee, the 33- year-old Issei spoke fluent German and French. He maintained his own studio apartment at 10 rue Erlanger.

The two mature students had an interest in French literature in common. Because Renee's command of the French language was stronger than Issei's, she offered to assist him with difficult translations.

Unknown to Renee, her new friend had things on his mind which had nothing to do with French translations. For years, this intelligent academic harbored fantasies, horrible fantasies. He wanted to make love to and consume portions of a female body — not just anyone, but someone he really liked and cared for. Unknown to Renee Hartewelt, she was that girl.

Issei planned well. The weapon he would use was already at hand. He had purchased a .22 caliber rifle for protection upon arrival in Paris. He purchased two cheap imitation leather suitcases and a wire carrier with wheels. In addition, he bought plastic garbage bags and sharpened knives.

On June 11, Renee was helping Issei with his studies in his apartment. Issei could contain himself no longer. He told Renee he loved her, and quickly added that it would be pleasant if they could have sexual intercourse right then and there. Renee, who had absolutely no romantic feelings toward her companion, suggested he concentrate on his French translations.

Issei rose, walked to a cabinet, extracted his .22 and shot Renee in the back of the neck, killing her instantly. He then had intercourse with the dead body.

Methodically, Issei went about spreading sheets of plastic on the floor. His pre-sharpened knives and razor were used to mutilate and remove portions of the dead girl. Nose, lips, breasts and parts of the buttocks were removed.

Although Issei was meticulous in most of his endeavors, he had neglected to purchase a saw, which everyone in the dissection business knows is almost a necessity. However, diminutive Issei took his time and completed his task, occasionally stopping to take photographs of his handiwork.

The strenuous task completed, Issei ate portions of the body. Some parts were cooked, others were eaten raw. Still other portions were neatly wrapped in plastic and placed in the freezer compartment of his refrigerator.

Two days later, on June 13, 1981, a small Oriental man was seen on the streets of Paris, lugging two cheap suitcases on a wire carrier. It was later learned that the man had planned to dispose of the suitcases in a nearby lake, but he lost his nerve. People seemed to be staring at him. Was it his size? Was it his macabre cargo? Whatever, Issei simply walked away, leaving his suitcases on the street.

When curious onlookers noted blood oozing from one suitcase, the police were called. An eager gendarme opened the suitcase, peered inside, and came face to face with a noseless and lipless head. He hastened to call the Surete, the Paris Criminal Investigation Dept.

An autopsy was performed on the hapless victim. A .22 caliber bullet was removed from the skull. The girl had been ravished after death. Above all, parts of the corpse were missing. Even at this early stage of the investigation, cannibalism was suspected.

A check of missing girls revealed that students at the Université Censier had reported one Renee Hartewelt missing from classes. She proved to be the victim. Although Renee's parents were wealthy, she had taken a room in exchange for baby-sitting services. Detectives searched her room, believing that the murder may have taken place there. However, the contents of Renee's room proved to be in perfect order.

Although Renee had been in Paris only four months, it was believed she would have come in contact with other foreign students at the university. A survey of foreign students was about to be undertaken when a taxi driver came forward and told police that he had picked up a passenger at 10 rue Erlanger on the evening of June 13.

By the time the cabbie had arrived at the address, a tiny Oriental man was standing on the sidewalk. He had two large suitcases at his feet. They proved to be heavy and it was only with some difficulty that they were placed inside the trunk of the taxi. The taxi driver left his fare off not far from where the suitcases were found.

Detectives checked out the occupants of 10 rue

Erlanger. They discovered that one studio apartment was rented to Issei Sagawa, a brilliant Japanese student at Université Censier. There seemed little doubt that they had their man, but there were obstacles. If the dissection had taken place in the studio apartment, the killer would have had plenty of time to dispose of the murder weapon and clean up any incriminating evidence.

Besides, the unspeakable actions of the killer didn't fit Issei's profile. Here was an intellectual with a clean record, both in his native land and in Paris. It was difficult to believe that he could have perpetrated the horrible crimes attributed to the mad cannibal. However, when police learned that Issei had rented a rug shampooer the day after the murder, they swooped down on 10 rue Erlanger.

There, leaning in a closet, where it had obviously been placed immediately after the murder, was the .22 caliber rifle used to take Renee's life. Ballistic testing proved it to be the murder weapon. But there were more surprises in Issei's flat. The missing portions of Renee Hartewelt were found in the refrigerator, neatly wrapped in plastic.

Issei confessed immediately to detectives. He related in detail how he had fantasized about what it would be like to have sex with an attractive girl and then eat portions of her body. When he had told Renee on a previous occasion of his feelings toward her, she dismissed his intentions as frivolous. That's when he decided to have her, alive or dead.

This was no spur of the moment murder. Issei had carefully planned the entire operation which, to his way of thinking, had gone very well, right up to the disposal of the body. He admitted that he had lost his nerve on the streets of Paris, but had still felt he was safe enough when he abandoned his cargo.

Despite his claim of being perfectly sane and his articulate manner in relating his repulsive deeds, Issei underwent extensive psychiatric examination. He was found to be incompetent to stand trial and was incarcerated in an institution for the criminally insane.

Three years later he was returned to Japan, under condition that he be confined to a mental institution. After spending fifteen months in a Tokyo psychiatric hospital, he was discharged. Doctors said he was normal.

Since being discharged, Issei has written several books on his favorite subject — cannibalism!

THE DOCTOR
HAD A MOTIVE

Doctors Merrill and Laverne Joss were the most respected young couple in the town of Richmond, Maine. Not that much ever happened in Richmond, but all that changed on the evening of March 27, 1941.

That was the night the town's chief of police was called to Dr. Merrill Joss' impressive old colonial home. Dr. Joss met the chief at the door. To say he was distraught would understate the case.

"It's my wife," the doctor explained. "She's been attacked by a dope addict or at least that appears to be the case. A bearded stranger appeared at my door demanding narcotics. Naturally, I turned him away. A doctor's house is an easy target, you know."

When the chief asked for a description, the doctor quickly replied, "The man was about five feet eight, had shaggy unkempt hair, wore a beard and had a dark coat and cap."

The doctor went on to hurriedly explain that he had left the house to complete an errand and was as far as the railroad tracks when he heard his dog Trixie barking. He returned to the house to find his office burglarized. Alarmed for his wife's safety, he searched the house for her. When he noticed that the door leading off the kitchen into the cellar was open, he dashed downstairs to find his wife lying on the cellar floor, bludgeoned about the head.

All of this was blurted out to the chief as they made their way through the house and down the cellar stairs. The chief noted blood on the stairs, wall and the floor. There was Laverne Joss, unconscious. In minutes, Dr. Edwin Pratt joined Dr. Joss, peering over Laverne's still form. Dr. Pratt dressed the head wounds as best he could with some gauze. Joss said that he would drive his wife to the hospital. Pratt insisted that an ambulance be called immediately. There was a tense moment, but Pratt prevailed.

An ambulance sped away to hospital with Laverne, while a horde of detectives and citizens joined in an effort to apprehend the man described by Dr. Joss. In a community the size of Richmond, everyone knew the victim of the wild attack. Both she and her husband were beloved by their friends and neighbors. Both were on a first-name basis with many of the police officers now investigating the burglary and the assault on Laverne. That same night, Dr. Laverne Joss died of her wounds.

Dr. Merrill repeated his story to detectives in detail. Probably it was state police Lieutenant Leon Shepard who first privately doubted his story. The seasoned detective had never heard of a dope addict knocking at a door and asking for drugs. Buying dope, stealing dope, yes — but walking up to a doctor's residence and simply asking for dope just didn't sit well.

As the extensive search for the shaggy stranger continued, detectives were provided with another piece of information concerning Merrill Joss. Evidently, when Laverne was brought into hospital, a blood transfusion was immediately ordered. Merrill objected, insisting upon a blood cross-matching. Laverne died before any transfusion was attempted. It was noted she had 27 head wounds and that her wedding ring was missing.

When Merrill was questioned about the ring, he confirmed that his wife always wore her ring and he had no idea how it had disappeared. Astute Lt. Shepard had his own theory. He got down on his hands and knees on the Joss' kitchen floor and, in true Columbo fashion, searched for the ring. Sure enough, there, underneath the refrigerator, was Laverne's ring.

Now, hot to trot, Shepard examined the cellar. In nearly empty bins of vegetables, he found a watch belonging to Laverne. The wily detective reconstructed the crime in his mind.

Shepard dismissed Merrill's story as a fabrication to cover his own tracks. He theorized that Merrill and Laverne had not been getting along, possibly there was another woman. The pair had argued in the kitchen. Laverne had taken off her ring and had thrown it at her husband. The ring had lodged under the refrigerator.

Merrill had picked up something and struck out at his wife. She had slumped to the floor, unconscious. He then threw her down the cellar steps. As she tumbled down, her wrist hit the wall, flinging the watch into a bin of carrots. Merrill cleaned the blood off the kitchen floor, ransacked his own office and either hid or destroyed the murder weapon before calling police. Shepard's theory accounted for all the known facts, except the 27 wounds on Laverne's head.

Shepard continued his investigation. Laboratory technicians were brought into the house. From the kitchen floor, they extracted tiny cotton threads almost invisible to the naked eye. Elsewhere in the house, they found a cloth which proved to be of the same fibres as those taken from the floor. Someone had wiped the floor clean. Certainly, a dope addict wouldn't have stopped to clean the floor after throwing his victim down the stairs.

Lt. Shepard's suspicions had first been raised by the doctor's implausible story. Now, he checked out the doctor's friends and discovered that Merrill was keeping company with a winsome cook at a local eatery. Elizabeth Mayo was questioned and readily co-operated with police. It was true. She and the doctor were seeing each other on the side, so to speak. Merrill had talked of divorce, but Elizabeth had never thought he would go as far as killing his wife. She produced love letters written by Merrill only hours before his wife's death. That's called motive, folks.

Detectives made a moulage cast of Laverne's head. They then proceeded to make a cast of the crude cellar floor. They found that by placing the head cast against the cast of the rough floor, they could match the two. Eerily, the wounds on the head cast fit the rough edges of the floor. Laverne had received some of her wounds when she was thrown down the stairs onto the floor.

An examination of the steps uncovered a lone eyebrow hair and minute pieces of flesh. The eyebrow hair matched those taken from Laverne's skull. The impact of her head against the steps may have accounted for several of the head wounds.

The entire case against Merrill was circumstantial, but it added up the way Lt. Shepard figured at the beginning, when boy scouts and police were scouring three counties for a man who didn't exist.

Most of the community were gathered at the Methodist Church for 37-year-old Laverne Joss' funeral. Merrill Joss was supported by a galaxy of friends as he dabbed at his eyes with a white handkerchief. As Merrill left the church, he was taken into custody by state police Chief Henry Weaver. Charged with his wife's murder, he was incarcerated in the Sagadahoc County Jail.

A few weeks later, while awaiting trial, Merrill borrowed a razor blade from another inmate. He cut the skin of his right arm and, using his fingernail, raised an artery. He then cut the artery with the blade. A guard found him unconscious and immediately summoned a physician. He was rushed to hospital and given blood transfusions. Attending physicians managed to save his life.

On June 23, 1941, Dr. Merrill Joss stood trial for his wife's murder. The trial lasted 10 days. Prosecuting attorneys dramatically revealed the history of the Joss' marriage. Both had been married before and had become attracted to each other while working together in a hospital. They had divorced their respective spouses and married each other.

Merrill admitted from the witness stand that he and his wife had not been getting along and had discussed divorce. Although married for over five years, they had never lived as man and wife. Laverne had undergone an operation just before marrying him, which made normal sex impossible. Their married life had been more of a brother/sister relationship than one of husband and wife. He further stated that his wife had been aware of his love for Elizabeth Mayo. Their talk of divorce had been amicable.

Merrill Joss got off relatively easy. The jury evidently felt that the crime did not contain the necessary "malice aforethought" and so reduced their verdict to one of guilty of manslaughter.

On July 5, 1941, Dr. Merrill Joss was sentenced to not less than 10 years and not more than 20 years imprisonment in the state prison at Thomaston, Maine.

WITCHCRAFT

Adolfo Constanzo could easily have passed for a youthful executive who had made it to the top rung of the corporate ladder. Tall, good-looking Constanzo excelled in his chosen professions of witchcraft, smuggling and murder.

Born in Miami on November 1, 1962 to a Cuban immigrant mother, he was raised in Puerto Rico, where his mother married for the second time. When his stepfather died, Adolfo and his mother returned to Miami. The attractive youngster left school after completing Grade nine and took odd jobs to help support his mother and his four brothers and sisters. Drawn to the big money being made in the drug trade, Constanzo left Florida in 1984 for Mexico. Here, the charismatic Constanzo earned his spurs in the drug business. Before long, he was the leader of a gang of smugglers based in Matamoros. It is believed that Constanzo's take was 50% of everything the Hernandez gang took in from their illegal operations.

Geographically, the gang's base of operations couldn't have been located more advantageously. Matamoros is situated on the U.S.-Mexican border. The International Gateway Bridge across the Rio Grande separates Brownsville, Texas and Matamoros, Mexico.

Despite his youth, Constanzo demanded respect, and

with good reason. He mixed fear with cold, hard cash. His followers soon had more money and a better life than they ever had before their young leader came on the scene. He organized the marijuana trade, shipping it from distant farms to where it was stored in a barn on the Rancho Santa Elena near Matamoros. From there, it was smuggled across the river into the U.S., eventually reaching Houston and Miami.

Followers of Constanzo practised a form of witchcraft in which animals and human parts were used to ward off evil spirits. In time, his followers believed that Constanzo could foretell the future and was a kind of devil. He was called El Padrino, the Godfather. Constanzo told his close cult followers that the police would never harm or harass them, and they never did. It wasn't really witchcraft. Constanzo was paying off the officials.

Constanzo often ordered his followers to pick up a human to be sacrificed to the gods. There, in a tiny shack on the farm, the blindfolded victim, in many cases unknown to the abductors, would be killed. Often, the heart and brains would be removed and placed in a cauldron with spices. By candlelight, strange rituals were enacted.

Mark Kilroy lived in a different world than Adolfo Constanzo. Mark was a junior at the University of Texas in Austin. He dated girls, cheered for the Longhorns and studied hard, with the intention of becoming a medical doctor. He was looking forward to the March break when he and buddies Bradley Moore, Bill Huddleston and Brent Martin planned on travelling down to South Padre Island near Brownsville. Over a quarter of a million young people had the same idea.

Mark and his friends made the trip. After two days of ogling girls and drinking beer in South Padre, the boys crossed the bridge to Matamoros. They were enveloped by wall-to-wall pedestrians, mostly American students like themselves. The boys had a beer at several of the inviting pubs. They met other students and had fun swapping stories until it was time to return to the other side of the

Rio Grande.

At 2 a.m., the crowds had thinned out. The loosely-knit group of four boys made their way toward the International Gateway Bridge. Sometimes one or two strolled ahead of the others, sometimes one lagged behind.

Mark Kilroy lagged behind the other three as they passed Garcia's restaurant. Then he was gone — vanished. The three boys retraced their steps, thinking that Mark might have turned around for some reason. Eventually, they returned to their car and drove around looking for their friend. The streets were deserted when they reported Mark missing to the Mexican police.

Next morning, in Matamoros, they advised the American consulate of their missing friend, after which they called Mark's parents in Santa Fe and told them their son was missing in Mexico.

Unknown to all, Mark Kilroy had been hustled away in a truck and taken to the Rancho Santa Elena. His head was split open with a machete. His brains and heart were extracted and used in Satanic rituals by Adolfo Constanzo and his followers. Then he was buried. Authorities on both sides of the border were soon conducting a massive search for the missing American student.

Sara Aldrete, 24, was an honors student at Texas Southmost College in Brownsville. A dark beauty, she stood six feet one inch tall. Sara was also El Padrino's girlfriend and constant companion, even thought she knew he was a homosexual and had two male lovers. She willingly took part in the Satanic rituals.

Rumors concerning the Rancho Santa Elena as the drug dropoff point had come to the attention of the police on several occasions. Nothing was ever done. It is alleged that those in authority accepted bribes totalling millions of dollars in return for allowing the drugs to flow.

Now, a new officer, Juan Benitez, headed the Matamoros police. The honest, 35-year-old policeman swept clean. He had a drug shipment traced to Rancho Santa Elena. On April 9, 1989, the police swooped down and took into custody Serafin Hernandez, a courier and cult member. In quick succession, Elio Hernandez, David Serna and Sergio Martinez were arrested.

Benitez was cracking down on the drug trade, but he also had a photo of Mark Kilroy, the missing American student, which he showed to everyone during the course of his drug investigations. Always, he received the same answer. No one had seen Mark Kilroy. That is, until he showed the photo to a farmhand at Rancho Santa Elena. His name was Domingo Reyes.

Without hesitation, Domingo told the officer, "Yes, I remember, I gave him a drink of water. Later they took him down to the shack and after that I never saw him anymore."

Police, accompanied by Domingo, went to the shack. A lock was broken, revealing the horror of what had gone on in that shack. There, in three pots, was a stew containing a human brain. An iron cauldron held dried blood, a roasted turtle and another human brain. In the general area of the cauldron were melted candles, a goat's head and part of a chicken.

The police now knew that the infamous drug smuggling activities of El Padrino included murder, but even with the evidence of stark horror, they had no idea of the scope of the killings they were about to uncover. The four men lodged in jail were questioned regarding murder.

All confessed, adding horror upon horror to the unbelieving police. Eventually, the accused men directed police to gravesites on the ranch and close by, where a total of 15 bodies were brought to the surface. One body was that of Mark Kilroy.

The hunt was on for Constanzo, Sara Aldrete, and other cult members. They were traced to Mexico City, holed up in an apartment. A veritable army of 80 plainclothes men and 110 uniformed police officers surrounded the building. Inside were Constanzo, Sara, Alvara de Leon, Omar Orea and Martin Quintana. A shootout ensued. Realizing the futility of his situation, Constanzo entered a tiny closet with his lover, Martin Quintana. He ordered

Alvara de Leon to shoot them both through the flimsy closet doors. Alvara sprayed the closet with machine gun fire.

El Padrino, the Satanic drug king, was no more. The rest of his drug smuggling Satanic worshippers were taken into custody.

SALT LAKE CITY BOMBER

Mark Hofmann was born to a religious Mormon family in Salt Lake City, Utah. In 1973, he graduated from Olympus High School and, as is the custom in his faith, left home for two years missionary work. Mark served his mission in Portsmouth, England and it was there that he became interested in old books and documents pertaining to the Church of Jesus Christ of Latter-Day Saints.

His interest in such material is not altogether unusual. The Mormon church has always cherished authentic documents dating back to the founding of the faith by Joseph Smith. Church officials often pay well for additions to their archives. In fact, a flourishing market exists for such material.

In 1976, Mark, having completed his mission, returned to the U.S. and entered Utah State University. While at university, he delved deeply into the history of his religion.

Mark wed pretty Dori Olds on September 14, 1979. Dori dropped out of school to help support her husband, who was pursuing a medical career. Mark contributed a few dollars from the occasional sale of old Mormon coins and documents.

About a year after his marriage to Dori, Mark purported to find an ancient document in an old 17th-century

Cambridge Bible. It was signed by Joseph Smith and contained hieroglyphics which Smith said he had copied from the Golden Plates of the Book of Mormon. Mark took it to the church archives department where the discovery caused quite a stir. After testing by experts, the document was deemed to be authentic.

Mark became the darling of the collectors' world. He gave lectures, granted interviews and received wide acclaim as the man who found what became known as the Anthon Transcript. Mark gave up his studies to devote full time to tracing, trading and selling valuable documents pertaining to the Mormon faith, as well as other original material.

By 1981, Mark had a wide reputation as a tracer of extremely rare documents. Some individual sales to the church brought as much as $52,000. To finance his purchases, he often borrowed heavily. When the sales went through, everything came up roses. When there were delays or if the deals went sour, he often had difficulty meeting his obligations. Over and above his business debts, Mark and his wife lived well. On the surface, money didn't seem to be a problem.

In 1983, Mark Hofmann consummated the biggest deal of his career. He had in his possession a letter written by Martin Harris. The letter contained the startling information that, in 1823, when Joseph Smith found the Golden Plates on which the Book of Mormon is said to be transcribed, he came upon a salamander that turned itself into a spirit. The discovery of the Salamander Letter, as it came to be known, caused great controversy among church leaders, as it differed from official Mormon theology, which held that Smith had received the tablets from the Angel of God. Harris' signature on the letter was believed to be the only one in existence.

Steven Christensen and his associate, Gary Sheets owned a large real estate firm. Devout Mormons, they both became deeply involved in authenticating the letter which went to the very heart of the Mormon religion. In time, Christensen purchased the Salamander Letter from

Mark for $45,000. On April 12, 1985, he donated it to the church.

Meanwhile, Mark wheeled and dealed, often in partnership with investors. He purchased letters written by Daniel Boone, describing his trek into Kentucky. On several occasions, Mark paid off his investors with large profits.

Mark slowly got in deeper and deeper. Deals had gone sour. The partnership of Christensen and Sheets also suffered from poor investments. Mark picked this time to leak the story that he had located a group of documents called the McLellin Collection. This ancient documents were hot. They cast doubt on basic church doctrine. Steve Christensen, acting for the church, would purchase the documents from Mark on behalf of investors who would donate the controversial documents to the church.

Mark desperately needed cash. He had a large amount of money invested in documents and had just purchased a $650,000 home. At wit's end, he contacted Hugh Pinnock, a devout Mormon, high church official and a member of the board of directors of the Bank of Utah. Mark managed to borrow $185,000, giving the promise that the McLellin letters would be given over to the bank for collateral. All this came to the attention of Christensen, who was owed $100,000 by Mark and who had been promised the valuable collection.

Try as he might, Christensen couldn't contact Mark. He even parked outside his home for a few nights, without results. Payments on Mark's home came due, as well as payments on the bank loan from Pinnock.

Around 8 a.m. on Tuesday, October 15, 1985, Mark walked up to Steve's office. He was carrying a parcel and passed Bruce Passey, an employee in the same building. Bruce noticed that Mark's parcel was addressed to Steve Christensen. Mark proceeded to Steve's office, which wasn't open. He left the parcel outside the door.

A few minutes later, Steve Christensen arrived at his office. He picked up the parcel. The building shook with the explosion. It blew away half his chest and killed him instantly. Detectives found thousands of nails in the vicinity of the Salt Lake City businessman's body.

Gary Sheets' wife, Kathleen, 50, had already completed her banking and was driving up her driveway at about 9:30 a.m. when she observed a cardboard box beside her garage. After parking her car in the garage, she picked up the box addressed to Mr. Gary Sheets. The motion sensitive bomb exploded, killing Kathleen instantly. Neighbors heard the noise and peered out windows. When they observed leaves flying in all directions, they assumed a tree had been felled. Kathleen's body was found by a friend an hour later.

No one could remember anyone ever being killed by a bomb in Salt Lake City. Now, two victims in under two hours — unbelievable.

Initially, police interviewed everyone who may have seen the man who took the box to Steve's office. They came up with Bruce Passey. Bruce was able to describe the man — medium height and build, moustache, wearing a green Olympus High School track team jacket with the letter missing. That night, several friends jokingly thought that Mark Hofmann fit the description to a "T." He often wore his old high school jacket with the ripped-off athletic letter. All dismissed the idea as being ridiculous.

The next day, Wednesday, the main topic of discussion in Utah was the Salt Lake City bombings. It was arranged that Mark Hofmann would turn over the McLellin Collection to church officials that afternoon. They were assured that the two bombings, tragic though they were, were in no way connected with the controversial documents. Mark never showed up.

At precisely 2:41 p.m., a bomb went off as Mark entered his Toyota. Tossed into the street, he was severely injured in the chest, head and legs. Near death, he was questioned in the hospital. He told detectives that when he opened his car door, a box had fallen onto the floor. He could tell them little more.

The focus of the entire bombing investigation now pointed to a connection with the buying and selling of historically valuable documents. Soon, Mark's precarious financial position was known to police. Bank and church officials informed police of the impending delivery of the valuable McLellin Collection to the church by Mark Hofmann.

Bruce Passey identified Mark as the man who had placed the package outside Steve Christensen's office. Police located a friend of Mark's who had purchased blasting caps for him. Mark, who was recovering in hospital, became the prime suspect in the murders of Steve Christensen and Kathleen Sheets. Still, authorities didn't feel they had enough to prosecute.

On October 31, Mark was released from hospital. By the end of the year, experts revealed that the Salamander Letter, his springboard to a new career, was now thought to be a fake. Mark was taken into custody and charged with double murder as well as 27 charges of fraud and forgery concerning phony documents.

On January 7, 1987, prosecution and defence lawyers met. A deal was struck. Mark pleaded guilty to two counts of second degree murder and to a theft-by-deception count concerning the sale of the Salamander Letter. In return, all other fraud charges against Mark were dropped. In addition, the charge concerning the Sheets' murder would be reduced to manslaughter if Mark revealed all details requested by authorities. Mark agreed.

He told how he made the bombs. Mark confessed that he killed Steve Christensen so that the McLellin deal would not be finalized. He had meant the second bomb for Gary Sheets so that authorities would believe the killings were connected to real estate business transactions, rather than his phony documents. He had attempted to kill himself when he became depressed over what he had done and was sure he would be apprehended. He wanted to spare his family.

Mark Hofmann was sentenced to life imprisonment in Utah State Prison with the recommendation by the presiding judge that he spend the rest of his natural life in custody.

SURVIVAL

Glen Stanley was a youngster from Kentucky who, in a matter of ten months, was drafted, trained and sent to Vietnam to fight a war he really didn't understand. While in Vietnam, he celebrated his twentieth birthday.

This is his story, but it is also the story of the terrible crime of man's inhumanity to man. The Vietnam War, with its tens of thousands of casualties, accomplished nothing.

On July 12, 1967, Glen was situated on a hilltop near the Cambodian border, together with 35 comrades. He was one of two communications men on the hill that day when the North Vietnamese forces struck. They came in waves out of the jungle, receiving heavy casualties. There was no stopping their advance. Scores died, but relentlessly the enemy moved forward, killing Americans with small arms fire and mortars. Glen Stanley, together with fellow radioman, Hugh Lucas, continued to report back to headquarters as the battle raged.

By sheer force of numbers, the North Vietnamese encircled the hill. One by one, the Americans were killed until, finally, only Hugh and Glen were left. They destroyed their communications equipment and picked up their M-16 rifles. The raging enemy ran directly toward the two Americans. Glen figures at least ten of the enemy fell before he emptied his rifle. He threw the rifle to the ground and drew his .45 automatic pistol. Three more of the enemy fell. The pistol jammed. Hugh Lucas was shot dead. Shrapnel tore into Glen's legs, but miraculously he was alive, the only American survivor on that hilltop in Vietnam.

Today, Glen Stanley assures me he was positive he was going to die. Twenty years old, bleeding on a hilltop, thousands of miles from home, surrounded by the bodies of his comrades as well as those of the enemy, rifle discarded, pistol inoperable, he awaited death.

Somewhere, in the deep recesses of his mind, he felt he had one chance for survival. He slumped to the ground. He would play dead. The gunfire ceased. All the Americans were dead. All except Glen Stanley from Kentucky.

Glen held his breath as enemy soldiers walked among his 35 dead comrades. He could hear the soldiers turning over the bodies, stripping them of anything of value. Surely they would discover he was alive when they searched his uniform. Surely he would die. Glen Stanley prayed to his god. All the while, he intermittently held his breath, inhaling and exhaling in a slow, even rhythm.

Glen could sense that the corpse next to him was being searched. A North Vietnamese soldier's foot scraped against his open wounds. The pain was excruciating. Glen stifled a scream. To move at all would mean death. Somehow, he overcame the pain and lay still.

Rough hands ripped the dog tags from his neck and extracted the wallet from his inside coat pocket. They reached under his limp form to remove his utility belt. Glen couldn't help it. His body gave an involuntary twitch. The voices seemed more angry now.

A wire was wrapped around Glen's wrist. Two soldiers struggled to bring his limp form to a standing position. Glen decided that no matter what, he would continue his charade to the end. He had no choice. Suddenly, his captors dropped him to the ground. They truly believed he was dead. For the first time, Glen felt he might survive, but his elation was short-lived.

A North Vietnamese soldier leaned over one of the dead Americans. He placed a pistol to the man's head and pulled the trigger. The .45-calibre pistol roared. Glen felt terror envelop his very soul. The enemy was delivering the coup de grace to all the fallen American soldiers.

Glen's mind raced. There was no escaping his fate. He thought of his home in Kentucky. He thought of the good times with his friends. As he lay on the jungle floor, amidst the broken bodies, he could smell nothing but the stench of death mixed with gunpowder. It would all be over soon. He thought of Christmas and how he and his family decorated their tree. He thought of opening presents on Christmas Day. It was another world, far removed from the hill of death in Vietnam.

A Vietnamese soldier leaned over the body of Lt. Henry Ransom. Glen's hand lay against Ransom's face. The muzzle blast seared his hand and inflicted a cut. Now, it was Glen Stanley's turn to die. He felt a hand in his hair pulling his head upright. A click of the trigger and a .45-calibre slug coursed along his skull. The pain ricocheted through his head.

Expecting death, Glen's will to play dead didn't desert him. He didn't scream. He did nothing but lie limp and endure the overpowering pain in his head. He fought the urge to drift into unconsciousness. There was no doubt his tormentors believed him to be dead. Blood trickled down Glen's face, across his nose and into his mouth. The enemy proceeded to fire more shots into the heads of his dead comrades. Then it stopped. The voices grew dimmer. No doubt the enemy was retreating across the Cambodian border.

Glen Stanley was alive, but there was one more hurdle to overcome. He had to remain conscious. If he didn't, he might very well be buried with his companions when American troops advanced to the hilltop.

There he lay, fighting to retain consciousness. His seared hand throbbed. Shrapnel was encased in his legs. He could only guess as to the condition of his head. Rain, a delicious, ever so light rain fell on Glen. At last he opened his eyes. He was alive. Painfully, he crawled to the base of the hill, over and around the bodies of the fallen, until he came to a small creek. Glen splashed water on his face. He lay in the drizzle. Would he live to see Kentucky? Would he open presents on some future Christmas?

For over four hours, Glen lay on the jungle floor beside the creek. Then he heard the familiar twang of an American voice. Glen called as loudly as his strength allowed, "Medic, medic, down here!" Then the response, "Jesus Christ, one of them is alive!" After hearing those words, Glen Stanley slipped into unconsciousness.

Glen was taken to hospital in Pleiku, Vietnam. Doctors discovered that the bullet fired from the .45-calibre weapon had made a deep crease across his skull but had not entered his head. Had the weapon been held at a slightly steeper angle, there is no doubt the shot would have been fatal. In all, Glen would spend over a year in hospitals in Japan and in Fort Knox, Kentucky.

Today, Glen is in his forties. He is in the horse business in his native state of Kentucky. Glen and his wife Susan have three daughters — Leni, Kendra, and Mary Elizabeth.

Glen assures me he suffers from none of the psychological trauma so common among Vietnamese veterans. He blames no one for the useless war which took so many American lives. He has been left with a permanent limp from the shrapnel in his legs. When the cold weather comes, his wife Susan massages them each evening.

Glen's hair covers the crease across his skull. He chuckles as he relates how strange barbers are always amazed when they come across his unusual wide part.

This year, as he decorates his Christmas tree and purchases presents for his family, his mind sometimes wanders back to that time years ago when he lay so close to death, on a blood-soaked Vietnamese hill, wondering if he would ever celebrate another Christmas.

MISSING BABY

Up until November 22, 1960, not that much had happened to Doreen and Gordon Jeffs. The young couple and their three-week-old baby, Linda, lived in an airy, comfortable home in Eastbourne, England. Gordon made a fine living as a butcher.

The day started like most days since the baby's arrival. Doreen prepared breakfast. Gordon left for work, after which Doreen attended to her housework and the baby's needs. Doreen was known by the couple's close-knit circle of friends to be a meticulous housekeeper. That afternoon, she decided to take Linda out for a walk in her carriage. At the same time, she would attend to a few errands. Since the baby's birth, Doreen had often felt depressed and liked to get out in the cool, fresh air.

At 10 minutes after four, Doreen walked into Dale and Kerley's Furniture Store in the centre of town. She inquired about the price of a vacuum cleaner. Outside, sleeping peacefully in her gleaming new carriage was three-week-old Linda. Three minutes later, Doreen left the store and was shocked to discover that the carriage and Linda were nowhere in sight.

The distraught woman ran up and down the street screaming, "My baby, my baby, where is she?" Passers by could do little but comfort her. Hysterically, Doreen ran back to the store entrance. She stood there shouting, "Please, have you seen my baby, a little girl in white woollens with a pink bow?" Busy shoppers paused, shook their heads and attempted to comfort Doreen. No one had seen her baby.

Seven minutes later, police and civilians were actively searching for the missing child. Hours passed. Kidnapping for ransom was eliminated. The Jeffs were not a wealthy family. The dreaded thought that the child had been kidnapped by professionals who sold children to illegal adoption agencies was considered, as well as the possibility that some deranged woman, who wanted a baby of her own, might be the abductor.

All theories were discarded at 8 p.m., about four hours after the kidnapping, when a police officer peered into some bushes in a park in Hartfield Gardens, about a half mile from the furniture store where the child went missing. There lay little Linda Jeffs in her carriage. She had been strangled to death.

Upon being told of her daughter's death, Doreen Jeffs collapsed. Her husband Gordon was devastated. An intensive investigation into the murder was immediately launched. A house to house survey was conducted in an attempt to find anyone who may have noticed someone wheeling a carriage away from the front of Dale and Kerley's store. No one volunteered any useful information. About the only clue the police had to work with was a very faint footprint found in grass near where the baby's body was recovered. The print was believed to have been made by a shoe with a stiletto heel, but there was no guarantee that it was connected with the murder.

So distraught was Doreen Jeffs over the murder of her daughter that it was four days before she could be fingerprinted in order to eliminate her fingerprints. Unfortunately, no other prints were found on the carriage, leading detectives to believe that the killer wore gloves.

Gordon Jeffs accepted the cruel hand he had been dealt. Doreen didn't seem to be recovering from the trauma of losing her only child. Her eyes were bloodshot from weeping. Seldom was she seen without a handkerchief.

As the investigation wore on, Scotland Yard detectives became troubled by one undeniable fact. It didn't seem reasonable that not one person could be located who had seen the baby carriage outside the furniture store at a few minutes before four. After all, the streets had been crowded. Several people were located who swore they were there at that time, yet no one had seen a thing. Detectives measured off the distance from the furniture store to where the body was found. It was a 15-minute walk. Several shoppers were in the area at the time. Not one had noticed a woman wheeling a baby carriage.

Realizing they were treading on sensitive ground, Scotland Yard detectives became convinced that the baby carriage had never been placed outside the furniture store by Doreen Jeffs. Could this woman, who was genuinely heartbroken, have murdered her own child?

Discreetly, Gordon Jeffs was questioned. Without revealing their suspicions, detectives learned that Doreen had been terribly depressed since the baby's birth. They also discovered Doreen's obsession with keeping her house in an almost antiseptic condition. Was it possible that her depression, coupled with the ordinary disruption of caring for a newborn child, could have caused Doreen Jeffs to become mentally deranged and to have killed her own child?

Detectives approached Gordon once more, this time revealing the possibility that Doreen might be the killer. They also explained that she would receive a great deal of sympathy from any court, as she was obviously suffering from a mental illness. Gordon agreed that it would be in the best interests of his wife for him to co-operate with police.

A meeting was held in which Gordon urged Doreen to tell her story one more time in an effort to assist police. Once again, Doreen repeated the story she had related on the day of the disappearance. Gently, police explained that they previously had had cases where mothers, mentally ill after giving birth, had killed their own

147

children. They told Doreen that none had been convicted of murder.

For the first time, Doreen wavered. She indicated that she was afraid of being condemned by her husband. Gordon assured her he understood. Doreen broke down. She told police she had been burping the baby that day when the child turned blue and stopped breathing. She placed Linda in the carriage and went out. Doreen couldn't remember going into the park, nor could she account for the baby's fractured skull, which had been discovered in a post-mortem. She had no memory of concocting the phony kidnapping, but remembered going through with the made-up story.

Doreen Jeffs was charged with the murder of her daughter. On November 28, she was released under custody to attend Linda's funeral. Weeping uncontrollably, Doreen collapsed at graveside.

The murder charge was soon dismissed and Doreen was charged with infanticide. She was allowed bail, conditional on her being confined to the Hellingly Mental Hospital until March 17, 1961, the scheduled date of her trial.

The trial was brief and to the point. Doreen pleaded guilty to infanticide. She was sentenced to one year probation, again conditional upon her remaining in Hellingly Hospital for the full year.

Gordon and Doreen Jeffs resumed their life after Doreen's release from hospital, but Doreen never fully recovered from the horror of taking her own child's life. On January 6, 1965, Doreen disappeared. Two days later, police found her coat folded on the edge of a cliff near Eastbourne. Days later, her body washed ashore at Folkestone, Kent.

WEB OF
INTRIGUE

The New Jersey patrol officers thought the young man behind the wheel of the sleek black Buick sedan had been drinking. He was weaving down the highway as if he owned both sides of the road. The officers pulled him over and received the shock of their lives.

It isn't every day that what appears to be an impaired driver turns out to be the suspected killer of two elderly citizens. Inside the car sat 18-year-old Paul Dwyer. Paul was in the front seat. The back seat was occupied by Mrs. J.G. Littlefield. The trunk was occupied by her husband, Dr. Jimmy Littlefield. The elderly Littlefields of South Paris, Maine, were very dead.

Two days prior to the officers' discovery on that November day in 1937, Dr. Jimmy and his wife had been reported missing from their home in Maine. The elderly doctor hadn't kept an appointment to see a patient. When the patient called the Littlefield residence, expecting to hear Mrs. Littlefield answer the phone as she always did, there was no answer. The Littlefields were reported missing to police, but not for long. Two days later, they popped up in their own car driven by Paul Dwyer.

Maine police scampered to the Littlefield residence. Originally, they thought the doctor and his wife had taken a trip without telling anyone. Now they knew better. An examination of the doctor's appointment book revealed that he had a house call to make at the Dwyer summer residence. Paul's mother, a nurse, lived and worked in Hebron. Paul was occupying the house for a few days while he closed it for the winter months. Before police had a chance to drive to the Dwyer residence, Paul confessed to the double murder to New Jersey officials.

According to the teenager, he had called at the doctor's office. He believed that he had contracted a venereal disease and suggested an examination. However, he told the doctor he wanted it done at his home because he was afraid that somehow his mother would find out about his suspicions from Mrs. Littlefield. Dr. Jimmy agreed and drove to the Dwyer summer home. He started to examine Paul in an upstairs bathroom. At some point, Dr. Jimmy suggested that Paul had fathered a local girl's baby. Paul said he had lost his cool, had wrapped his belt around the doctor's neck and had choked the elderly medic. He ran from the bathroom, but upon hearing the doctor moan, he dashed back, picked up a handy wrench and hammer and proceeded to beat his hapless victim to death. The police officers sort of looked at each other. Not every bathroom is equipped with hammers and wrenches.

Paul said he pulled the Littlefields' car up to the back door. He then carried the doctor's body down to the car and stuffed it into the trunk. Realizing that Mrs. Littlefield was at home and would soon be missing her husband, he decided to trick the woman into accompanying him. Paul drove to the Littlefield residence and told the startled Mrs. Littlefield that her husband had hit two men with the Buick. He had helped Dr. Jimmy hide the bodies in some bushes. The good doctor had then hopped a train for Boston.

Paul went on. Mrs. Littlefield became hysterical and insisted that he drive her to Boston. Paul then pretended to make a phone call, returning to tell the distraught woman that her husband would meet them in Concord, New Hampshire, at the train station.

That whole day, with her husband's body peacefully

reposing in the trunk, Mrs. Littlefield was chauffeured around New Hampshire. They met the appointed train in Concord but, of course, we all know Dr. Jimmy didn't show up. Mrs. Littlefield became despondent, believing her husband may have committed suicide. She urged Paul to take her home to South Paris.

Paul, who had been driving a good many hours, was dead tired. Around New Gloucester, Maine, he was so exhausted he almost drove off the road. He pulled over to sleep. As he dozed off, Mrs. Littlefield asked him questions. He must have slipped up in his web of lies, because suddenly Mrs. Littlefield wanted to get out of the car. She even had the gall to suggest that Paul may have harmed her husband.

Evidently, this was all too much for Paul's sensitive disposition. He whipped off his trusty belt and proceeded to strangle Mrs. Littlefield. After the nasty deed was done, he placed the body in the back seat. Later, he was stopped by those traffic-wise New Jersey cops, who discovered his rather unique cargo.

Paul was flown back to Maine to face the music. Meanwhile, Maine officers descended on the Dwyer residence. The bathroom was blood-spattered from floor to ceiling. Hardened officers cringed as they imagined the desperate fight the elderly doctor had put up as he was strangled and beaten to death. Dr. Jimmy's false teeth were found under the bathtub. Detailed footprints were lifted from the hardened blood. They were matched to Paul Dwyer's shoes.

A couple of things bothered detectives investigating the murder. Could such a vicious attack have been initiated by a mere suggestion that Paul had been responsible for a local girl's pregnancy? Would Dr. Jimmy have violated a patient's confidence to Paul? These minor riddles were solved when Paul changed his story. He now told police that the motive had been money. He had lured the doctor to the bathroom as previously stated, but had killed him for the contents of his wallet. The rest of his story regarding Mrs. Littlefield was true in every detail.

For all intents and purposes, that tied up the case. In November 1937, Paul Dwyer pleaded guilty to the murder of Dr. James Littlefield. He was sentenced to life imprisonment in Maine's state prison.

A few weeks after being incarcerated, Paul Dwyer asked to see the warden of the institution. He told the warden a most unusual tale, which was to have far-reaching consequences. According to Paul, another man, Francis M. Carroll, a 48-year-old resident of South Paris, was the real murderer of Dr. Jimmy. Carroll had been a deputy sheriff and was the father of 18-year-old Betty, who happened to be Paul Dwyer's girlfriend. To complicate matters, Carroll had recently been discharged from his deputy sheriff's position and had been charged with having an incestuous relationship with his daughter, Betty.

Paul told the warden that Betty had sent him letters, informing him that her father was carrying on an incestuous relationship with her. She told her father that Paul had the damaging letters. Carroll badgered Paul for their return, hinting that his daughter was pregnant and that Paul was responsible.

Into this web of intrigue entered Dr. Jimmy Littlefield. Paul and Betty had arranged to meet at Paul's house, where Dr. Littlefield would examine the girl to discover whether she was pregnant. Daddy Francis Carroll had been asked to the meeting, but had no idea Dr. Littlefield would be there. When he arrived and saw the doctor, he flew into a rage. According to Paul, Carroll said, "What the hell is this, a trap? Why are you messing into this, Littlefield?"

Dr. Jimmy responded that he knew plenty about Carroll's incestuous relationship with his daughter. With that, Carroll started to hit Dr. Jimmy with anything that was handy. Paul claimed that he attempted to intervene, but the much bigger man knocked him out. When Paul came to, Dr. Jimmy was dead. Carroll was about to kill him, but Paul pleaded for his life. Finally, he convinced Carroll that the doctor's wife knew where he was going. If his life would be spared, he would pick up Mrs.

Littlefield, leave town and never be heard of again. Naturally, he would be blamed for the murder. Carroll agreed, and the rest, as they say, is history. But not quite.

Paul had to account for Mrs. Littlefield's murder. He now stated that he had picked up the doctor's wife after telling her the phony hit-and-run story. He decided to tell her all, adding the little white lie that her husband's body was back at the house in South Paris. Mrs. Littlefield demanded to see Carroll. They parked outside his house, waiting for him to drive up. Spunky Mrs. Littlefield faced Carroll and was promptly strangled to death by him.

Unbelievably, based mainly on Paul's statement and Carroll's terrible reputation, Francis Carroll was arrested. On June 24, 1938, he was charged with murder. Later that summer he was tried, convicted and sentenced to life imprisonment for the murder of Dr. Jimmy Littlefield.

Both Francis Carroll and Paul Dwyer languished in Maine State Prison. After Carroll had served 12 years, his conviction was overthrown as being unconstitutional. The court ruled his conviction was obtained through "fraud and deception" and that the case "seethes with inadmissible evidence and hearsay evidence."

Carroll was released in 1950 and died of natural causes in 1956.

In 1960, Paul Dwyer's sentence was commuted to time served. He was released after having spent 22 years in prison. Within the year, dapper Paul, 41, became a bridegroom.

No one was ever tried for the murder of Mrs. J. G. Littlefield.

THE BLACK DONNELLYS

They came from County Tipperary in the mid-19th century to settle in a new land. Most made their way to Lucan, Ont., about 14 miles north of London, to be with their own countrymen and to carve small farms out of the wilderness. It was a tempting proposition. Land could be purchased for a mere 13 shillings an acre. The new immigrants worked hard and they played hard.

One of their number was Jim Donnelly, a small, handsome man, who preceded his wife Johannah and son James to the new land. Two years after Jim's arrival, Johannah and her little son joined him in Lucan. A year later, Johannah gave birth to a second son, William, who was born with a club foot. In the years to follow, five more boys, John, Patrick, Michael, Robert, Thomas, and a lone girl, Jenny, would bless the union.

Whatever reputation Jim Donnelly was to later attain, no one has ever claimed that he was a lazy man or that he lacked ambition. He settled on a piece of vacant land along the Roman Line, so called for the large number of Roman Catholics whose farms faced the road. The lot that Jim settled on belonged to John Grace. In 1855, Grace sold half the site to Michael Maher, who, in turn, leased it to Patrick Farrell.

Patrick Farrell wanted his land and therein lies the

crunch. One must take sides when studying the saga of Jim Donnelly and his family. At every turn he could be painted either as a moody bully or a man justified in fighting for his rights and maintaining his principles. It is for the reader to decide.

The Irish had brought with them to the new world all the superstitions and feuds which had been passed down through generations back in Tipperary. Alliances were soon formed along the Roman Line. Neighbor fought neighbor. Disputes about land boundaries, livestock and rights of way were sometimes settled in court. More often, they were settled with fists outside Keefes Tavern, one of 12 watering holes which prospered in the small town.

Now, Patrick Farrell wanted the land which he legally owned. There was Jim Donnelly. He and his wife, with the help of their small boys, had worked year after year, from dawn to dusk, clearing the land until it was a functioning farm. By all that was holy, it was his property. After all, others had squatted on land with little regard for legal formalities.

Farrell rode up to the Donnelly homestead. Jim came out of the barn, which still stands, 111 years later, grim witness to the events which were to follow. Farrell gave Jim an hour to get off his property. Words were exchanged. Blows were struck. Farrell towered over Jim and outweighed him by at least 40 pounds. Despite these inequalities, Jim is reported to have given Farrell a severe beating, as Johannah and the boys cheered him on.

Farrell took his case to court. The results of the court action didn't sit well with Jim Donnelly. Farrell was awarded the south 50 acres, while Jim was given legal title to the north 50.

The two men became blood enemies. Donnelly is said to have taken a pot shot at Farrell, who lived close by his farm. The shot missed, but Farrell was convinced that his enemy had attempted to kill him. He formally charged Jim with "felonious shooting". Just before New Year's 1856, Jim stood in the Goderich Courthouse and swore to keep the peace for one year and not to molest Patrick Farrell.

For the next two years, Farrell would claim that Jim was responsible for the string of misfortunes which befell his farm. Cows took ill and suddenly died. Farrell's barn mysteriously caught fire. Legend has it that it was Farrell who first coined the phrase 'Black Donnellys.' As things turned out, he had good reason to be the originator of the derogatory description.

The second confrontation between Jim Donnelly and Patrick Farrell took place on June 27, 1857.

In pioneer days it was the custom to hold bees to clear land or raise a barn. The menfolk of the community donated their labor and animals to complete the work in record time. On that fateful hot day in June, several men were engaged at a logging bee on the small property of William Maloney. Some of the men brought jugs of whisky. Others relied on Maloney to provide the sauce for the day's labor. Big Pat Farrell was there. So was Jim Donnelly.

Oxen grunted and chains were pulled taut. Sweat-stained men stripped to the waist. It was hard work, conducive to taking long deep slugs of whisky from Maloney's liberal supply.

According to reports of the events which transpired, it is certain that both Farrell and Jim were drinking that day. Most likely, Farrell was intoxicated. Each time the two men came close to each other, a nasty remark would pass between them. Jim and Pat teed off against each other, but were separated before any harm was done. Jim is reported to have taunted Farrell into continuing the fight. Big Pat grabbed the nearest weapon, a big hand spike. The hand spike, a three-foot-long piece of hardwood, was used as a lever to move large logs. It made a formidable weapon.

Within minutes, Farrell faced Jim, who had also picked up a hand spike. Once again, cooler heads prevailed. The two adversaries were separated. It is reported that Big Pat fell to his knees, either from a push or from the effects of Maloney's whisky. At that precise moment, Jim raised his hand spike and brought it down full force on Farrell's head. A few moments later, Patrick Farrell died. The logging bee came to an abrupt halt. Ashen-faced men looked at Jim Donnelly. Jim slowly left the scene and walked home.

Two days later, an inquest was held into Farrell's death. Jim Donnelly didn't show up, but the inquest jury managed just fine without his presence. They came to the conclusion that Jim had murdered Pat Farrell and a warrant was issued for his arrest.

Jim was nowhere to be found. He had fled, but not far. Tough Jim was hiding out in woods, which skirted the rear of all the farms along the Roman Line. Jim's older boys — James, 15, Will, 12, and John, 10 — brought their father provisions. Sometimes Jim donned women's clothing and managed to work his distant fields while being sought by the law.

With the coming of winter and the severe windswept snows which swirled along the Roman Line, Jim had much more difficulty staying at large. Often he would spend the cold nights in a farmer's barn. There is some evidence that friends of the Donnellys allowed him to stay in their homes for short periods of time.

Still, life in hiding was no life at all. Johannah needed her man. Jim's children needed a father. On May 7, 1858, after being at large for a year, Jim Donnelly turned himself in to the local sheriff. Jim was tried, found guilty of murder and sentenced to hang.

Johannah Donnelly's nature wouldn't allow her to sit back while her husband's life was in jeopardy. She went about getting signatures on a petition for clemency. Some of the citizenry's hatred of Jim Donnelly was overcome by their sense of fairness. The death had taken place during a drunken brawl. Had Pat Farrell's wild swings connected with Jim's head, it would be Farrell who would be in the shadow of the hangman's noose.

Johannah wandered far afield to London and Goderich in search of men who knew her husband and regarded him quite differently than his enemies in Lucan. No less a personage than Attorney General John A. Macdonald, who would later become prime minister of Canada, commuted Jim's sentence from death to seven years imprisonment.

The cold iron gates of Kingston Penitentiary closed behind Jim Donnelly. Two months later, Johannah gave birth to Jenny, her only daughter.

One can only imagine the plight of Johannah Donnelly, with seven boys and a baby daughter to care for and a farm to run, living amongst many who hated the Donnelly clan with a passion. It is a tribute to this remarkable woman's resolve that she was successful in running and improving the farm during her husband's absence.

Seven years passed. Despite petitions, Jim served every day of his prison term. Now 48 years old, he returned to his family. His oldest son, Jim, was a young man of 23.

Jim Donnelly was back in town and life in Lucan would never be the same.

After Jim's return, every mishap which befell those who had testified at his trial seven years earlier was laid at the feet of the Donnelly family. The boys could scrap like hellions and there is no record of them ever losing a fight. The Donnellys prospered. In the 1860s, they went into the stagecoach business. Will and young Jim discovered they had a knack for business. From all reports, their small line was the cleanest, most efficient of any in service in the area. Their competition, old Bob Hawkshaw, planned to retire. Will and Jim offered to purchase his line, but Hawkshaw sold out to John Flannigan. Big John was well-liked and was confident that customers would patronize his stagecoach line rather than the Donnellys'. He was right.

Then, as if willed by the Devil himself, strange and unusual misfortunes befell Flannigan's stagecoach line. One day an axle broke, shaking up the passengers, severely damaging the coach and injuring a horse. Accident, maybe. Sabotage, possibly. One of Flannigan's barns burned to the ground. Five days later, another Flannigan barn inexplicably caught fire. A stagecoach was burned beyond repair, but eight horses were rescued from the blazing building. It is even reported that on one occasion Flannigan found his horses with their tongues cut out.

Flannigan was understandably incensed at the Donnellys. Together with 17 men, who believed that the Donnellys had gone too far, he advanced toward the Donnelly farm. Will and James were preparing the stagecoach for the run to London. The unruly mob stopped in front of the Donnelly barn. Jim, Sr. and all seven sons looked at the mob and rolled up their sleeves. Jim, Sr. spoke first, "You gentlemen seem to be looking for trouble. If so, the boys and I will be pleased to oblige you."

Flannigan hesitated at the cockiness of Jim Donnelly. That hesitation was to cost him dearly. The eight Donnellys tore into the 18-member mob. Several witnesses observed the Donnelly boys as they clubbed and punched until their enemies lay prostrate on the ground or took flight. It was all over in 10 minutes, but the scene of the fearless family fighting against better than two to one odds remained indelibly etched in the minds of the witnesses, who never tired of telling the story of the epic battle.

To gain some perspective into the terror that was the Donnelly family, one has only to scan the criminal charges placed against them in the first three months of 1876. It is an impressive list of 33 charges, including assault, arson, wounding, robbing and shooting with intent.

Like all pioneer families, the Donnellys had their share of personal tragedies. Jim, Jr., is reported to have died of pneumonia. Like everything about the Donnellys, his death is shrouded in mystery. Some say he was shot to death and the shooting was kept secret by the family. Whatever the truth, he lies today in the country graveyard beside St. Patrick's Church. Later, brother Michael was stabbed to death in a barroom brawl. He is buried beside his older brother.

The feuds continued, fiercer and crueller than before.

Word of the acts of terrorism and the law's inability to cope with the Black Donnellys slowly trickled to the outside world. Inside the tight pocket of pioneer Canada, desperate men had had enough. If the law couldn't tame the Donnellys, they would mete out their own brand of justice.

Jim Carroll was the catalyst which was required to ignite the local citizenry into action. Jim was born in the area, but had moved to the U.S., returning in 1878, at age 26. He was quickly made aware of the scourge known as the Black Donnellys. Big Jim let it be known that he had no fear of the Donnellys.

Robert Donnelly was hustled off to Kingston Penitentiary for taking a pot shot at Constable Sam Everett. Everett was given a severe thrashing soon after Robert's conviction. He couldn't or wouldn't identify his attackers and, soon after, resigned his position.

Big Jim Carroll became a Lucan constable with the promise, "I will drive the Donnellys out of Lucan." In a way, he did just that.

On the night of February 3, 1880, grim-faced men met at the Cedar Swamp Schoolhouse. They called themselves the Biddulph Vigilance Committee. The stone schoolhouse had been the gathering place for socials and political meetings, but this was different. By lantern light, jugs of whisky were passed from man to man. Although the weather was not overly cold, the whisky was necessary for the task at hand.

Some say there were 31 men in attendance, some say over 40. It matters little. They walked down the road toward the home of Jim Donnelly. Other men joined them en route. Into the Donnelly home they marched. Patrick "Grouchy" Ryder was among their number. Grouchy's barn had been burned. After many postponements, Johannah and Jim, Sr.,were to appear in Granton to answer to the charge of arson the next day.

Farming is a demanding occupation. Chores must be carried out and farm animals must be fed. To that end, the Donnellys had a neighboring youngster, 11-year-old

Johnny O'Connor, sleeping over that night. Johnny was to take care of the animals the next day, while the Donnellys drove to Granton to appear in court. A niece, Bridget, was visiting from Ireland. Tom was at home with his parents.

Constable Jim Carroll led the group. He sighted Tom Donnelly asleep in a tiny bedroom off the kitchen. Big Jim snapped handcuffs on his wrist. Tom awoke with a start and cried out, "What the hell!" Carroll responded, "You're under arrest."

The noise woke up Johannah, who in turn woke up her niece Bridget. Jim, Sr., was sleeping with Johnny O'Connor. He pulled on his trousers and joined the rest in the kitchen. He saw his son in handcuffs, "What? Tom, are you handcuffed?" he asked.

"Yes," Tom replied. "He thinks he is smart." By candlelight, Jim, Sr., went back to the bedroom for his coat. Johnny O'Connor had been using the elder Donnelly's coat for a pillow. Now he held it out for Jim, who returned to the kitchen.

There, in the eerie glow of the candle, Johnny O'Connor's eyes met Jim Carroll's. Later, Johnny would state there was no way Carroll was unaware of his presence. In light of future events, it is a minor mystery that Johnny O'Connor's life was spared.

Did the men intend only to beat up the Donnelly clan? Bill Ryder, a great great great nephew of Grouchy Ryder, says, "I believe the intent was to rough up the Donnellys, but something went wrong and, once started, the mob got out of hand."

All but one of the inhabitants of the house that night were beaten and clubbed to death. Tom Donnelly fell. So did his parents and so did his cousin Bridget. Johnny O'Connor, trembling with fear, hid under a bed, where he could see a shovel being brought down time after time on a Donnelly skull.

The house was set ablaze and in moments the mob was gone. Johnny O'Connor escaped from the burning house and ran barefoot to a neighboring farm. The mob's work wasn't completed. Down the road they marched to the home of Will Donnelly. It was his brother John who answered the door. Silhouetted in the light of the doorway, he was an easy target. John died moments after being shot. The mob thought it had killed the hated Will. Now the carnage came to an end. The men dispersed, leaving five members of the one family dead in their wake.

Next day, word of the tragedy spread. Initially, 13 men were held on suspicion. Of these, six were charged with murder — James Carroll, John Kennedy, Martin McLaughlin, Thomas Ryder, James Ryder and John Purtell. The six men were lodged in the jail behind the London courthouse.

On January 24, 1881, Jim Carroll stood trial for the murder of Johannah Donnelly for the second time. This time, he was found not guilty. Because the case against Carroll had been so strong, it was felt that it would be futile to try any of the remaining men. They were all released from custody. No one has ever been convicted of the five murders which took place in the wee hours of the morning of February 4, 1880.

In the years which followed the massacre of the Donnelly family, members of the Vigilance Committee were buried in the little graveyard beside St. Patrick's Church. Ironically, they rest forever beside the Donnelly family, victims of Canada's most infamous crime.

WHERE'S LUCKY?

My God, where's the Lord? That's the question every Englishman was asking back in 1974. The unanswered question has puzzled the entire world ever since.

Richard John Bingham, better known as Lord Lucan, was born with a sterling spoon between his tender gums. At the age of 13, he was packed off to Eton, where he excelled at rowing. Five years later, he joined his father's old regiment, the Coldstream Guards.

Lucky Lucan, as he was now called, took up bobsledding and continued to row while in the army. Upon rejoining civilian life, the handsome six-footer became an international playboy. Let's see, there was the winter season in St. Moritz, golf in Scotland, and, above all, gambling in the Bahamas, as well as back home in London.

Lucky Lucan was a familiar sight at London's better gaming establishments. Just before his 29th birthday, he married Veronica Duncan. Veronica was a tiny, beautiful woman who had been a teenage model. On November 28, 1963, the two were married at Holy Trinity Church, Brompton. Two months later, Lord Lucan and his bride moved into their home in Belgravia. Eleven months later, a son Francis was born, to be followed in three years by a second son, George Charles. The Lucans third and last child, Camilla, was born in 1970.

In the early seventies, Lucky Lucan wasn't lucky at all. His incessant gambling over the years had dissipated his inheritance. It wasn't unusual for him to drop the equivalent of $25,000 in one night. Being plagued constantly by creditors was bad enough, but there was another fly in the ointment. Lady Lucan had had enough of the Lord and his playboy ways. The couple separated.

To add insult to injury, the courts awarded Lady Lucan custody of the three children. Lucky was furious and developed an absolute obsession concerning his children. He wanted them back with a passion.

At 10 p.m. on November 7, 1974, the patrons of The Plumbers Arms were startled out of their bitters when the front door of the pub flew open and a woman entered, screaming, "Help me, help me! I have just escaped from a murderer! My children, my children...he's in the house... he's murdered the nanny...help me..."

No one took the plea lightly. The woman was bleeding profusely from head wounds. The barman of The Plumbers Arms, Art Whitehouse, and his wife rushed to the woman's aid. As Mrs. Whitehouse washed the stricken woman's wounds, she found that she was tending Lady Lucan, who lived but a short distance from the pub.

An ambulance was dispatched to The Plumbers Arms and the police to the Lucan residence. Police found the house in darkness. They had to force the front door to gain entrance. Inside, they found fresh bloodstains on the hall wallpaper. At the bottom of stairs leading to a breakfast room, they observed a large pool of blood.

Two flights upstairs in a bedroom, police spotted a bloody towel lying across a pillow. Two further flights up, on the fifth floor, they entered the nursery. Here, seven-year-old George and four-year-old Camilla were peacefully asleep in their beds. Francis, 10, was standing in a confused state beside her brother and sister.

One of the officers proceeded down into the basement. At the foot of the stairs was another pool of blood, strewn with broken cups and saucers. Inside the breakfast room, the officer observed a U.S. canvas mail bag. Blood oozed out on the floor from the canvas bag. The top of the bag was folded over, but not tied. As the officer unfolded the bag and peered inside, his colleague joined him. It was a sight they would not soon forget. A female body was doubled up inside the bag. The body was still warm to the touch.

The victim in the canvas mail bag was identified as Sandra Eleanor Rivett, the Lucan's 29-year-old nanny. Sandra had been in Lady Lucan's employ for only a few weeks before the murder.

Soon, Lord Lucan's mother appeared on the scene. She had received a telephone call from her son, asking her to come to his wife's home. He told her there had been "a terrible catastrophe."

That same evening, the Dowager Countess took her three grandchildren to her own home. A police officer accompanied her. No sooner did they arrive at her home in St. John's Wood than the phone rang.

The officer heard only one side of the conversation. He heard the Lord's mother inquire, "Where are you? Are you all right? Yes, they are all safe here and are asleep." When the caller was asked if he wanted to speak to the police officer, he hung up. The Lord's mother told the officer that it had been her son on the phone. He said he would call them in the morning. He never did.

The morning after the attack, Lady Lucan was questioned in hospital. She reconstructed the events of the night before. Sandra Rivett usually took Thursdays off, but on this fateful Thursday she chose to remain at home. Between 9 and 9:30 p.m., Lady Lucan was watching television with her eldest son, Francis. Sandra asked her mistress if she cared for a cup of tea and proceeded downstairs, carrying cups and saucers which had been used earlier in the evening.

Sandra never returned. Twenty minutes passed. Wondering what was keeping her, Lady Lucan proceeded downstairs. She peered into the basement, which was in darkness. She called Sandra's name. Without warning, a man appeared out of nowhere and hit her over the head. While she was stunned, the man attempted to strangle her. She managed to fight him off and run to The Plumbers Arms.

On the morning after the murder, William Shand-Kydd, who was married to Lady Lucan's sister, received two letters from Lucky. One asked that certain assets be disposed of to take care of pressing creditors. The other letter stated that he had interrupted a fight between his estranged wife and an intruder. He had fought off the intruder.

Lady Lucan had accused him of hiring an assassin to kill her. He claimed that he had attempted to take care of her wounds, but when he went to the bathroom, she ran to The Plumbers Arms. He said he believed the circumstantial evidence against him was strong and that his wife's version of the events would be believed.

If Lord Lucan's recital of the events of that night is to be believed, the intruder must have had a key, as there was no sign of forced entry into the home. Why would anyone want to kill Sandra Rivett? A check of her boyfriends and acquaintances exonerated them all. Sandra was a cheerful, good-looking woman who had no enemies. She had not been sexually assaulted, nor had any valuables been removed from the Lucan residence.

Detectives found it hard to believe that an outsider had perpetrated the crime. On the other hand, Lord Lucan knew that Sandra usually took Thursdays off. He had a key to the house. He wanted his wife out of the way so that he could have custody of his children.

On November 10, police found a Ford Corsair parked in Newhaven, Sussex. The interior of the car was bloodstained. Inside the trunk of the Ford, police recovered a piece of lead pipe two feet long with adhesive tape wrapped around one end, forming a type of handle. A similar piece of pipe had been found at the murder scene and was assumed to be the murder weapon.

The Ford Corsair belonged to a friend of Lord Lucan's,

Michael Stoop. When questioned, Stoop revealed that he loaned the vehicle to Lucky Lucan two weeks before the murder. Stoop volunteered that, at the time, he had offered his friend a loan of his Mercedes, but Lucky had insisted on the Ford.

Detectives noted that the Ford had a much larger trunk than the Mercedes. They theorized that Lucan had planned to transport his wife's body in the trunk of the Ford. All his plans went awry when he encountered nanny Sandra Rivett on her way to fetch tea for Lady Lucan. To fortify Scotland Yard's theory, Lady Lucan identified her husband as her attacker from the witness stand at an inquest which took place some time after the murder.

November 8 was fixed as the day Lord Lucan abandoned Stoop's vehicle. Two trawlermen later told police they had seen a well-dressed gentleman walking along a nearby pier on that day. Another man was checking out his boat the same day, when he saw a man, whom he later identified as Lord Lucan, walking on the pier.

Did Lucky Lucan take the big plunge or was he cunning enough to plant the seeds of his demise by suicide? Some believe him to be innocent of murder and still on the run. Others believe that he murdered Sandra Rivett and made his way to North America.

Guilty or innocent? Dead or alive? The mystery of whatever became of Lord Lucan has never been solved.

THE PERFECT
CRIME

Josephine Medina, 17, a student at Haaren High School in New York City, was in love with 18-year-old William Sanders. During the summer of 1943, she was employed at a factory which manufactured artificial flowers on West 18th St. Billy liked Jo well enough, but love — that was another matter altogether.

Billy invited Jo to his parents' cottage at Candlewood Lake, Connecticut. Jo was thrilled. This could be the real thing. They would elope and live happily ever after.

On August 28, Jo wrote a letter to her mother and left it with a girlfriend. It read, "Dear Mum, I have gone away. Please don't worry. Will take care of myself. Your daughter, Jo. P.S. : Will send you money every month."

The letter sounded as if Jo had no intention of returning. Such was not the case for Billy Sanders. He was planning on a weekend of lust and sin with an attractive girl and nothing more.

On the night of the 28th, Jo and Billy walked into Danbury for groceries. They returned to the lake for a swim. While there, they met several teenagers and chatted with a merchant marine sailor, after which they returned to their one-room cottage.

Jo and Billy stayed overnight. Next day, they sought adventure and a better site for lovemaking. They looked over the various larger cottages and found one that was locked up for the season. The young couple broke into a cottage owned by Mr. and Mrs. Nick Noce. They headed for the master bedroom and made love.

Everything was turning out just swell for Billy Sanders. There he was, away from the hustle and bustle of New York City, with a cool lake to swim in and a lovely young thing at his beck and call.

Then the roof caved in. Jo suggested marriage. Nothing was the same after that. The day, which had begun with sweet lovemaking, deteriorated into bickering. Billy tried to reason with the girl. They were too young. What would they live on? Where would they live? Jo wouldn't listen. They would go away, get jobs and live happily ever after.

No, insisted Billy. Things just don't turn out that way. They had to get an education first. Jo put her hands over her ears. She retaliated by screaming that if he didn't marry her, she would go to both her own parents and his and tell them how she had succumbed to his lovemaking under the impression that they would get married.

The two young people didn't spend a pleasant night. Next morning, Jo prepared breakfast and retired to the livingroom. For his part, Billy was frightened out of his wits. If Jo's parents didn't kill him, his own parents would do the job. There was no way he could allow Jo to expose their affair. He had to do something. Who knows exactly when he began to think of murder.

Billy had noticed a .22-calibre rifle in the cellar. Was there ammunition somewhere? He went into the cellar and noticed a box of bullets on a shelf near the rifle. Quietly, he loaded the weapon and made his way upstairs. Silently, Billy sneaked up behind Jo, aimed the barrel of the rifle close to her head and squeezed the trigger. Jo Medina fell to the floor, dead.

Billy had some difficulty lugging Jo's body into the cellar. Once there, he attempted to dig a hole in the hard packed earth which hadn't been disturbed for years, but it proved to be too difficult a task. Finally, Billy gave up and placed Jo's body just below the surface. He put ashes over the body in order to conceal his handiwork.

Jo's clothing was hastily burned in the back yard. Billy then sprinkled fuel oil all over the cellar and set it afire. He walked into Danbury in time to catch the 3:30 p.m. train to New York City.

Back at Candlewood Lake, the Noces' cottage burned to the ground. There wasn't much of an investigation. Fire sometimes destroyed a cottage in the lake area. Maybe, a bum had broken in and had thrown away a lighted cigarette. Maybe, spontaneous combustion was responsible.

One of the firemen found a .22-calibre rifle amidst the debris. The stock had been burned away and the various metal parts had been bent and twisted from the heat. The fireman tossed what remained of the rifle in a garbage bin.

Josephine Medina was reported missing by her parents. They showed her letter to police. It certainly appeared as if the young girl had run away from home. Nothing much was done. Girls leave New York City every day. Nine months later, on May 31, 1944, Mr. and Mrs. Noce drove to Candlewood Lake to survey their burned-down cottage. Mrs. Noce decided to rake away the burned embers and ashes, which were strewn over what had once been the earthen cellar floor. Her rake caught on something. That something was the badly burned body of Jo Medina.

An autopsy indicated that the young girl had been shot in the head with a single bullet fired from a .22-calibre weapon. An anthropologist estimated the girl to be five feet six inches, slim, brown-haired and a teenager. When it was reported that a body had been found in the remains of the fire, the fireman who had discarded the rifle informed police that he had tossed it into a garbage bin. Although it had been nine months since the gun had been placed in the bin, police discovered that the garbage had been removed from the bin only six weeks before the body was found.

Several policemen were assigned the disagreeable task of sifting through the Danbury city dump. Four days later, they found the .22-calibre rifle. Mr. Noce identified the weapon as the one he had left in his summer home.

Now the authorities had a body and what was apparently the murder weapon, but they hadn't identified the victim. Because most of the residents of the cottage country around Danbury are New Yorkers, it was decided to check each teenager reported missing in New York. While this task was being addressed, a strange coincidence took place.

Two police officers were having lunch at a Danbury diner. Close by, two sailors were discussing the Candlewood Lake murder. The murder was understandably the main topic of conversation in the area. The officers overheard one sailor tell the other that he had a friend who had spent some time at Candlewood Lake the previous summer. The officers' ears perked up. They introduced themselves and learned that the sailor's friend had told him he had chatted with a girl from New York who said she worked in an artificial flower factory.

With this information to go on, New York detectives were immediately able to locate the missing persons report on Josephine Medina, which had been filed on September 1, 1943.

Classmates at Haaren High School told police about Jo's love affair with Billy Sanders. Jo's mother confirmed the romance. The Sanders had moved to the Bronx, but were soon located. When Billy was questioned, he admitted to being at Candlewood Lake himself, but claimed he had never been there with Jo. However, when Jo's badly burned clothing and the burnt rifle were brought into the interrogation room, Billy wilted. Finally, he blurted out, "All right, I did it."

Billy had almost committed the perfect crime. By sheer luck, he had not been connected to the murder until two sailors chanced to sit near two police officers in a diner in Danbury, Conn. On September 20, 1944, William Sanders pleaded guilty to murder in the second degree. He was sentenced to life imprisonment.

YOU BE
THE JURY

Okay, folks, pay attention. I'll set out the pertinent facts in a murder case for you to peruse, much as they were laid out for a British jury back in 1923. You have only two verdicts to consider: Guilty or not guilty.

The murder itself lacked those qualities which contribute to a celebrated case. It was the trial which produced high drama.

Ready? Here we go.

Taxi driver Jacob Dickey was parked in London's West End, in anticipation of picking up a fare out of the hundreds of individuals and couples leaving the busy entertainment district. Before this night in May, the 39-year-old Dickey had led an exemplary and relatively anonymous existence. All that was to change within 40 minutes. A fare entered his taxi and Dickey drove away.

Jacob Dickey was next seen struggling desperately with a man on Baytree Rd. in Brixton, some distance from the bright lights of London's West End. The doors of his cab were wide open. The residential street was quiet except for the struggling men. The sound of shots broke the still night air. Dickey fell to the street. His assailant ran away.

The police were at the scene in moments. Dickey lay dead beside his taxi. Nearby, on the road, police recovered a recently fired gun, which the killer had hurriedly thrown away. They also found a cane with a distinctive gold knob, a pair of suede gloves and a blackjack. Dickey's fare had been well-prepared to rob the unsuspecting taxi driver.

Police attempted to trace the flight of the killer. They found a flashlight in an open residential garage at 28 Baytree Rd. There were footprints and broken shrubbery in the garden behind the house. The trail led to a wall, enclosing the backyard of 15 Acre Lane. Two ladies lived in the house at 15 Acre Lane. They were surprised to see a man jump over the wall onto their property. The desperate man, who they thought was a burglar, faced the two women, who had not heard the shots. "I must get through to the street," he said. The terrified women let the stranger go through their house and out onto Acre Lane.

Scotland Yard didn't take long to trace the distinctive cane to a small-time transplanted American crook named Eddie Vivian. Eddie was well-known around Soho and often carried a gun in his chosen line of work, namely house breaking.

Eddie was located in lodgings at Charlwood St., Pimlico. More specifically, he was located in bed with his lady friend, chorus girl Hettie Colquhoun. When shown the distinctive cane, Eddie immediately admitted ownership. He also agreed that the flashlight found near the scene of the crime belonged to him. However, Eddie proclaimed that he had been home in bed at the time of the crime and all that day with stomach trouble. Hettie had taken care of him and would vouch that he had never left his room.

Eddie stated that a friend, 22-year-old Scottie Mason, had been released from prison only a few days before Dickey's murder. The two men had spent time in prison together and had planned to pull a few "house jobs" when Mason got out. Sure enough, on the Sunday before the murder, Mason had shown up. They had looked over a few likely houses to burglarize.

When the night for the planned robbery arrived, Eddie

173

was too ill to take part. Scottie had borrowed his walking stick, flashlight and blackjack. According to Eddie, Scottie had left at 7:30 p.m. and had returned at 11:30 p.m. in a dishevelled condition. His shoes and clothing were dirty and had bloodstains on them. Scottie had told his friend, "I've made a mess of things. I've shot a taxi driver."

Eddie told Scotland Yard detectives that he had put Scottie up that night, telling Hettie that his friend had been roughed up by some thugs. The next morning, Scottie left. Eddie hadn't seen him since.

Eddie was detained. The very next day, Scottie Mason was spotted on the street by an alert police officer and taken into custody.

Scottie was placed in a police lineup. The two women who had had the disconcerting experience of showing a killer through their home were brought in to see if they could pick their visitor out of a lineup. Without hesitation, both identified Scottie as the man.

Eddie Vivian was released from custody and Scottie Mason was charged with the murder of Jacob Dickey. All Scottie would say was, "I cannot understand it. I was nowhere near Acre Lane that night. I know nothing whatever about the murder. You are making a mistake. I did not do it." More than that, Scottie Mason would not say. When he wanted to give a statement, he was told that because he hadn't had legal advice, he had better wait until a legal aid lawyer was appointed to represent him.

On July 11, 1923, Scottie Mason stood trial for murder without ever really giving his side of the story. Eddie Vivian was rigorously cross-examined by Scottie's legal aid counsellor, A.C. Fox-Davies. The defence put it to Eddie that his story of being sick had been concocted to conceal from Hettie the fact that he and Scottie were planning a robbery.

Fox-Davies revealed that Scottie had left the Vivian love nest at 7:30 p.m., Hettie had left at 8:30 p.m., leaving Eddie plenty of time to meet Scottie at Baytree Rd. Fox-Davies accused Eddie of being the man who was Dickey's fare that night and of being the murderer of Jacob Dickey. Eddie vehemently denied all.

The accused man took the witness stand in his own defence. Scottie told the court that Eddie's illness had been contrived between them to allay Hettie's fears that they would pull a robbery that night. They had planned to meet at Baytree Rd. Eddie had told Scottie that he knew a shady taxi driver who would drive for them.

Scottie went to Baytree Rd. to wait for Eddie and the taxi. As the taxi approached, Scottie heard the two men arguing. The doors flew open and the taxi driver and Eddie began fighting on the street. Shots were fired. Scottie didn't wait around. He took off, jumped a fence and stood for a few seconds before an open house garage. It was here he left the flashlight.

Eddie jumped over the same fence. Frantically, he looked at Scottie and said, "My God, Scottie, help me, I can't walk! My legs are gone. I can't move!" Scottie wasn't in any mood to help anyone. He jumped over a wall, where he was seen by the two women who let him go through their house. He then made his way back to Eddie's lodgings and found Eddie already there.

Scottie's story had the desired effect on the court. Many believed he was telling the truth. He had placed Eddie in Dickey's taxi. He had accounted for Eddie's cane, flashlight and blackjack being found near the scene. Above all, his story accounted for the two women identifying him.

Now, it's your turn. You are faced with two unsavory characters. Both had spent time in prison for burglary. Both admitted to planning a burglary on the night of the murder. Yet both told far different stories.

What is your verdict? Did the jury find Scottie Mason guilty or not guilty?

Despite his plausible story, the English jury took only 17 minutes to find Scottie Mason guilty of murder. He was sentenced to death. Five days before his execution date, he received a reprieve. The home secretary, William Bridgeman, later revealed that Mason's story had placed a lingering doubt in his mind, which resulted in his issuing a reprieve.

An interesting aspect came to light when the prosecuting attorney, Sir Richard Muir, revealed that throughout the trial he had consulted an old ordinance survey of the area where the crime had been committed. It was his practice to visit the scene of every murder where he acted as prosecuting attorney. However, on the day he drove down to look at the Dickey murder scene with the intention of making sketches, a terrific rainstorm, accompanied by thunder and lightning, took place. As a result, he didn't get out of his car, but relied on the old survey drawings.

In the years between the time of the survey and the date of the murder, several buildings and walls had been erected. The escape route described by Scottie as the one taken by Eddie was an impossibility. Scottie had made up the story incriminating Eddie. He was indeed the guilty party, but his life had been spared because of a thunderstorm.

Scottie Mason spent 14 years in prison before being paroled in 1937. He served as a merchant seaman in the Second World War and was lost at sea when his ship was torpedoed.

CYANIDE KILLINGS

Frumpy 44-year-old Stella Nickell first saw the light of day in Portland, Oregon. Her family was poverty stricken and Stella was left pretty much to her own devices during her formative years. By the time she was 16, she was married and the mother of a bouncing baby girl, Cynthia.

Stella got into minor scrapes with the law. Let's see now, there was the silly scam the law called fraud, and the small-time wallpapering operation, which an inconsiderate prosecuting attorney deemed to be forgery.

Eventually, Stella shed her teenaged husband and married Bruce Nickell, a heavy equipment operator with a drinking problem. For a while, Bruce and Stella had fun barhopping their lives away. It was kind of a shock to Stella when Bruce took the cure. To Stella's way of thinking, the good times stopped and boredom set in.

In the early 1980s, Stella and Bruce lived in a trailer in Washington state. Money was scarce. Bruce was unemployed for long stretches of time. Daughter Cynthia, who had married and divorced, was bringing up her child in Stella's trailer. Right beside the Nickells' trailer lived Stella's elderly mother. All in all, Stella had her hands full. Life was a bowl of cherry pits.

In 1982, Stella confided to her daughter that she would like to get rid of hubby Bruce. She vaguely told Cynthia that she was thinking of insuring his life and collecting on the insurance. Then she would purchase the land the trailer was on and open a tropical fish store. Cynthia listened to her mother, but dismissed the conversation as the ramblings of a woman who had missed the boat.

But mother wasn't kidding.

In 1985, Stella took out a $40,000 insurance policy on Bruce's life, with herself as sole beneficiary. Bruce, who often worked for the state, had an employment policy which paid his wife $136,000 in the event of accidental death. The same policy paid only $31,000 if death was due to natural causes.

One fine day in June, Stella took a bottle of Excedrin capsules down from a shelf in the kitchen. She laced several of the capsules with cyanide. Just like in an Agatha Christie novel, Bruce came home from work complaining of a headache. He reached for the Excedrin and gulped down four pills. Stella watched. Bruce turned on the TV. Nothing happened.

He then got up and went outside. Bruce screamed, "I feel like I'm going to pass out!" True to his word, Bruce bit the dust. Stella did the wifely thing. She called paramedics and watched as a helicopter flew her seriously ill husband to Harborview Medical Center in Seattle. A few hours later Bruce was dead.

When informed of Bruce's death, Stella had the distasteful duty of breaking the news to Cynthia. She felt obliged to tell her daughter that she had nothing to do with the unexpected tragedy.

A coroner failed to detect any poison in Bruce's body and attributed death to pulmonary emphysema. Stella had committed the perfect murder. But our Stella was far from pleased. In fact, she was downright depressed.

Remember those insurance policies? Stella stood to collect $40,000 and $31,000, for a total of $71,000, which everyone will agree is a tidy sum. But darn it all, if only the death had been accidental, the payoff would have been a whopping $176,000. There simply had to be a way to get at the big bucks. Stella thought and thought. Then the idea came to her. Why not murder someone else? Authorities would be convinced that her husband had been killed by some nut who ran around killing strangers.

Stella opened three bottles of Extra-Strength Excedrin and Anacin-3 and emptied some of the capsules. She refilled them with cyanide. The poisoned headache remedies were surreptitiously placed on the shelves of three nearby stores.

Within a week, one of the bottles was purchased. Sue Snow, 40, was the assistant vice-president of the Puget Sound National Bank branch of Auburn, Washington. She had recently married for the third time. Husband Paul Webking, 45, was a truck driver, who dearly loved his new wife.

Somewhere along the line, Sue had heard that caffeine in Extra-Strength Excedrin would give you a boost to start the day. It was her habit to take two capsules each morning. On June 11, 1986, Sue got up around 6 a.m., took her capsules and collapsed on the bathroom floor. Six hours later, Sue was dead.

This time, Stella's handiwork was uncovered. Doctors stated Sue had been poisoned by the administration of cyanide placed in Excedrin capsules. That same morning, Sue's husband Paul, who suffered from arthritis, had taken Excedrin from the same bottle as Sue. He suffered no ill effects, no thanks to our Stella. By sheer luck, his capsules had not been doctored.

Now Stella went after those accidental death insurance dollars. Exhibiting more gall than brains, she informed authorities that her husband had also taken Excedrin the day he died. An examination of skin tissue indicated that Stella's suspicions were well founded. Bruce Nickell had been poisoned.

The Bristol-Myers Co., manufacturers of Excedrin, acted swiftly in removing hundreds of thousands of bottles of their products off store shelves. Paul Webking filed a wrongful death suit against Bristol-Myers. Bold as brass, Stella Nickell filed a similar suit.

In all, five poisoned bottles of headache remedy were

uncovered. Because two of the five were found in Stella's home, she received close attention from detectives attempting to crack the case. It wasn't long before they discovered the insurance policies on Bruce Nickell's life. Stella was given a lie detector test, which indicated she was not responding truthfully.

The case was solved when Stella's daughter Cynthia, now 28 years old, came forward and agreed to testify against her mother. Stella was taken into custody.

At Stella's murder trial, Cynthia was the state's star witness. From the witness stand, she reviewed the family history. She revealed that her mother had told her that her life had become empty and boring when Bruce stopped drinking. Her mother had stated that she was contemplating killing Bruce. Why had Cynthia not revealed her mother's intentions before Stella committed double murder? For one thing, Cynthia never dreamed that her mother would actually kill anyone.

Defence lawyers suggested that Cynthia had been tempted by the $300,000 reward for the killer's identity put up by the Non-Prescription Drug Manufacturers Association. An official of this organization has informed me that, as of this date, no one, including Cynthia, has applied for the reward.

After deliberating for over five days, the Washington jury found Stella guilty of causing death by product tampering. She was the first person convicted in the U.S. under a new law covering product tampering, instituted in 1983 after seven people were killed in the Chicago area by poisoned bottles of Tylenol. The Tylenol killer has never been apprehended.

Stella Nickell was sentenced to 90 years imprisonment. She will be eligible for parole in 2018, when she will be 74 years old.

"COMPANY"
SLAVE

Outwardly, there was nothing strange about Cameron and Jan Hooker. Cameron, who stood six feet four inches tall, was a conscientious 24-year-old lumbermill worker down at Diamond International. The young couple had been married in 1975 and had a baby girl. They lived quietly in a rented house at 1140 Oak St. in Red Bluff, California. Cameron was considered a quiet, laid-back sort of guy, who never caused any trouble, never made any waves.

When the truth was revealed, Superior Court Judge Clarence Knight would call Cameron "the most dangerous psychopath I have ever encountered."

What no one knew, not neighbors, not relatives, was that Cameron had become obsessed with bondage. It was really nothing new. He and Jan had practised bondage before they were married, when she was 17. They would go to an isolated area outside town, where Jan would let Cameron tie her up. Jan didn't like the practice, but Cameron was always so nice to her afterward that it sort of made up for the temporary pain and indignity.

After the baby was born, Cameron talked to Jan about capturing a female victim so that he could act out all his fantasies on her. At first, Jan objected. She simply didn't need another woman around the house. Gradually,

Cameron convinced Jan that it would be fun. He would take care of all the details in advance. There would be no risk of being found out. Slowly, Jan was won over. They would capture a woman all for themselves.

Colleen Stan, 20, left Eugene, Oregon, on May 19, 1977 to hitch-hike to the small northern California town of Westwood. A girlfriend was celebrating a birthday and Colleen had promised to attend. By 4 o'clock that afternoon, she had made her way to Red Bluff. Several cars stopped to give Colleen a ride, but she was a careful hitch-hiker and refused rides that didn't seem right.

When Cameron and Jan Hooker drove up with their baby on Jan's knee, Colleen didn't hesitate. She jumped right into the Hookers' Dodge Colt. She had no way of knowing that Cameron and Jan had been making dry runs for weeks, searching for a victim. Colleen would do nicely.

Cameron drove off the highway onto a dirt sideroad. Without warning, he was in the back seat, pressing a knife against Colleen's neck. He handcuffed and blindfolded the helpless girl. Everything happened at double speed. Cameron had the tools of his trade at hand. A leather strap was placed around Colleen's head and under her chin, locking her mouth closed.

Cameron proceeded in an organized manner. He undid a strange-looking wooden box, which Colleen had noticed on the back seat when she first got into the Hookers' car. It proved to be what Cameron called a head box. The 20-pound plywood box was placed over Colleen's head. It fit tightly around her neck. Cameron snapped the hinged opening shut.

When it became dark, Colleen was transferred to the basement of the Hooker residence on Oak St. Once there, Jan busied herself putting the baby to bed. Cameron had other ideas. He handcuffed Colleen to an overhanging pipe. A Coleman ice chest was placed under her feet. She was undressed and made to stand on the chest on her toes. Cameron kicked away the ice chest.

Pain shot through Colleen's wrists and shoulders. Still

gagged with the leather strap, she couldn't cry out in pain. She kicked frantically for some support for her legs, but there was none. The kicking angered Cameron. He proceeded to whip his helpless victim. Finally, the chest was replaced under Colleen's toes, giving her some relief from the excruciating pain.

Cameron undid Colleen's handcuffs and forced her into a three-foot high box with an opening at one end. She didn't know it at the time, but this was to be her new home.

For a few days no one missed Colleen. Her friends believed she was attending a birthday party, while her pals at Westwood thought she had decided not to show up. In time, she was reported missing to police.

Cameron didn't miss a day's work down at the mill. He remained the quiet, unassuming employee he had always been. Jan tended house and cared for her baby. Neighbors liked the quiet young couple. No one ever suspected that they had a human plaything living in a box in their basement.

Cameron fed his victim scraps of food left over from his and Jan's meals. When the mood struck him, he took Colleen out of the box and performed any sexual fantasy which entered his warped mind.

Weeks turned into months. Colleen Stan was totally cut off from the world. Her world consisted of torture when outside the box and total darkness when confined. There was no night, no day, no days of the week, no weather, no news. She lived in a vacuum of pain.

Six months after capturing Colleen, Cameron got the bright idea that she should be put to work. He constructed a closet in the basement. Each night, he removed Colleen's handcuffs and let her out of the box. He placed her in the closet and instructed her to unhook her gag. Colleen did macrame work and knitted during the night. Each morning, before going to the mill, Cameron picked up Colleen's finished products and returned her to the box. Cameron sold the wares at a flea market in San Jose. Colleen Stan had become the

Hookers' slave.

The change in Colleen's status wasn't lost on Cameron Hooker. He read somewhere of a slavery contract and thought it a great idea. With Jan's help, he made up an impressive looking document and approached Colleen. He told the hapless girl that an organization known as "The Company" dealt in slaves. She listened to the weird tale.

Cameron told Colleen that The Company was aware he had captured her. As a member of the sect, he had to register her or face death. Colleen signed the slave contract, which in essence stated that Cameron, who would ever after be addressed as Master, owned her body and soul. Should she attempt to run away, the company would send out patrols to kill her parents and hunt her down. Colleen had been brainwashed. She believed every word.

The Hookers moved to a trailer outside of Red Bluff. Cameron proceeded with his usual efficiency. He constructed a box under his and Jan's waterbed for their slave. The move was accomplished without a hitch. Colleen crawled into her new home.

In 1979, Colleen turned 23. She had spent well over two years in captivity. Cameron, for reasons known only to him, showed his first act of kindness toward his slave. He allowed her out of her box for longer periods of time. She was even permitted to put on scraps of clothing. Sometimes, if the mood struck him, Cameron would let Colleen work in the garden outside the trailer. Neighbors chatted with Colleen. She gave no hint of her predicament. Later, they said that the Hookers' roomer was a pleasant young girl, if a bit shy. Little did they know that Colleen firmly believed that if she spoke out or ran away, she would be hunted down and killed.

In 1980, Colleen was able to go to a roadhouse with Jan. They danced with boys and had a few beers. Not once did Colleen attempt to run away, so completely was she under the control of Cameron Hooker. Colleen had one wish, and that was to let her parents know that she was alive. She often begged Cameron to let her call them. Eventually, he relented. With Cameron at her side in a phone booth, she spoke to her dumbfounded parents and her sister. She revealed nothing about her plight or location. When instructed by Cameron, she hung up.

Cameron now felt he had full control over his slave. The ultimate test would be to let Colleen visit her parents. He made his usual elaborate preparations. He told Colleen that her parents' phone had been tapped by The Company. Every word uttered in their home would be recorded. If anything went wrong, all members of her family would be slaughtered.

On March 20, 1981, accompanied by Cameron, Colleen visited her parents. He dropped her off at the door and drove away. Colleen's parents were understandably thrilled to see their long absent daughter. They noticed that Colleen was thin and pale, yet she seemed happy enough. There would be plenty of time for questions later.

Colleen slept in the house, went to church with members of her family next morning, and spent a total of 24 hours free outside the presence of the Hookers. Cameron drove up, was introduced to the family with a phony name and, as suddenly as she had appeared, Colleen was gone.

As the years passed, a relationship developed between Jan and Colleen. They seemed to like each other. Jan's friendship with Colleen coincided with her misgivings about her husband. Sometimes, the two young women discussed their roles in Cameron's life, but never once did Jan reveal that the dreaded Company was a total lie.

Cameron's ultimate mastery over his slave would be complete if he could control her while she worked independently at an outside job. In a short time, Cameron fattened up his slave to a robust 120 pounds. It was now seven long years since Colleen had been kidnapped. She had no difficulty obtaining employment as a maid in the nearby King's Lodge Motel. It was the best thing that had happened to Colleen since her capture. She was out of the hated box all day and was free of Cameron's harassment and torture.

Colleen was thrilled when Cameron granted her and Jan permission to go to church. They became regular church-goers. Eventually, Jan grew to fear for her own life. Could something occur which would change her status from wife to slave? Was her husband capable of killing her?

On August 7, 1984, Jan decided to tell Colleen the truth. There was no Company out there ready to kill her or her family if she ran away. Colleen was devastated by the news and made immediate plans to escape the clutches of the man who had held her captive for over seven years.

A call to her father for $100 travelling money was hurriedly made. A day or so later, Colleen was back at her parents' home. She never revealed details of her ordeal. She received a call from Cameron, begging her to return. He even promised to give up bondage. Jan, who had left at the same time as Colleen, succumbed to her husband's phone calls and returned to him.

Things were never the same in the Hooker residence after Colleen escaped. Husband and wife argued incessantly. Finally, Jan sought psychiatric and spiritual help. It was her minister who listened to her story and called police.

Cameron was taken into custody. Janice Hooker was granted immunity from prosecution in return for her testimony. Cameron Hooker was found guilty of seven charges ranging from kidnapping to rape. He was sentenced to a total of 104 years in prison. The various sentences making up the 104 years are to run consecutively.

JAKE AND
THE MISTRESS

Oil field roustabouts would walk into Millers Dry Goods and buy yards of calico just to have a chat with Clara Smith. Well, that's not exactly true. They didn't mind gazing at Clara's figure as well.

The 16-year-old dry goods clerk had all the proper feminine assets on the right side of the ledger. She came complete with sensuous lips and large brown eyes. No question about it, Clara was one of the best-looking young women in Lawton, Oklahoma.

One day in 1910, a young lawyer, new in town, walked into Millers to purchase some buttons. Life was never the same for Jake Hamon after that. You see, Jake had a wife, Georgea, a daughter with the great name of Olive Belle and a son, Jake Jr. The Hamons were Kansas folk who had moved lock, stock and barrel to Oklahoma, where Jake planned on making his mark. Construction was booming and oil was gushing out of the ground in abundant quantities. Oklahoma was a good place for an ambitious man to plant his roots.

Jake, an old smoothie with a line that would tumble robins out of the trees, just had to have Clara for his very own. The 16-year-old virgin was flattered. The local yokels were a crude lot who didn't know how to treat a girl. Jake was different. He didn't mind telling Clara his innermost thoughts — how he would invest in railroads and oil, how he would dabble in politics, how she would be at his side.

Let's let Jake tell it in his own words, "Someday I'll be the biggest man in this country and I'll take you with me to the White House." What was a girl to do? Clara's other boyfriends talked about the corn growing as high as an elephant's eye. Jake talked about being president of the U.S.

Clara thought; Clara softened; Clara relented. Finally, Clara went to bed with Jake.

In pursuit of his dream, Jake opened new law offices in Ardmore. Mrs. Hamon kept house in Lawton. Clara was enrolled in a business course in Ardmore. Jake also enrolled her in the Hotel Randol, where he had an adjoining room. It didn't take long for rumors to reach Georgea Hamon's ears. Her husband was playing the old hanky panky game with a sweet young thing named Clara Smith. Mrs. Hamon was one of those patient women who decided to let the romance take its course. She would wait for her husband to return to her side. Georgea had made one big mistake. Jake had no intention of leaving Clara, and Clara stuck to Jake like glue.

On the business front, Jake, backed by John Ringling of circus fame, bought into the Mexico and Pacific Railroad and made a fortune. Jake became a multi-millionaire within three years. He invested heavily in oil and made a second fortune.

As the years passed, Jake gave vent to his political aspirations. In 1919, he was the driving force behind the nomination of Sen. Warren Harding for president of the U.S. All the while, Clara was his companion and lover.

Jake had done it all. He was now a political force to be reckoned with. There was one problem. Clara could prove to be an embarrassment. Not to worry. Jake had an answer. He had his nephew, Frank Hamon, marry Clara. They were married in name only, but the marriage allowed Clara to pose as Jake's dutiful niece, who acted as his secretary. For years, Frank received a $100 cheque each month from Jake for going through with the marriage of convenience.

Clara's marriage covered the prolonged affair for a while, but the big boys in the Republican party let it be known that Jake had to do something more. After all, there was talk that in eight years hence he would be considered as Republican nominee for president of the country. It was one thing for the inner circle to know he was carrying on with Clara. It was quite another for the common folk to get wind of the fact that a presidential hopeful travelled and slept with one woman while the potential first lady was back home tending to her knitting.

It was time for Clara to exit gracefully. Folks, we all know things don't happen that way. Here was the former dry goods clerk, who for nine long years had been the constant companion of Jake Hamon, one of the most powerful and richest men in Oklahoma. Clara no longer wore calico. She was now draped in furs and jewelry. She entertained some of the most influential men in the U.S. Now that her Jake was vying for the brass ring, she was to be dropped. Not on your life!

On November 2, 1920, Sen. Warren Harding became president of the U.S. Jake had his man in office. In eight years it would be his turn. Jake brought the ever patient Georgea to Chicago to entertain his political cronies. After nine years of waiting, she was finally taking her place beside her husband. Georgea was beaming. She had won.

It happened on Sunday evening, November 21, 1920. Who knows the exact thoughts which went through Clara Smith's mind? She remembered when Jake was a struggling lawyer and she was a clerk at Millers Dry Goods. Now, with the doors of the White House within reach, she was to be cast aside like an old shoe. In fact, Jake had seen to it that her trunks were packed. They stood in a corner of her room at the Randol Hotel, a room which held so many memories.

For one last time, she walked through the adjoining room which Jake had maintained for appearance's sake. For company, she lugged along a steel .25-calibre revolver.

A few minutes later, Jake Hamon staggered down the hotel hallway, leaving a trail of blood on the carpeted floor. He made his way to the hotel's dining room, where he enlisted the aid of Dr. A.J. Cowles. With the help of Dr. Cowles, Jake managed to walk to the Hardy Sanitarium, about a block from the hotel. Jake whispered that he had shot himself accidentally while he was cleaning his gun. He asked for his business manager, Frank Ketch.

Jake was in a bad way. The .25-calibre slug had entered his right side, plowed through the right lobe of his liver and rested about an inch to the right of his spinal cord.

The morning after the shooting, Clara was ushered into Jake's hospital room. She stayed only a moment before rushing off to Frank Ketch's office.

Two stories about the shooting flashed across the nation. One was Jake's version — that it had been a tragic accident. The second was not so kind. Jake had had a terrible argument with his mistress, which had ended with him at death's door. Five days after being shot, Jake Hamon died.

Jake's highly-placed friends attempted to have the shooting officially labelled an accident, but it was no use. Rumors persisted that Clara had plugged her lover. Attempts by law enforcement agencies failed to locate Clara, but Sam Blair, a Chicago newspaper reporter, together with Clara's 19-year-old brother Jimmy, tracked her down. It took a month. On December 20, 1920, Sam and Jimmy found Clara in Chihuahua, Mexico.

Clara's return caused a sensation. She claimed that she had fled the country because Jake and his influential friends had wanted her to leave. She had no idea at the time that Jake was going to die. Once back in Oklahoma, Clara was arrested and stood trial for murder.

Mrs. Georgea Hamon took the witness stand and told the story of her ruined marriage. She gave vivid details of how Clara had stolen her Jake with her cunning sexual charms. She testified that when Jake came to his senses, Clara shot him.

Clara was the star of the show. She related how she had been Jake's right-hand girl for nine years before he attempted to discard her. On the day she was to leave him forever, Jake hit the bottle. They had planned to spend one last night together.

When she entered his quarters, Jake shoved her into a chair. She abruptly left, but Jake followed and threw her down on her own bed. He slapped her face repeatedly and cursed at her. According to Clara, Jake kicked her in the back and tried to choke her. She struggled free, but Jake lunged drunkenly toward her, clutching at her blouse. Frantically, Clara reached into her open purse, which lay on the window sill. Her hand closed on her revolver. Out it came. Clara levelled the weapon at Jake to scare him. Jake ignored the gun, picked up a chair and swung it at Clara. The chair hit the gun, which discharged.

Clara went on. "Jake fell to the floor, but his wound didn't make him unconscious. It sobered him, though, for he talked quite rationally as he tried to sit up. 'Clara, you've hit me,' he moaned. I tried to lift him onto the bed and told him I'd run for a doctor. But he kept saying, 'No, Clara, it wouldn't be wise. I'm all right. I'll walk to the hospital and make believe I shot myself.'" Clara watched as Jake staggered out the door.

The prosecution presented a far different version of the shooting. A personal friend of Jake's, W.B. Nichols, the Oklahoma City chief of police, testified that Jake told him from his hospital bed that he had been lying on Clara's bed. She had been stroking his hair with one hand when she shot him in the stomach with the other.

Dr. Walter Hardy, head of the Hardy Sanitarium, told the court that as the days passed, Jake's condition deteriorated. He took Dr. Hardy into his confidence. The doctor disclosed, "He told me that Clara, the girl about to be put out of his life, shot him ruthlessly as she caressed him."

The Oklahoma jury retired to reach their verdict. It took them only 39 minutes to find Clara Hamon not guilty. Our

Clara walked out of court a free woman. Shortly after her trial, she moved to California. On August 22, 1921, she married film director John Gorman.

WHY KILL
ALICE?

Lee Orsini wasn't your average little girl from Little Rock. Lee was pretty enough, but was a bit of a diamond in the rough. You know what I mean.

Lee married Douglas Sudbury in 1963, when she was only 16. They were divorced soon after, but remarried on July 14, 1966. A year later, Lee, who obviously couldn't quite make up her mind, divorced Doug for the second time and went home to Mama. Never one to stay on the shelf on a permanent basis, Lee married David May in 1971. This latest go round in the rodeo that is matrimony lasted only six months.

On September 17, 1976, Lee sashayed to the altar for the fourth time. She brought her daughter Tiffany, a product of her very first marriage. Her spanking new husband was Ron Orsini, 34. By this time, Lee was an experienced 29.

The Orsinis purchased a large home on Pontiac Drive in North Little Rock. From that moment on, they were house poor. They not only had a hefty mortgage to carry, but were strapped with large furniture payments. All their troubles were dwarfed by the events which occurred on the night of Wednesday, March 11, 1981.

On that night, Ron went to bed alone. Lee fell asleep with Tiffany, who was ill. It was close to midnight when the sound of a shot broke the still night air. Some inconsiderate person had blown Ron's brains all over the bedroom.

Next morning, Lee discovered her husband's body and called police. Ron had been killed by a .38-calibre bullet fired from a pistol which had been placed against his head. He was asleep when he was murdered.

Police studied the bed carefully. It appeared from the indentations that someone had slept beside Ron, although Lee insisted that she had fallen asleep in Tiffany's bedroom. The murder weapon was never found, but police learned Ron had reported his .38-calibre pistol stolen from his truck some time earlier. The house showed no signs of forced entry and nothing had been stolen. Fortunately for Lee, Ron had insurance which paid off the mortgage on the house.

Understandably, Lee Orsini was a suspect in her husband's murder. She retained well-known Little Rock lawyer Bill McArthur, advising him that she thought her husband had become involved in drug dealing. She called on McArthur often, telling him that her house was being watched and of other suspicious activities directed toward her. McArthur probably believed his new client, but couldn't understand how Lee had not heard the shot which had taken her husband's life.

Lee Orsini seemed to bask in the celebrity status which her husband's death had thrust upon her. When the media tired of writing about her, she would come up with another choice bit of intrigue. Once she claimed she saw men leaving her house with plastic bags of a white powdery substance.

After investigating the Orsini murder, a grand jury returned a verdict of "no true bill," which meant Lee would not be tried for murder.

A year later, the Orsini case had been dropped from the front pages of the Little Rock newspapers. Other crimes and world events had supplanted the killing. Still, there were many who felt that Lee Orsini had succeeded in getting away with murder.

On Friday, July 2, 1982, two men called at the home of

lawyer Bill McArthur. They knew that Bill's wife Alice would be at home alone. Alice peered out a window. She saw a man with a bouquet of flowers and a clip board.

Alice was careful about strangers, and with good reason. Weeks earlier, when she had jumped into her Olds Cutlass and turned on the ignition, the car had blown up. She had been lucky to escape with only minor scratches to her legs. Police investigating the bombing told her that had the entire bomb detonated, she and her car would have been blown to bits. The identity of the bomber was a mystery. In conjunction with his law practice, Bill McArthur was part owner of a western-style bar in town. No doubt he had enemies and the bomb could have been intended for him.

Alice opened the door. It was a mistake. Maybe she ran the moment the man gave her the bouquet and reached into his pocket. As she ran, a shot whizzed past her head. Alice made it to an upstairs closet with the stranger in pursuit. She knew her husband kept a gun in the closet somewhere. She groped frantically for the weapon, but it was no use. The gunman had caught up to her. Another shot missed, but a third found its mark. Alice McArthur fell dead in her upstairs bedroom closet.

When Bill McArthur arrived home that afternoon, he found the family dog outside. The door to the house was open. He couldn't locate Alice. He called one of Alice's girlfriends, Anita Prather, but Alice wasn't there. Bill called police. Anita arrived at the house around the same time as Patrolman Robert McNeely. While Bill was explaining his wife's absence, Anita strolled through the house. It was she who found her friend's body in the upstairs closet.

Bill McArthur was devastated at his wife's death. Who would do such a thing? There was talk that a rival bar owner might be responsible, but nothing of a tangible nature developed from this avenue of investigation.

While Alice McArthur's murder occupied the front pages of the two Little Rock newspapers, a small-time criminal, Yankee Hall, inquired of his acquaintance, Forrest Parkman, if the police had any clues to the murder.

Forrest Parkman was a member of the Little Rock Police Department.

The bouquet of flowers left at the scene of the crime had been traced to a local flower shop. The woman who had sold the flowers gave police a detailed description of her customer. Parkman immediately thought the description fit Yankee Hall. That same day, police received an anonymous phone call informing them that a man named Larry McClendon was the trigger man in the Alice McArthur murder.

Yankee Hall was nervous. He asked another police officer if police would have enough evidence for a conviction if they located the man who had purchased the flowers. When he received an affirmative answer, he inquired if the man would get life or be executed. Hall had good reason to be apprehensive. He had spent one year in prison on a cocaine dealing charge and was out on parole. He feared being sent back to prison, but he feared death even more.

Little Rock detectives played on his fear. They told him that they had found a small card attached to the bouquet. On it were printed the words, "Have a Nice Day." They let him know that the police lab was endeavouring to lift a fingerprint from the card. The only reason the card hadn't been checked earlier was because the lab had been closed for the weekend.

Yankee Hall was held for questioning and later charged with the murder of Alice McArthur. A flower shop employee picked him out of a lineup as the man who had purchased the bouquet found at the crime scene. Two of his fingerprints were found on the incriminating card.

Faced with this evidence, Hall confessed. He and Larry McClendon had been hired by Lee Orsini to kill Alice McArthur. He believed she had been commissioned by Bill McArthur to do the job.

During the course of the multi-pronged police investigation, officers learned that Lee Orsini had solicited a friend to make the anonymous call to police naming McClendon as the killer. She, too, was taken into custody

196

and charged with murder.

Only Bill McArthur was able to prove himself devoid of any guilty knowledge concerning his wife's murder. He was not romantically involved with anyone and had nothing to gain from Alice's death. McArthur was exonerated only after being arrested and investigated by a grand jury.

In return for his confession and a guilty plea, Yankee Hall was assured by the state that he would receive a life sentence. He revealed how he and Lee Orsini had been responsible for planting the bomb in an attempt to kill Alice. Lee had told him that McArthur would pay them $20,000 to do the job, which would be enough money to set them up in the cocaine dealing business.

On the day Alice McArthur was shot, Hall was waiting beside the car. When he heard the shots, he walked up to the front door. He was met by Larry McClendon and frantically asked Larry what had happened. Larry replied, "Let's go, let's go." The two men dashed from the house. McClendon had panicked and had left the bouquet behind, although he had strict instructions to take the flowers with him when he left the house. That's what made Hall so nervous after the murder. He knew there was a good chance his fingerprints were on the card attached to the bouquet.

An Arkansas jury deliberated eight hours before finding Lee Orsini guilty of capital murder. She was sentenced to life imprisonment without possibility of parole. Only a gubernatorial pardon can save her from spending the rest of her life in prison.

Larry McClendon was found guilty of murdering Alice McArthur. Larry was out of prison on parole at the time of the murder. Now he must complete his original sentence of 31 years imprisonment. He was sentenced to another 20 years confinement for the McArthur murder. In all, McClendon stands to serve a total of 51 years in prison.

Yankee Hall, who is not eligible for parole, is serving his life sentence in an Arkansas prison. He works as a barber in the institution.

Bill McArthur has been married, divorced and remarried since Alice's murder. He continues to practise law.

MYSTERY
HOUSE
MURDER

On November 29, 1909, when Dr. Herbert Simmons walked up the steps of the old frame house at 89 North 14th St. in East Orange, New Jersey, he had no idea he was to become a character in a murder scenario which was to fascinate aficionados of the macabre for months to come.

Ocey Snead wasn't fascinated. She lay dead in the bathtub. But let's get back to the good doctor.

A woman dressed entirely in black opened the front door and announced that she was none other than Virginia Wardlaw. She led Dr. Simmons to the bathroom. There, lying in a small, half-filled tub of water was beautiful Ocey Snead. Her body was in a crouched position, with legs doubled up at the knees. Ocey's head was submerged under the faucet.

After assuring himself that his new patient was beyond help, the doctor noted a pile of clothing lying beside the tub. A note was pinned to a blouse. The doctor read the note: "Last year my little daughter died; other near and dear ones have gone before. I have been prostrated with illness for a long time. When you read this I will have committed suicide. Do not grieve over me. Rejoice with me that death brings a blessed relief from pain and suffering greater than I can bear. O.W.M. Snead."

Dr. Simmons questioned Virginia and learned that the deceased was her niece. Ocey had been despondent, having lost her first child about a year before. Virginia also volunteered that her niece had lost her husband seven months earlier. Her four-month-old son was ill in St. Christopher's Hospital in Brooklyn. As if all that wasn't bad enough, Ocey herself had been in failing health.

Dr. Simmons smelled a rat. He asked Virginia when she had found the body. The elderly lady replied that she had discovered Ocey just before she had called him. Simmons knew that something was rotten in the state of Denmark. From his examination of the body, he could tell Ocey had been dead for at least 24 hours. When he imparted that information to Virginia, the lady in black had a ready response. She hadn't seen her niece for over 24 hours.

The doctor was amazed that an aunt could live under the same roof with her sick niece and not inquire of her well-being. It wasn't natural. Even more unnatural was the fact that the big house was practically devoid of furniture and was extremely cold. Virginia said that the house was only a temporary arrangement.

Dr. Simmons left and immediately called police. Sgt. William O'Neill was the next to enter what was later to become known as the Mystery House. Virginia showed him around, including a view of the body in the bathtub. O'Neill felt a chill go through his bones as the 60-year-old Virginia led him through the cold, empty house. She repeated her story much as she had told it to Dr. Simmons, adding that she and her niece had only been living in East Orange ten days. She had accompanied Ocey to nurse her while she was ill.

O'Neill was immediately suspicious. Who would bring a sick person to an unheated, unfurnished house in East Orange? Virginia told him they had previously lived on East 48th St. in Brooklyn. Sgt. O'Neill informed Virginia that she would have to accompany him to the police station. He believed that it was possible this strange woman, heavily veiled in black, had held her obviously feeble niece under water until she drowned.

An autopsy revealed that Ocey had indeed met her death by drowning. The deceased woman had suffered from starvation, weighing only 80 pounds at the time of her death.

Detectives found out that another physician had been called to the Mystery House five days before Ocey's death. Dr. Charles Teeter had examined Ocey and had found her to be suffering from bronchitis. He, too, had commented on the lack of furniture, but was told that aunt and niece had just moved in and furniture was on the way.

Police visited Virginia's previous residence in Brooklyn. Neighbors there remembered her well. They told investigators that the older woman, who dressed only in black, kept to herself. They seldom saw her beautiful niece outside the house.

The janitor of the building explained to detectives that about a year and a half earlier, Ocey and her husband Fletcher, who was her first cousin, had moved into the house. Ocey was rather frail, but very beautiful. Fletcher was a real Southern gentleman.

A few months after their arrival, three older women moved in with the young couple. All wore only black. In March 1909, Fletcher left. That August, Ocey gave birth to a baby boy. The women had difficulty paying the rent and finally were told to move. Early in November, they placed their furniture in storage. Virginia and Ocey moved to the empty house in East Orange.

Police learned that Ocey's life was insured for $24,000. The policies had been borrowed against until they had very little real cash value. However, Ocey owned a valuable parcel of land in Virginia, where the entire Wardlaw clan had originated. In times past, the family had been an influential one in the South. However, they had lost their wealth and had moved north to the New York area.

Police were now certain that Virginia Wardlaw, possibly with the aid of her two sisters, had starved Ocey to the point where she was helpless. They then had placed her in the bathtub and held her head under the water until she drowned. When handwriting experts stated they were certain the dead woman had not written the suicide note, Virginia was taken into custody and charged with murder.

The hunt was now on for the two elusive sisters. One sister, Caroline Martin, was Ocey's mother. Caroline and her husband had divorced years earlier and the dear man subsequently had died. She was found living at Manhattan's Bayard Hotel, heavily veiled and dressed totally in black.

A clerk at the hotel had found her behavior so strange he had called police. Caroline was kept under surveillance while police attempted to find the third sister. Mary Snead, 61, was located in New York City. She and Caroline were arrested and charged with Ocey's murder. Enough evidence was gathered to indicate that all three sisters had acted in concert. They were lodged in adjoining cells.

The strange murder case attracted attention throughout the United States and Canada. Because of the publicity, there were those who said that Fletcher Snead, Ocey's supposedly dead husband, was alive and well. Newspaper reporters tracked down Fletcher in St. Catharines, Ontario, employed at the New Murray Hotel as a cook. He was using the name John Lucas.

Fletcher had quite a story to tell. He had worked for a firm in New York, where his boss and best friend, William Earthman, had been indicted for stealing from the company. Fletcher had been summoned to testify at Earthman's trial. Rather than appear against his friend, he had skipped. Fletcher told police it was hard for a northerner to understand, but it was a matter of southern pride. He had even told his wife, aunts, and mother what he was about to do. They had said they understood.

On December 22, a grand jury brought in indictments of murder against all three sisters. On August 8, 1910, after months of living in jail, Virginia Wardlaw took ill. She had been refusing to eat for days. After lying comatose for 36 hours, she died. She had succeeded in starving herself to death.

Caroline Martin's lawyers fought desperately to have their client judged insane, so that she would be confined to an asylum. If found sane, she would be tried for murder. The court found her sane and fit to stand trial. She was allowed to plead guilty to manslaughter. The 65-year-old woman was sentenced to seven years' imprisonment. In prison, her condition deteriorated, becoming so serious she was transferred to the State Hospital for the Insane. On June 21, 1913, she suffered a heart attack and died.

Mary Snead fared best of the three sisters. It was explained to the court that since her sister had pleaded guilty to manslaughter and, as there was no charge of accessory to manslaughter in New Jersey, Mary could not be brought to trial as an accessory to her sister's action. The prosecuting attorney moved to quash the indictment against her. Mary Snead was set free. She lived out her life on a ranch in Colorado.

Fletcher Snead, whose southern pride allowed him to desert his wife, children, mother and aunts, drifted into obscurity.

MURDER
ON THE
GOLF COURSE

Ray Smith, 18, was the new boy on the block. He had arrived in Eau Claire, Wisconsin with his parents at the beginning of October 1948. Tall, handsome Ray was employed at the American National Bank. Within three weeks of his arrival, the outgoing, pleasant young man was well-liked at the bank and in the limited social circle he had managed to cultivate.

The Smiths had moved from Superior, Wis. to their comfortable home on Keith St., just two doors removed from the Baumann family. On his way to and from his employment at the bank, Ray often bumped into attractive Gertrude Baumann. Seventeen-year-old Gertrude was flattered when Ray stopped to chat. In the three weeks she had known him, the pretty high school student considered Ray her new friend.

On October 23, Gertrude was lingering on her front porch. Ray stopped to talk. After the usual pleasantries, he invited Gertrude to take a walk with him down by the golf course. Gertrude ran inside the house to fetch her camera. Together, the two young people made their way to the golf course. It was autumn, a crisp, clear day. Leaves crackled underfoot.

By 6 o'clock, Paul Baumann wondered why his daughter hadn't returned for dinner. It wasn't like her to be late. At 7 p.m., he phoned the Smiths, whom he knew slightly as new neighbors. James Smith was worried as well. Ray was not at home and, he too had never been late for dinner before.

As darkness fell, the Baumanns and the Smiths phoned every friend of their respective offspring. No one had seen the missing pair. Next morning, the distraught parents advised police that Ray and Gertrude were missing.

Police had to consider the obvious. Did the pair elope? Had Ray abducted Gertrude? A cursory investigation put both those suspicions to rest. The young people hadn't known each other that well. Both were responsible individuals who were well-liked at school and work. Ray Smith and Gertrude Baumann were not the type to leave home for any reason without informing their parents.

Local officials organized a massive search of the Eau Claire Country Club. At 4:15 p.m., James Smith, an older brother of Ray's, was searching a weedy area just north of the 14th green when he came across the body of a girl. James ran to the nearest phone. By coincidence, at precisely that moment, two other searchers, M.D. Miller and Charles Richards, found Ray Smith's body nearby, half-submerged in the Eau Claire River.

Local police cordoned off the murder area. Gertrude's body was partially clothed. She lay on her back. Bloodstains covered her head. The tall grass and weeds around Gertrude's body were bent and trampled, indicating a struggle. A discernible trail of bent underbrush led to the riverbank, 175 feet away, where Ray's body had been found.

Detectives were certain both victims were murdered while they were together. For some reason, Ray's body was dragged down to the river. A few items of Gertrude's clothing were found in the river, where the killer had obviously thrown them. Coroner E. Wallace Stokes stated that Gertrude had been shot three times and Ray four. Normally, the shots would have attracted a lot of attention, but the hunting season was in full swing and the report of gunfire was a common sound in the wooded area around the golf course.

That night, the 30,000 citizens of Eau Claire didn't rest easy. Double murder just didn't take place in their community. Who had killed two young people who, by pure chance, happened to be walking on the local golf course? The murders could not have been planned.

The day after the murders, 16-year-old Jack Hanson walked into the police station and told detectives, "I think I heard the shots that killed those two people." Hanson explained that he had been hunting in the area when he had seen Gertrude Baumann with a boy. He knew Gertrude well and recognized her, but didn't know her companion.

The pair had been walking along the Eau Claire River. They had disappeared from Hanson's sight behind some trees. That's when he had heard the shots and thought he heard a scream. He had looked up, but had seen nothing. Then, there were more shots. When asked why he didn't report the shots earlier, Hanson quickly responded that there were a lot of hunters around and it had occurred to him that Gertrude might have been laughing, not screaming.

When he learned of the murders, he figured the shots he had heard were the ones which had taken the young couple's lives. Hanson had heard the shots at 4:15 p.m. and had seen one fellow in the general area around that time. He hadn't paid much attention to the man, but believed he was wearing a leather jacket.

In the few days following the murder, all possible acquaintances of the two victims were eliminated as suspects — all except one.

A year earlier, a young classmate of Gertrude's had fallen madly in love with her. He begged her to go steady with him. Finally, he became a nuisance and was told in no uncertain terms to stop pestering her. Frustrated, the young man went home, loaded his .22-calibre rifle and attempted to kill himself. His aim was poor and he suffered a minor flesh wound. The youth's family had since moved to Chicago. They were traced and proved without a doubt that their son was in Chicago at the time of the murders.

As days passed, other men became prime suspects. Recently released convicts were given special attention. So were hunters known to have been around the golf club area at the time of the murders.

A local man, Arthur Thompson, told police that he had encountered a hunter on the golf course on the day of the murders. Thompson knew the man. He was Marshall Johnson, 32, a man who had served time in prison. Detectives had Johnson on their list of ex-cons living in the area. Inquiries were made. It was learned that Johnson had not reported for work on the day after the murders. He had left for Minneapolis. The suspect was traced to Seattle and flown back to Eau Claire.

Johnson denied any knowledge of the murders. He had left town, because, as an ex-con, he was being harassed by police for every illegal act which took place around Eau Claire. Johnson admitted that he had been hunting with his .22-calibre rifle on the day of the murders but, then again, so were a lot of people. When asked for his weapon, Johnson said he had met a man on the course who had bought the rifle for $20. Johnson had no idea as to the stranger's identity.

Officers were convinced they had their man. To solidify their case, they used every available means, including mine detectors, in an attempt to find the murder weapon. They had no luck finding the rifle, but kept questioning Johnson, letting him know they didn't believe he had sold his rifle. Finally, Johnson blurted out, "I don't know why I did it!"

Johnson went on to say that he had been hunting on the golf course when he had spied the young couple. The crime had been sexually motivated. He wanted Gertrude. When she objected and screamed, he shot her. When Ray attempted to intervene, he shot him as well. He had planned to drag both bodies to the river, but after lugging Ray's body into the water, he spotted two men walking nearby. He panicked and ran away. As an afterthought, he added that he had not sold his rifle. "I threw it into Dell's Pond on my way home," he stated.

Two professional divers were hired to scour the bottom of Dell's Pond. They were successful in retrieving Johnson's .22-calibre rifle. Ballistic tests proved that the slugs found in the bodies of the two victims had been fired from Johnson's rifle.

On March 31, 1949, Marshall Johnson pleaded guilty to first-degree murder. He was sentenced to two life terms in the Wisconsin State Prison at Waupun. Johnson spent 23 years in prison before being paroled in 1972.

MACABRE
CARGO

This is the story of two losers. One, abused in prison as a teenager, turned out to be a sexual sadist, pedophile and murderer. The other, a tragedy of our times, was his 12-year-old victim.

Douglas Robert Worth was born on January 7, 1952 in New Glasgow, N.S., just down the road from his parents' home in Stellarton. Times could be tough in that part of Nova Scotia when the coal mines were down or the Trenton Steel Works were operating part-time.

Doug, one of 10 Worth children, got into trouble at age 16 when he stole a car and received a two-year jail sentence. A month before his sentence was up, while out on a day pass, he stole a car and raped a girl in New Glasgow. He received two years for breach of prison regulations, two years for stealing a car and two years for rape. Doug Worth was well on his way to a lifetime of crime.

In 1974, Worth was released from prison on mandatory supervision. Now a bitter young man who claimed that he had been sexually abused while incarcerated, he left the Atlantic provinces to roam the rest of Canada. Worth made his way to Oakville. In August 1975, he assaulted a police officer. For this offence he was jailed for 30 days.

Upon release, Worth travelled to Kenora, where he tried

his luck at breaking and entering. His luck was out to lunch, as it had been all his life. He was convicted of two counts of breaking and entering and found himself once more behind bars, this time for 90 days.

The displaced Maritimer made his way to Edmonton. It didn't take long. In 1979, he was convicted of raping a 19-year-old girl and was sentenced to eight years in jail.

While serving time in a Fort Saskatchewan, Alta., prison, Worth met Mary Kelly, who was visiting a relative in the pen. When Worth received a day pass, he spent it with Mary. He didn't return on schedule and was transferred to a maximum security prison in Edmonton and later to Kingston Penitentiary.

Doug Worth spent every day of his eight year sentence in prison. He was released on June 11, 1987, exactly eight years to the day he was sentenced. Kingston penal authorities placed him on a plane to Edmonton and told Edmonton officials that one bad apple was headed their way.

In Edmonton, Worth moved in with his old flame, Mary Kelly, a divorced mother of three. Her daughter and son, both in their twenties, moved out when Worth moved in. The third Kelly offspring, a boy of 14, stayed with his mother.

Although he had taken a meat cutting course while in prison, Worth obtained work as a roofer. Kelly worked in a restaurant. At home, she was physically abused by her common-law husband. Worth beat her at the least provocation. Sometimes he choked her. But she never left her man, nor did she report the abuse to authorities.

In September 1987, Worth and Kelly quit their jobs, sold their belongings and, together with Mary's teenaged son, moved to Orangeville, Ont., where Kelly's adult daughter lived. The very next night, a Friday, Kelly and her daughter went to a bingo game. They won $600. Worth was elated. He confiscated the winnings, as well as $800 they had received for their belongings back in Edmonton and took off to visit his family in Nova Scotia. A month later, he returned to Orangeville minus the $1,400.

Worth tried his hand as a laborer with a construction crew. A month after returning from Nova Scotia, he decided to leave Kelly and move into a rooming house at 244 Main St. N. in Brampton. Mary Kelly, despite the beatings, was very upset at Worth moving out. She and her son moved back to Edmonton.

Trina Campbell stood 4-foot-11 and weighed 85 pounds at the time of her death. If ever a youngster was born to a life of hard knocks, it was Trina.

Born in Melford, Sask., to an alcoholic mother and father, she and her two brothers were taken by child welfare workers when her parents parted company. Trina was nine years old when her mother was killed jumping from a truck while intoxicated.

In 1984, the Campbell family of Streetsville adopted all three children. Trina was enrolled in school and did well enough, but she was a troubled youngster. She often stole things from her home. When confronted, she ran away. In short, she was a problem child.

Finally it was decided that Trina would function best in a group home located in Brampton. She often ran away from the group home as well. In the wee hours of the morning of December 11, 1987, she was found in a local doughnut shop and was taken back to the group home by Peel Regional Police.

That day, it was decided that Trina would attend school as usual. She was picked up by a bus and returned around five in the afternoon. There is some evidence that Trina spent the next few days in a dilapidated house often frequented by vagrants and runaways. The 12-year-old was reported missing to police.

A few days later, a man who had spent time in prison with Doug Worth spotted him on the street in Brampton. Worth had a young girl in tow. He was leading her by the arm. It appeared to the man that the girl was being coerced by his old prison buddy.

Later, he and Worth met in a tavern and had a few beers. The friend noted that Worth had blood on his hands and shirt. When he inquired, Worth said he was in

211

a fist fight. The friend asked, "What about the girl I saw you with earlier?" Worth replied ominously, "She got everything she deserved."

What had happened to Trina Campbell? According to later testimony, Worth told Dr. Robert Woodhill, a psychiatrist, that he had met Trina in a store and figured from her actions that she was a runaway. He befriended her, took her to his rooming house, where he sexually attacked and killed her.

On December 14, 1987, Doug Worth took the body of Trina Campbell out of his room to a field behind the house. He covered the body as best he could with bushes. That same day, he sought a new place to stay. A few days later, he found a room in a private home. Worth moved in, then took off for Stellarton, N.S. to spend Christmas with his family.

During the holidays, Worth drank more than usual and was notably depressed. He was a man with a problem and that problem lay in a field behind a rooming house in Brampton, Ont. Worth had to tell someone.

Worth's sister Sharon was married to Wayne Lewis. Worth confided in his brother-in-law, but he didn't tell the exact truth. He told Lewis that he had been in a fight with a man he had met in a bar. He had been forced to kill the man, a drifter with no family.

Something within Worth's psyche wouldn't let him admit that he had murdered a child. Worth went on to tell his brother-in-law that he had been seen with this man and if the body were discovered he would be apprehended. He planned to return to Brampton to bury the body.

On January 2, Worth returned to Brampton. Two weeks later, Mary Kelly returned from out west and moved into her own accommodations. She started seeing Worth again, but he hadn't changed. He still beat her.

The pair rented a car to visit relatives in St. Catharines. During the visit, Worth attacked Mary and tossed her out of the car. This time, Mary reported the beating. Worth was picked up, but soon released. He patched up his difficulties with Mary.

By mid-February, Worth had fed Mary a string of lies to cover his latest plan. He told her, "I've done something really bad. Don't get the wrong idea. It's not a body, it's not a woman, it's not a man. I just stole some guns." Worth went onto explain that he had to move the guns from their hiding place because there was a witness who knew where he had stashed the weapons.

There were no guns, only the tiny nude body of Trina Campbell, which had been lying behind his rooming house under some bushes for over two months.

On March 4, 1988, Doug instructed Mary Kelly to rent a Dodge Colt from Budget Rent-A-Car in Brampton. They would move those guns he was always talking about. Instead of acting immediately, the urge to return to his native Nova Scotia overcame him. He and Mary made a quick trip and returned March 11.

Two days later, Mary drove Doug to the field behind his old rooming house. He left the car carrying an empty hockey bag. Mary waited in the parked vehicle. About a half hour later, Doug returned with a bulging hockey bag and placed it in the trunk. He was perspiring and appeared to be nervous and pale.

All the while, Peel Regional Police were trying to locate the missing Trina Campbell. Ten thousand flyers describing Trina were distributed throughout the country.

Doug and Mary, with their macabre cargo, made their way to the Orangeville area. It had been a hard night's work. Doug was tired. He and Mary parked and soon fell asleep. One can only imagine what went through Doug Worth's mind when he was awakened by an Orangeville police officer.

The officer, who had no idea that he had stumbled upon one of the most bizarre killers in Ontario's history, advised the occupants to move on. Doug mumbled to Mary, "We're all right, long as he doesn't look in the trunk."

The Dodge Colt made its way to Terra Nova, where Doug told Mary to park until daylight. When dawn broke, they were noticed. A customer walked into the Terra Nova general store at 7:50 for coffee. He told Mr. Bernier, the owner, that there was a suspicious-looking couple parked down the road. Mr. Bernier called the OPP detachment at Shelburne, but when he was placed on hold, he grew impatient and hung up.

Only months later did the folks of Terra Nova learn they had had a murderer among them that morning.

It was time. Doug took the hockey bag out of the trunk and lugged it into a nearby field. Mary observed what she thought was blood oozing out of the bag. When she mentioned this to Doug, he told her it was transmission fluid.

Police believe Doug visited the body behind his rooming house many times. When he discovered it wouldn't fit into his hockey bag, he systematically dissected the body with his hacksaw. Doug had taken a meat cutting course while in prison and so knew something about what he was doing.

Now divested of the body, the pair made their way back to Brampton. Realizing that blood had dripped out of the bag staining the trunk, Doug had Mary's young son and another lad wash out the trunk. They noticed blood stains and they too were told the stains had been caused by transmission fluid. The boys couldn't remove the stains from the rug.

Next day, Doug asked Mary to cut out the stained portion of the rug. She told him she had done as he had instructed, but in reality she hadn't bothered. The vehicle was returned to the car rental agency.

On March 30, 1988, Doug, Mary and her young son left both their rooms in Brampton, stealing anything of value. They made off with jewelry, towels, cigarettes and loose change. Once again, Doug Worth was going back to Nova Scotia in a rented car.

Doug discussed his most pressing problem with his sister, Sharon, and his brother-in-law, Wayne Lewis. He admitted he had dismembered a body and moved it from behind his old rooming house. Doug was curious about how long it would take a body to decompose. He also told his sister he thought teeth were the only way police could identify a decomposed body.

Without funds, it was impossible for him to get back to Ontario to dispose of the head. He thought it would be a good idea to bring his victim's head back to Nova Scotia and bury it deep in the woods.

Usually, Doug referred to his victim as a man, but a few times in relating his story he slipped up and called his victim a girl. Somewhere along the line, he saw a poster of Trina Campbell. Doug almost flipped out, not for what he had done, but from the urgency to dispose of his victim's head.

Doug and Mary moved from Stellarton to their own apartment in Pictou. On April 22, a teenage lad overheard Doug, Mary and the Lewises discussing a murder and the moving of a body. He related the story to his guidance counsellor, who took the tale seriously and contacted the RCMP in Pictou. They, in turn, contacted Peel Regional Police. Was there anyone who had been reported missing around December 14 of the previous year? There was only one outstanding missing person — 12-year-old Trina Campbell.

Under the direction of Insp. Rod Piukkala of the Peel Regional Police, an investigation into Doug Worth's background was conducted. It was soon discovered Doug had a long police record which included rape. The vehicle used to transport the body was located at Budget in Brampton. Inside the trunk were the telltale bloodstains. Laboratory analyses of the most sophisticated nature were conducted at the Forensic Sciences Centre, which determined that the stains had been made by decomposed human blood.

Everything fit: the missing Trina, the bloodstains and the youngster's story in Pictou. Still, police had no body, no confession and no real proof murder was committed.

Piukkala dispatched Det.-Sgt. Edward Toye and Det.-Sgt. Len Favreau to Nova Scotia. With the help of the RCMP, they would learn more about Doug Worth without revealing to friends and relatives that he was the prime suspect in what they felt certain was a murder case. The undercover officers learned of Doug's hatred of women and his reputation in the area, but as no new developments took place, it was decided that the RCMP would keep tabs on Doug while the Ontario officers returned home.

Toye and Favreau were scheduled to fly back to Toronto on the night of May 6, 1988. Unexpectedly, at 10 a.m. that same day, Wayne Lewis walked into the local police station and told the whole story. He revealed Worth wanted to return to Ontario to retrieve the head of a person he had murdered and dissected. Doug hadn't left because he was broke. Toye and Favreau cancelled their flights. When Wayne Lewis' wife, Sharon, was informed that her husband had told what he knew, she corroborated his statement.

The Lewises agreed to co-operate with investigating officers. Outfitted with recording equipment, they engaged in conversation with Doug in which he gave what amounted to a confession. Police rented an old car and gave Wayne $300. Wayne, under instructions, gave the car and the money to Doug so he could return to Ontario to complete the task of disposing of the head. Doug thanked the Lewises profusely. He inquired if they had a spare shovel. They didn't.

Within 45 minutes, Doug and Mary were on their way to Ontario. With Piukkala acting as anchor man, the pair was tailed all the way to Quebec City, where fresh surveillance officers were put on the job of following them. In Port Hope, Doug unsuccessfully attempted to purchase a shovel. In Brampton, he scoured through a few construction sites, obviously looking for a shovel.

The man with the gruesome mission made his way north and parked close to the spot where the body had been placed. He was waiting for daylight, unaware he was under surveillance by police. He left the car carrying a gym bag, while Mary waited. He wasn't long returning with the bag, which was placed on the back seat. Doug stopped at a Shell station to dispose of a pair of gloves, which were immediately picked up by the trailing officers. Down Hwy. 10 he and Mary proceeded. Ironically, they drove past the Peel Regional Police Headquarters before being pulled over. Inside the gym bag was the decomposed head of Trina Campbell.

During his trial, it was revealed that Doug had often bragged in prison that after his release he would "go to a public school in Kingston with an axe and chop as many children as he could." He once told prison psychologist Sharon Williams he would "wreak havoc on society" as revenge for his years in prison. On another occasion, he stated he would "make serial killer Clifford Olson look like a choir boy."

Doug pleaded innocent by reason of insanity. He was judged to be sane and guilty of second-degree murder. Before being sentenced, he yelled from the prisoner's box, "First of all, I'm not a cold-hearted son of a bitch! You're all saying I'm a monster. I've got feelings. I feel for people. I've got to get this out before I kill somebody up at the detention centre with my pent-up emotions."

Doug Worth was sentenced to life imprisonment with no possibility of parole for 23 years.

On June 1, 1990, in a Brampton courtroom the charge of being an accessory after the fact of murder against Mary Kelly was dropped.

TERROR IN
ATLANTA

Can it be that 13 years have passed since Atlanta, Georgia was held in a grip of terror for 22 long months? Seldom has a city, its inhabitants and its officials come under such critical scrutiny. Someone was systematically murdering the city's black children. As the number of victims grew, the case became known around the world as the Atlanta Child Murders.

On July 28, 1979, a woman pushed back shrubs and rubbish along Campbellton Rd. in Atlanta. She was looking for returnable bottles. The unwary woman recoiled in horror at the sight of a human leg sticking out of the foliage. Police were soon on the scene. They were in for a surprise. Barely one hundred yards from the first body, they uncovered a second victim. The boys were identified as Edward Hope Smith, and Alfred Evans, both 14.

In itself, two teenaged boys found shot to death on the same day in the same place was unusual. But there was more to come. Much more.

Six weeks after the bodies of Edward and Alfred were found, another 14-year-old boy disappeared. Milton Harvey had one possession he loved above all others and that was his bicycle. It was found abandoned along a dusty road. Investigators discovered that Milton had skipped school on the day of his disappearance because he was embarrassed to wear his worn-out tattered shoes. Three weeks later, his decomposed body was found in a dump in the Atlanta suburb of East Point, not far from where the first two bodies had been discovered.

Little Yusef Bell, 9, was running an errand for a neighbor when he dropped out of sight. His body was found by a vagrant in the heart of Atlanta. Four children had been murdered. All were poor and all were black.

In retrospect, the Atlanta police have been criticized for not intensifying their efforts to apprehend an obvious madman who, for some perverted reason, was killing black boys. Would more effort have been put into the investigation if the victims had been white?

The story soon drifted out of the local area. These killings were different from anything which had preceded them. The murders continued.

The Christmas season of 1979 passed without incident. The following March, 12-year-old Angel Lanier was found dead. She had been raped and strangled with an electrical cord. A pair of panties not belonging to the dead child had been stuffed down her throat. Angel's murder was a departure from the killer's usual pattern. For the first time, he had murdered a female, and for the first time, sex was involved in the killing.

A week later, 10-year-old Jeffrey Mathius left his home to pick up a pack of cigarettes for his mother. He was never seen alive again. Jeffrey's skeletal remains would be found months later.

Camille Bell, little Yusef Bell's mother, probably did more than anyone to bring the series of murders to the public's attention. She gave statements to journalists, accusing police of laxity in apprehending the killer. She insisted that one person was responsible and had to be apprehended before he killed again. Mrs. Bell's concern was well-founded. The killings continued, but now the terror which had enveloped Atlanta was being reported by the world press. Strange details concerning the murders became public knowledge. Some of the victims

219

had been washed after they were killed.

Eric Middlebrooks, 14, was stabbed and beaten to death. Christopher Richardson, 11, disappeared on his way to a swimming pool. His skeleton was found eight months later. La Tonya Wilson, 7; Arron Wynche, 10; and Anthony Carter, 9, were murdered in quick succession.

The effect on Atlanta was devastating. Racial tension ran high. Rumors spread throughout Georgia. Some claimed a white man had taken it upon himself to wipe out black children. Others said the killings were not the work of one individual, but a diabolical scheme initiated by the Ku Klux Klan to kill black children so they would not grow up to propagate their race.

The city of Atlanta is reported to have spent a quarter of a million dollars a month conducting the extensive investigation. Funds poured in from the public and from private interested parties. Frank Sinatra and Sammy Davis, Jr., headlined a benefit concert at Atlanta's Civic Centre, raising $250,000 for the investigation. Schoolchildren and the public in general staged fund raisers. Actor Burt Reynolds contributed $10,000. Atlanta's first black mayor, Maynard Jackson, announced that the city had instituted a reward of $100,000 for the apprehension and conviction of the killer. Several corporations, with the help of heavyweight boxing champion Muhammad Ali upped the reward to half a million dollars.

Still, the litany of murder continued: Earl Lee Terrell, 11; Clifford Jones, 13; Darron Glass, 10; Charles Stephens, 12; Aaron Jackson, 9; Patrick Rogers, 16; Lubie Geter, 14; Terry Pugh, 15; Patrick Balazar, 11; and Curtis Walker, 13 — all under 16 years of age, all from underprivileged backgrounds and all black. By now, the list numbered 21 victims. Many thought the number to be far greater, claiming that other missing youngsters had fallen to the madman, but their bodies had not been found.

Ronald Reagan became president of the United States. He immediately allotted $1.5 million to help defray the cost of the investigation, as well as ordering the Federal Justice Department to assist in the case. That month, Jo Jo

Bell, 15, and Timothy Hill, 13, were murdered by the Atlanta Child Killer.

On March 30 and 31, 1981, the bodies of Eddie Duncan and Larry Rogers were plucked from the Chattahoochee River. These two victims were a departure from the now well-patterned category of victim. Both were 21 years old and both were mentally retarded.

The task force solely devoted to apprehending the killer had interviewed and released scores of suspects during the course of their investigations. One such man was Wayne Williams, a rather unlikely suspect. Williams was a bright young man, who lived with his parents, both retired school teachers, on Penelope Rd. in north-west Atlanta.

As a high school student, Williams had constructed and operated his own radio station in the basement of his parents' home. Currently, he was active as a freelance newspaper photographer, media consultant and music producer. It was this latter activity which first connected him to the child killing case. Involved in promoting musicians, Williams had flyers printed outlining his credentials in this field. These flyers had been found on, or in the possession of, four of the victims.

Was it possible that Williams had lured victims with promises of recording dates and stardom? Williams also had access to the city's streets. He often roamed the streets in his station wagon, ostensibly looking for the opportunity to take saleable photographs. Williams often showed up at accidents and fires. He was well-known to police.

While Williams was being investigated, the bodies of Mike McIntosh, 23, and Jimmy Payne, 21, were pulled from the Chattahoochee in the same week in April. That same month, John Porter, 28, was found stabbed to death on the streets of Atlanta. In May, William Barrett, was discovered strangled to death in a ditch.

On May 22, 1981, three Atlanta police officers and an FBI agent were on stakeout duty at the South Cobb Drive Bridge over the Chattahoochee River. Suddenly, there was a splash in the water. The police saw automobile lights on the bridge. As the car sped away, they radioed another member of the stakeout team in a vehicle.

The chase was on. The car, a green station wagon, drove away, stopped, turned, and reversed its course, driving back over the South Cobb Drive Bridge. A second police car joined the chase. Two miles down the road, the station wagon was stopped by police. The driver was Wayne Williams. He was taken into custody, questioned and released. However, he was kept under close surveillance while the FBI dragged the river for a body. Two days later they recovered the body of 24-year-old Nathaniel Cater. Two weeks later, Williams was taken into custody and charged with Cater's murder, as well as that of Jimmy Payne.

Williams' murder trial lasted nine weeks. Prosecution attorneys produced microscopic fibres and dog hairs taken from the Williams' residence and car, which matched fibres found on victims. It was the state's theory that Williams hated his own race and killed so that they wouldn't become parents. It was also believed that he exulted in the challenge of outwitting the combined police forces attempting to solve the case.

Williams testified in his own defence. He claimed he was on the bridge at 2:45 a.m. looking for a female vocalist he wished to interview before she auditioned later that day. He swore he hadn't killed anyone, nor had he any knowledge of the murders.

A jury of eight black and four white citizens found Williams guilty of two counts of murder. He received two life sentences to run consecutively. After the sentencing, police announced that Williams was responsible for over 20 other murders, but it would serve no purpose to have him stand trial on those charges.

Not everyone is convinced of Williams' guilt. In 1987, an attempt to reopen the case, led by the mothers of several of the victims, was quashed. They believe that a ring of pornographic profiteers used the children before killing them.

Wayne Williams is presently serving his sentences at the Georgia State Correctional Centre in Jackson.

SUNSET SLAYER

Carol Bundy was a rather frumpy middle-aged nurse who had just split up with her boyfriend. It was tough sledding for Carol. She had fallen hard for John Murray, a singer from Australia, who had left Down Under to seek fame and fortune in Hollywood, Calif. Murray hadn't found fame and fortune but had managed to get a part-time job at the Little Nashville roadhouse in North Hollywood. That's where he had met Carol.

Murray, who was booked as the Australian Cowboy, wasn't a great singer, but whatever he lacked in the vocal field, he more than made up for between the sheets. There was one little thorny detail — Murray was married. Pushy Carol suggested he obtain a divorce. She was devastated when the Australian Cowboy informed her that he had no intention of divorcing his wife.

Carol then did the unthinkable. She approached Murray's wife, which is a no-no in the triangle game. Murray immediately told Carol they were through. Carol was heartbroken, but although the affair was over, she remained friends with Murray. She was easy prey for the next man on the prowl.

That man was Doug Clark. Carol couldn't have done worse. Doug specialized in unattractive, overweight women, who were easy pickings for his well-practised line.

When they weren't available, he preferred prostitutes. Doug moved in with Carol after their first date.

It didn't take Carol long to realize that her new lover lived for sex. Their frenzied love making initially was welcomed by Carol, but as time passed she realized no one woman could satisfy her Doug. Gradually, she learned to accept the fact that every couple of nights Doug would go out patrolling for prostitutes along Hollywood's notorious Sunset Strip. She even learned to control her natural jealousy when Doug brought home young prostitutes and had her take photographs of him performing.

Doug's sexual fantasies became even more bizarre. He talked about the thrill of killing prostitutes. Carol dismissed his rantings, believing that even her weird Doug wasn't that weird. She changed her mind when, in June 1980, Doug drove her to a freeway off-ramp near Hollywood and showed her the bodies of two teenaged girls. Doug liked to describe his necrophilic activities with the dead girls. Carol was shocked, but she stuck with her depraved boyfriend. Later, she would state that she didn't tell anyone of her guilty knowledge because she was in love.

On June 12, 1980, the bodies of the two teenagers were found. They were stepsisters Gina Marano and Cynthia Chandler, both 16. They had been shot to death with a .22-calibre handgun — Gina in the head, Cynthia in the heart.

Eleven days later, Doug picked up 21-year-old prostitute Exxie Wilson. Exxie hailed from Little Rock, Ark. A vice crackdown in that city had forced her to move her business to Hollywood. Doug had sex with Exxie, shot her to death and decapitated her. The headless body was dumped in an alley. The head was taken home to be presented to Carol.

That same day, Doug picked up 20-year-old Karen Jones. Her body was disposed of behind a steak house in Burbank, where it was found the next morning. Later in the morning, Exxie's headless body was discovered in an alley by a man emptying his garbage.

Back at the Clark residence, Doug proudly displayed the human head he had brought home. He had Carol dress up the head with cosmetics. The abnormal behaviour of the two lovers was beyond belief. Carol later was to state,"I made her up like a Barbie with make-up."

Doug placed the head in a box and left it on a private residential driveway. The owner of the house opened the box, recoiled in horror and called the police.

By now the press had dubbed the perpetrator of the bizarre series of killings, the Sunset Slayer. More of the maniac's handiwork was uncovered. Earlier, on June 1,17-year-old Marnette Comer, a runaway from Sacramento, had disappeared from the streets of Hollywood. Her body was found in a ravine in the San Fernando Valley. Marnette had been shot four times in the head.

Carol was now quite accustomed to patrolling the streets with Doug, looking for runaways or prostitutes. When they picked up their sixth murder victim, Carol handed Doug the gun he used to shoot the girl. The victim was known to them only as Kathy. When her body was found months later, no one could remember her last name. Kathy has never been identified.

One girl escaped the clutches of the deranged pair. She had been lured into their vehicle from a shopping centre parking lot. The girl was repeatedly stabbed, but managed to jump from the car. Despite suffering 26 stab and slash wounds, she survived the attack.

Occasionally, Carol would drop into Little Nashville to chat with her old beau, the Australian Cowboy, John Murray. On one particular day, Murray told Carol that he believed her boyfriend might be the Sunset Slayer. He was even thinking of going to the police with his suspicions. John had spoken to the wrong person.

Carol made a date to meet John in the parking lot of Little Nashville at midnight. She was packing a knife and gun when she showed up for the rendezvous. The pair drove away in John's van.

Four days later, the Australian Cowboy's body, sans

head, was found. He had been stabbed to death by an impatient Carol. They had travelled only a few blocks from the roadhouse when she had attacked him. Carol had tossed the head into a ravine. Despite an extensive search, it has never been found.

Throughout the series of gruesome killings, Carol worked steadily as a nurse at a convalescent hospital in Burbank. One day she broke down. It was during a coffee break that she burst into tears and screamed, "I can't take it any more. I'm supposed to save lives, not take them." Carol became hysterical and blurted out the whole terrible story to her supervisor, who immediately notified police.

Doug Clark was picked up. Police recovered his .22-calibre handgun. Ballistic tests indicated that five of the Sunset Slayer's victims had been shot with Clark's weapon. Carol filled in all the details, admitting only to the murder of John Murray and to assisting in the murder of the unidentified prostitute named Kathy.

On January 28, 1983, Doug was found guilty on six counts of first-degree murder. Carol, who was the state's chief witness against him, pleaded guilty to one count of murder and one count of being an accessory to murder.

Carol Bundy was sentenced to 27 years to life for murder and 25 years to life on the accessory charge. The sentences are to run consecutively. Doug Clark was sentenced to death in San Quentin's gas chamber. For the past seven years, he has resided on that institution's Death Row.

CANADIAN KILLER

W as Robert Rae Cook guilty of murder? That was the burning question put before the jury back in 1960 when he stood trial with his life in the balance.

Bobby was born in Hanna, Alberta, on July 15, 1937. When he was only nine years old, his mother died while undergoing minor surgery. Within two years, his father married school teacher Daisy Gaspar and the family moved to Stettler, a small town about 200 km southeast of Edmonton.

In the following 10 years, Daisy Cook gave birth to five children. Who knows what effect this rapid expansion of the family had on Bobby? We do know that, at the age of 13, he stole a car. It was a criminal act he was to repeat time and again. A year later, he stole another vehicle and ended up in the Bowden Correctional Centre. Bobby continued his career as a car thief, as well as an inept break and enter artist. In all, between the ages of 13 and 21, he was convicted 19 times.

In 1959, the Queen visited Canada. Bobby Cook was one of those non-violent offenders who received amnesty in honor of her visit. On June 23, he and other released prisoners drank the day away in Saskatoon. Next day, he stole a car and drove to Bowden to retrieve $4,300 he had buried before being incarcerated.

Now well-fixed for cash, Bobby made his way to Edmonton, where once again he spent freely, buying drinks for several ex-cons. On Thursday, June 25, according to Bobby, he got a lift to Stettler, met his father and drank some beer with him. During their father-son chat, Bobby learned that his mechanic father was planning to purchase a garage in British Columbia. Bobby later claimed that he turned over about $4,000 to his father. He planned to move to B.C. with his family. His father urged him to relocate in an attempt to straighten out his life. Bobby agreed.

Rae Cook gave his son the family station wagon, with instructions to trade it in on a new car. Again, according to Bobby, his father gave him his driver's licence, insurance policy and registration for the family station wagon.

Father and son parted. Later that night, around 9:30 p.m., Bobby entered the Cook residence. He gave his father his prison issued blue suit. An hour later, at 10:30 p.m., he left Stettler for Edmonton.

At 1 a.m., Bobby ran into ex-con Sonny Wilson in Edmonton. Together they broke into a dry cleaning establishment, absconding with the paltry sum of $30. Bobby slept until 9 a.m., when he showed up at Hood Motors, where he traded the family station wagon for a 1959 white Chev Impala convertible. He used his father's credentials to purchase the vehicle and made up a history of steady employment. The salesman accepted Bobby at face value, but later that same day, an official at the garage recognized the fraudulent transaction and called the police.

Bobby took a spin in the convertible. He drove to Camrose, then on to Whitecourt and back to Camrose. On Saturday, June 27, he was given a ticket for having open liquor in his car and sent on his way. Bobby claims he then drove to Stettler, but found that his parents had left. He assumed they had started off for B.C. Bobby noticed two suitcases and a metal box containing the family's personal documents. He threw them in the car with the intention of taking them to British Columbia.

Not long after leaving his home that Saturday evening, Bobby was stopped by RCMP Constable Braden. He was told to report to the local RCMP detachment. Bobby proceeded to the detachment office, where Sgt. Thomas Roach advised him that he had used his father's ID to fraudulently purchase the new convertible. Bobby admitted using the ID, but claimed it was with his father's permission. Bobby went on to give an account of his movements, much as we have related here. He never deviated from his story in any detail in the months to follow.

Sgt. Roach visited the Cook residence, but found no one at home. The convertible was searched. Police found the suitcases and metal box. Inside the suitcases were the family's nightclothes. The box contained Mr. Cook's bankbook, the children's birth certificates and a marriage licence. Sgt. Roach visited the Cooks' house for the second time. The front door was unlocked. Roach went inside, using a flashlight, and found nothing amiss.

The next day, Sunday, for the third time, the RCMP visited the Cook residence. In an attached garage, under floor boards which covered a grease pit, they found the bodies of the entire Cook family.

Rae Cook's body was riddled with bullets. His wife Daisy lay beside him. A shotgun blast had blown away half her face. Underneath their bodies lay those of the children; Gerald, 9, Patrick, 8, Christopher, 6, Cathy, 4, and Linda Mae, 3. Their heads had been beaten with the stock of a single barrel shotgun. Someone had washed blood off the walls inside the house, but traces of the blood were still discernible. Inside the master bedroom, police found Bobby's prison issue blue suit under a mattress. It was bloodstained.

Bobby had a ready answer for all questions put to him. He had given his father the suit to make the trip to British Columbia. They were the same size and it seemed the right thing to do. He had come back to Stettler to wait for his parents' call, telling him where to meet them. Bobby was charged with the murder of his father and lodged in the Ponoka Mental Institution. He asked permission to attend his family's funeral. When permission was denied, he smashed through a wire mesh window and escaped. Four days later, a bedraggled, half-starved Bobby Cook was apprehended hiding in a barn not far from Stettler.

Meanwhile, the investigation into the mass murder focused solely on Bobby Cook. Medical examination of the bodies indicated that the murders had taken place at least 24 hours before they were found, but not more than 72 hours. This time frame proved to be ticklish. It put the time of the murders between 11 a.m. Thursday, June 25 and 11 a.m. on Saturday morning, June 27. During much of this time span, Bobby could prove he was nowhere near Stettler.

Police believed the murders took place sometime after 9:30 p.m. on Thursday, June 25 and 5 a.m. Friday, June 26. For Bobby to have committed the crimes at any other time would have been virtually impossible. Reliable witnesses placed him far away from the murder scene.

Unsavory witnesses, such as admitted thief Sonny Wilson, placed Bobby in Edmonton at 1 a.m. Friday. If these witnesses were to be believed, Bobby would have had to have left Stettler, a two and a half hour drive, at 10:30 p.m. Thursday, leaving him less than an hour to shoot two adults, bludgeon five children to death, carry bodies to the garage grease pit, replace floor covers, wash bloodstains off walls and get out of town.

The $4,000 Bobby claimed to have given to his father was never found. Police believe it never existed. However, several prison inmates were well-aware that Bobby had a cache of more than $4,000 buried somewhere on the outside.

Did Bobby Cook, a 21-year-old petty criminal who had never committed a violent act in his life, systematically slaughter his entire family? Is it possible that after Bobby left that Thursday night, someone else committed those murders for the $4,000 in Rae Cook's possession?

In November 1959, Bobby's murder trial opened at Red

Deer. It took 10 days to present, but the jury took only an hour and a half to bring in a guilty verdict. Bobby was sentenced to hang. His lawyers appealed the conviction and won a new trial. The results were the same. This time the jury took only 25 minutes to bring in their guilty verdict.

On Monday, November 14, 1960, Robert Rae Cook was hanged at the Fort Saskatchewan Correctional Institute.

THE LAST TWO
TO HANG

Before they met in jail, Arthur Lucas and Ronald Turpin never knew each other. In death, they would be united forever.

Art Lucas was born in Cordle, Georgia, on December 18, 1907. Both his parents died of natural causes before he reached the age of seven.

Art was raised by an aunt and uncle in Byronville, Florida. He quit school in the sixth grade and went to work. By the time he was a teenager, he was running errands for small time gangsters and making his living on the streets. Art had an IQ of 63, which is classified as borderline intelligence.

As the years passed, Art graduated to more serious crimes, specializing in narcotics and prostitution. While still a young man, he served a prison sentence in Leavenworth Penitentiary.

In 1953, Art married Dolores Chipps, a prostitute who originally hailed from London, Ont. Dolores presented Art with a son. Apparently Art was so overwhelmed by the event, he kicked mother and child out of the apartment, and ushered in Lillian Boykin, who followed the same occupation as Dolores.

In 1961, Art was making his living by procuring young girls to work in brothels in and around Detroit. He also wasn't above being paid to administer a beating to anyone who had crossed a fellow hoodlum. That's what he was doing in Toronto in November 1961.

A Detroit crook, Gus Saunders, had been fingered by an FBI informer, one Therland Crater. Crater, better known as Checkerboard, was to be a material witness against Saunders in an upcoming narcotics trial. Saunders loaned Art his pink Buick to drive to Toronto to teach Crater a lesson. Art taught well.

At 7 a.m. on Friday, November 17, 1961, a postman, Francis MacGuire, discovered Crater's body in the hallway of a Kendal Ave. boarding house. He called the landlord, Sygmant Turlinski, who entered Crater's apartment and found the nude body of 20-year-old prostitute Carol Ann Newman in a bedroom. Carol Ann, who sometimes plied her trade under the name Jean Rochelle, had been slashed across the throat. Crater had been shot in the back with a .38-calibre revolver. As an afterthought, his throat had been cut as well.

Toronto detectives were soon told by informants that the double murder had connections in Detroit. The word went out to the Detroit underworld for information. It wasn't long in coming. Red Thomas, a punk who had it in for Saunders, told police of Art Lucas' trip to Toronto in Saunders' pink Buick.

Detectives called on Art's wife Dolores, whom he still saw on a regular basis. She told police that Art had killed Crater and Newman. Dolores stated that Art had travelled back to Detroit on the day of the murders. He had come to her house in an agitated state and told her, "I just killed two people."

Art had also told Dolores that a man named Crater was one of the victims and that the murders had taken place in Toronto. He had not intended to hurt the girl until she had screamed. Carol Ann was simply in the wrong bed at the wrong time.

Dolores said that Saunders had been informed on by Crater and deserved a beating, but she never thought her husband capable of killing anyone. Art had washed blood from his hands and had even rinsed blood out of a pair of shorts in a pail of water, which Dolores was able to turn over to police. The pink liquid in the pail proved to be diluted blood. Art was also very concerned because he was sure he had lost his ring in the bedclothes on Carol Ann Newman's bed.

Less than 24 hours after the double murder, police picked up Art Lucas at Lillian Boykin's Burns Ave. house in Detroit. Art denied having murdered anyone. He claimed that he had called on Crater to find a position for one of his prostitutes. He had had some drinks with Crater and had borrowed money from him, leaving his ring as collateral for the loan.

On April 30, 1962, Art stood trial for the murder of Checkerboard Crater. He was found guilty and sentenced to death with no recommendation for mercy.

Ronald Turpin was born on April 29, 1933. His father was often away from home, working as a conductor with the Canadian Pacific Railway.

At age 13, Ronald was placed in a foster home. He dropped out of school in Grade 8 and, for a while worked as a clerk in Ottawa. In 1951, when he was 18, he stole a car. That little escapade earned him 18 months in Kingston Penitentiary. From that time on, Ronald earned his living as a small time thief and counterfeiter, spending short periods of time in prison.

On October 25, 1961, Ronald, together with his girlfriend Lillian White, arrived at 222 Wellesley St., home of prostitute Della Burns. Della was throwing a party.

The good times rolled for a while, but were abruptly interrupted around midnight when Della answered a knock at the door. Someone she had never seen before fired two shots at her, but missed. Della later told police that Ronald Turpin wrestled the gun out of the stranger's hands. He and Lillian left the party with the stranger's gun.

Unknown to Ronald, Della was under police surveillance in the murder investigation of one Lorne Gibson, an underworld character believed to have been killed by gambling competitors. Ronald and Lillian had run out the back door of Della's residence just as a police cruiser pulled up at the front. Della and the other guests told the officers what had transpired. Only one witness, Frank Benson, gave a different version. He claimed Ronald Turpin was the gunman.

Police felt that the weapon used in the attempt on Della's life might very well have been the one used to kill Lorne Gibson. In fact, it was theorized that Turpin might have committed both crimes. The hunt was on for Ronald Turpin. Officially, he was wanted only for discharging a firearm with intent to wound.

Ronald and Lillian hid out in Sudbury. They continued on to Buffalo, before succumbing to the urge to spend the Christmas season in Toronto. They decided to stay on in the city they knew so well. The month of January was uneventful. Ronald operated in the open using various aliases. In February, he decided that he and Lillian should move along to Northern Ontario. With this in mind, they purchased a beat-up old van.

On Sunday, February 11, 1962, Ronald and Lillian had a farewell drink with Della Burns. Ronald slipped away to raise a little money for the impending trip. He robbed the Red Rooster Restaurant of $632.84. The robbery had gone well, but now a police car was trailing him along the Danforth. Maybe, thought Turpin, it was because one of his headlights was damaged. Maybe the officer recognized him. We will never know the reason why Const. Frederick Nash had Ronald Turpin pull over.

Ronald identified himself as Orval Penrose and was asked to get out of his vehicle. An eyewitness, Leonard Boreham, saw the two men wrestle between the van and the police car. He watched as shots rang out and Const. Nash crumbled to the street. The other man jumped into the police car and attempted to drive away.

When a second officer arrived at the scene, Turpin was still behind the wheel of the police car. When the policeman approached, Turpin threw his gun at him and shouted, "Look after the police officer!"

Ronald was taken to hospital by ambulance. He was wounded in both arms and had a flesh wound in the cheek. Const. Nash died of his wounds. He left a wife and four children.

On May 28, 1962, Ronald Turpin stood trial for the murder of Const. Frederick Nash. He was found guilty and sentenced to death.

It was on Death Row in Toronto's Don Jail that Ronald Turpin and Arthur Lucas met for the first time. The two men who had been brought up in unstable environments and had led lives of crime, awaited death together. They got to know each other well. Both leaned heavily on the spiritual comfort given them by Brigadier Cyril Everitt of the Salvation Army.

On Monday, December 10, 1962, the condemned men were led to the gallows. Brigadier Everitt was with them to the end. He read the 23rd Psalm. The two doomed men stood back to back. The trap door swung open and they plunged to eternity.

Arthur Lucas and Ronald Turpin were the last men to be executed in Canada.

THE STUART
MYSTERY

It was the most dramatic phone call Dispatcher Gary McLaughlin had ever received. It would prove to be one he would never forget.

On the night of Monday, October 23, 1989, McLaughlin was manning the emergency line at the State Police Communications Centre in Boston. He picked up the phone and heard a male voice sob, "My wife's been shot! I've been shot!" The call emanated from a cellular car phone.

McLaughlin urged his caller to tell him his location. The man in the car couldn't be sure. McLaughlin begged the wounded man to hang on. He found out that his caller's name was Chuck Stuart and that he was driving a blue Toyota Cressida.

McLaughlin found out that the man and his wife had been shot and robbed. The robber had run off with the keys of the Toyota, but Chuck explained that he had another set. The Stuarts had been forced to drive to a secluded area of Mission Hill before the robber shot them and took off. Chuck simply didn't know where he was. He couldn't see a street sign or a recognizable building.

As they spoke, police cars were already scanning Mission Hill looking for the wounded man. What follows is a transcript of the taped conversation which took place between McLaughlin and Chuck Stuart.

McLaughlin instructed, "If you can drive, give me any street indication and stay there. I'll get someone right to you."

"I'll start the car. Oh man. I'm starting the car."

"Okay. Bear with me, Chuck. I'm going to get someone to you. Hang in with me now."

"I'm at a place but I can't read it."

"Just try to read it, Chuck. Just calm down. Stay with me. I'm going to get help to you. Help is on the way. Is your wife breathing?"

"She's still gurgling. There's a busy street up ahead, but I can't see where I am."

"Can you see a building?"

"I'm driving with my lights off. I can't reach forward, it's too painful."

"Just tell me what the street is, Chuck."

"Ahhh, man! I'm pulling over. It's Tremont St.," the wounded man replied in a whisper. "Oh, man, I'm going to pass out, and my wife has stopped gurgling. She's stopped breathing."

A short time later, Chuck Stuart heard police sirens. At last help had reached him. Carol Stuart, who was seven months pregnant, had been shot in the head. She was rushed to Brigham and Woman's Hospital, where her baby was removed by Caesarean section. The child was a three pound boy. A priest christened the boy Christopher, as the parents had planned months earlier. Six hours after being shot, Carol died without regaining consciousness.

Chuck was taken by ambulance to Boston City Hospital. His condition was extremely serious. A lone bullet had damaged his liver, urological tract, stomach and intestines. For the first few days he lingered between life and death, but as time went by it became apparent he would recover. In the next five weeks in intensive care he would lose 50 pounds. To add to his discomfort, he had undergone a colostomy.

When he regained consciousness, Chuck was questioned by police. He and Carol had been in the

Mission Hill district, not the safest area of Boston, to attend Lamaze classes. According to Chuck, they were waiting for a light to change when a black man, brandishing a silver pistol, jumped into the Toyota. He ordered them to drive to a dark, isolated street. He demanded their car keys, money and jewelry, which were quickly turned over to him.

The robber then demanded Chuck's wallet. When Chuck told him he didn't carry a wallet, the man went berserk. He shot Carol in the head and then pointed the weapon at Chuck's head. He fired and missed as Chuck scrambled for cover. The man then leaned over the front seat and shot Chuck in the side. The gunman took off into the night. Chuck dialled 911.

Chuck had an extra set of car keys and so was able to follow McLaughlin's instructions, which undoubtedly saved his life. He gave a detailed description of his assailant to the police. The killer was a black man with brown eyes, between 25 and 35 years old and stood five feet 10 inches, weighing between 150 and 160 pounds. He wore his hair in a short Afro. He was dressed in a black sweat suit with two or three red stripes on the jacket sleeve.

The story of the horribly wounded man, his murdered pregnant wife and the Caesarean section had a profound effect on the citizens of Boston. Were decent God-fearing folks not safe on a public highway waiting for a light to change? The heat was on to apprehend the killer. Most pressure was placed on the black community. Males faintly resembling Chuck's description were stopped on the streets and searched. Racial tension rose dramatically in Boston.

Chuck took on the role of a hero, Carol that of a saint. Their past lent credence to their "All American couple" image. Chuck Stuart was born to blue-collar Irish parents. He had three brothers, Michael, Mark and the youngest Matthew. After high school he had attended a vocational school and became a cook.

When he met Carol, a bright and cheerful university

240

student, Chuck believed he could better himself in some other field of endeavour. He applied for and was accepted as a trainee at Kakas and Sons, a prestigious fur store which had been in business since 1858. Chuck was an ambitious, valued employee. He received promotion after promotion until he became manager of the business, answering only to the owners. His income at the time of the shooting was well in excess of $100,000 per annum.

Carol also had progressed in her career. She graduated from university with a law degree and was earning a substantial salary at the time of the tragedy. The Stuarts lived in a comfortable split-level home in the Boston suburb of Reading. In four years of married life, the Stuarts had come a long way. The American dream had been fulfilled, but the future for Carol Stuart had been terminated by the squeeze of a finger against a trigger.

From his hospital bed Chuck wrote a eulogy to be delivered by a friend at Carol's funeral. Eight hundred people attended the service at St. James Church in Medford. There were no dry eyes among the mourners.

Meanwhile, the intensive police search for the killer had apparently paid off. Willie Bennett, a small-time hoodlum, was taken into custody. He fit the general description given by Chuck. An acquaintance of Bennett's informed police that Willie had told him that he had killed Carol Stuart.

On Thursday, November 9, 17 days after his birth, baby Christopher Stuart was near death. Chuck requested to see his child. He was transported by ambulance to Brigham and Woman's Hospital and saw his son before the baby expired.

On December 5, Chuck was released from hospital. Now with no wife, no child and lugging around a colostomy bag, he went about picking up the pieces of his life. One of the pieces was $82,000 life insurance money which had been carried at Carol's place of employment. Chuck inquired about the money shortly after his release.

While the glare of publicity had diminished appreciably

241

since the night of the shooting, there was one more function for Chuck to perform. He had to attempt to pick his wife's killer out of a police lineup. Chuck did so with little hesitation. He pointed at Willie Bennett and said, "He looks most like the guy." Willie Bennett was in big trouble.

Unknown to all was the fact that Willie Bennett had nothing whatever to do with the Stuarts. The man who knew the whole story was Chuck's brother, Matthew Stuart. Here is the story he told his brother Michael and eventually his entire family and his lawyer before informing the police.

About 10 days before the tragedy, Chuck had approached him about ripping off an insurance company by orchestrating a phony theft. The day before the shooting, the brothers met. Chuck drove Matthew to a deserted street in Mission Hill. He told Matthew he would meet him the following night at that exact spot between 8:15 and 8:30. At that time he would toss a package into Matthew's car. All Matthew had to do was dispose of the parcel.

The following night, Matthew showed up. Chuck threw a bundle from his car into Matthew's. Matthew was told to get rid of the parcel. Chuck drove away. Matthew claims he never saw Carol in the car. He then examined the bundle. It contained a nickel-plated revolver, a woman's purse, make-up and jewelry. Matthew threw the bundle into the Pines River.

And how did the police know this unbelievable tale was true? Matthew Stuart had saved one piece of jewelry he thought his brother might want to keep. It was his sister-in-law Carol's engagement ring.

Matthew, the ever dutiful brother, forewarned Chuck of his intention of going to the police. The world was closing in on the man who had once had more than most men achieve in a lifetime. What went on in his mind we don't know. What we do know is that early on the morning of January 4, 1990, Chuck Stuart committed suicide by jumping off the Tobin Bridge into the dark cold waters of the Mystic River. He left a note, the contents of which have never been divulged. The murder weapon was later recovered from the Pines. It proved to be a pistol stolen earlier from Chuck's employer, Kakas and Sons.

Why did Chuck Stuart kill his wife, child and seriously wound himself? The most prominent theory, according to acquaintances reviewing the case, is that Chuck wanted to become his own boss. Although he had been doing well financially, he longed to open his own restaurant. There is also some evidence that Chuck was involved with another woman. It is believed that by killing his wife and child, he would leave himself free to marry this other woman and at the same time collect the $82,000 insurance benefit to use as seed money for his restaurant. He had meant to wound himself superficially, but instead had by accident almost killed himself.

INNOCENT
BEGINNINGS

St. Thomas, Ont., is a peaceful community located south of London, just up the road from Lake Erie. But one day in the spring of 1934, guns blazed and bodies fell like a wild west shootout.

It all started innocently enough. Fred MacTemple, 21, was wanted for stealing a bicycle. Const. Colin McGregor and Sgt. Sam McKeown were dispatched to bring in the local youth for questioning. By chance, Detective Bert McCully of the Michigan police happened to be in the St. Thomas police station. He volunteered to give the officers a lift to 13 Queen St., where the MacTemples lived. The street was in the rougher part of town and the MacTemples were known as tough customers.

The officers decided to take the necessary precautions. They asked McCully to cover the back door as they approached the rather run-down house. They knocked on the front door. A young boy answered. When the officers asked to speak to Fred MacTemple, the lad was so frightened he could only point to the rear of the house.

The two officers entered. A door opened, and there stood Fred MacTemple, brandishing a wicked-looking blue/black U.S. Army issued .45-calibre automatic. "Stick 'em up!" he shouted.

Neither officer was expecting such a move. They had

felt at worst that their young suspect might try to run out of the house. Now they stared at a nervous young man waving around a dangerous weapon. McKeown tried talking his way out of a tough jam. "Just a minute," he said, "We've got a warrant against Fred MacTemple for stealing a bicycle. Why all the gunplay?"

The tall young man rasped, "No cops is going to take me!"

McKeown continued, "It's not that serious."

He was interrupted. "Shut that talk!" Fred shouted.

From a door leading off the kitchen, 55-year-old Frank MacTemple emerged waving a revolver in each hand. One was an ugly-looking German Luger, the other a white .38 Ivor-Johnson. He took command of the situation and shouted orders. "Shut that talk and both of you put your guns on the table! No tricks!"

McKeown couldn't believe he was facing a total of three handguns, all over a stolen bicycle. Once again he attempted to talk his way out of this unlikely predicament. "You're Frank MacTemple, I take it. Your son is wanted for bicycle stealing. It isn't a serious charge."

MacTemple would have none of it. He pushed a gun into McKeown's ribs and commanded, "Shut the talk and put your gun on the table! We're not going to be taken by any damn cop." Fred MacTemple grabbed Const. McGregor's gun. McKeown didn't respond to the elder MacTemple's orders. McGregor warned, "Be careful, Sam, the hammer of that Luger is up." For the third time, Frank cursed, "Put your gun on the table or I'll let you have it!" At that precise moment, McKeown jumped Fred MacTemple. Frank started cursing and shooting.

Const. Colin McGregor took a slug directly in his stomach and fell to the floor. McKeown, in a desperate struggle with Fred, was shot in the wrist. He grimaced in pain as his hand went numb. Frank was still shooting. A bullet entered Fred's neck, spinning him to the floor. MacTemple had missed McKeown and shot his own son.

Frank MacTemple, guns blazing, backed out a side door

and escaped. Det. McCully raced into the house but was too late to apprehend the crazed man. McKeown managed to get off one shot, which missed.

From upstairs, Mrs. MacTemple and her young son heard the shooting. When it stopped, she ventured downstairs and saw her son Fred lying on the kitchen floor with a bullet through his neck.

The two wounded officers and Fred MacTemple were rushed by ambulance to hospital. The day after the shooting, Const. Colin McGregor died of his wounds. Fred MacTemple lingered between life and death for some hours, but gradually recovered. McKeown's hand was bandaged and he was released from hospital.

As soon as Fred was able to talk, police questioned him. They wanted to know what had motivated the shooting. Fred explained that it was a grudge shooting, not particularly against McGregor, but against the police in general. Evidently, the threat of going to reform school for the theft of the bicycle and of the older MacTemple going to jail for other minor thefts had caused father and son to flee the area. Only after they had purchased guns in Erie, Pennsylvania did they return, swearing that the police would never take them.

Fred explained, "Police had broken up our home, separated our family and made it impossible for Dad and me to come home." After they procured the weapons, the MacTemples decided to chance returning to St. Thomas.

Now the hunt was on for Frank MacTemple. One of the largest manhunts ever conducted in that section of Ontario was quickly organized. Frank was spotted in several places, but the quarry always managed to elude the hunters.

On May 9, two days after the shooting, a 16-year-old farmhand, Clifford Anderson, was pitching hay from the haymow to the barn floor below. There was a scream and out popped a dirty old man in ragged clothing. The man implored Clifford not to tell his boss, Malcolm McNeil, that he was hiding in the haymow. Clifford, who suspected he was talking to the most wanted man in the province, was frightened out of his wits. He was relieved when MacTemple allowed him to leave the barn to go to his supper. Two hours later, Clifford told the McNeil family about the stranger in the barn. McNeil immediately called police.

MacTemple left the barn and stayed in nearby woods until dark. He then made his way to West Lorne, where he had a friend, Dick Carnegie, 58, who operated an antique store. Police felt the wanted man might seek refuge in his friend's sparse two-room shack. They decided to encircle Carnegie's home, but to remain hidden. Carnegie was told to expect MacTemple. He agreed to co-operate with police and do anything in his power to apprehend the suspected killer.

About 11:30 p.m. that same night, MacTemple showed up at Carnegie's door. He claimed he had been hunting squirrels and had accidentally shot himself in the hand. He showed Carnegie his slightly wounded hand, which he had acquired in the melee two days earlier. Carnegie washed and bandaged the wound.

About an hour after he entered the house, MacTemple jumped up. He thought he had heard a noise outside the shack. Before he could respond further, Carnegie exclaimed, "It can't be anything. I'll go out and see, though." With that, he dashed out the door. He was met by police officers, who were in position around the house. Carnegie confirmed, "I got him inside. What am I going to do with him? If anyone but me goes in that door, he'll shoot. He's got a gun and he's ready to use it." The courageous man continued, "I guess I'll hafta hold him so he can't use his gun while you boys come in."

Carnegie returned indoors and offered his guest a cigarette. After the man accepted the cigarette, Carnegie threw himself upon the startled MacTemple. He yelled for help and, within seconds, it was over. Carnegie was so exhausted and excited, he fell faint to the floor.

On March 26, 1935, Frank and Fred MacTemple were tried for the murder of Const. McGregor. Both were found guilty and sentenced to death. There was a great hue and cry to save Fred's life as he hadn't actually fired the murder weapon. However, all appeals failed. On June 27, 1935, father and son were hanged in the St. Thomas jail yard.

BIBLE STUDENT'S ORDEAL

It's been over 10 years since Karen Ann Phillips was raped and murdered in her apartment in Oak Park, Ill. One man, Steven Linscott, has lived with the murder all that time. You see, Steven has been accused of murdering Phillips, but many believe he had absolutely nothing to do with her death.

At the time of the crime on October 3, 1980, Steven was 26 years old; his wife Lois, 25. He lived at a Christian halfway house for ex-convicts called the Good News Mission. Steven was a supervisor at the mission, as well as a student at Emmaus Bible College in nearby Dubuque, Iowa. Phillips was murdered two buildings removed from the mission.

Had Steven Linscott ignored the murder as an unfortunate occurrence which took place in his neighborhood, it is unlikely that he would ever have become personally involved in the investigation into Phillips' death.

The day after the murder, police canvassed the Linscotts, inquiring if they had seen or heard anything unusual around the time of the killing. Both Steven and Lois told them that they had observed nothing out of the ordinary.

A few days later, Steven mentioned to Lois that he had

had a dream around 1 a.m., the exact time it is believed that Phillips was murdered. Steven told his wife and fellow students at the Bible college that he had awakened in a cold sweat after experiencing a nightmare. In the nightmare, he had witnessed a blonde man beating someone to death. The victim seemed to be resigned to her imminent death.

Steven's wife and friends were intrigued with his narrative and urged him to contact the Oak Park police. Initially, Steven felt a bit silly about the whole thing, but after thinking about his dream and the fact that it might in some way assist police, he decided to tell them his story. He told officers that in his dream he had seen a livingroom which contained a stereo system and couch. The killer was a blonde man who wore a t-shirt. He used a blunt instrument of some kind to beat his victim, whom Steven erroneously thought might be black. The entire room was blood-splattered when the killer finished his handiwork.

Detectives took Steven's dream seriously. They advised him that he had provided their best clue and that he might have psychic powers. Steven was flattered. In the past, he had often felt that he had been somewhere else when he woke up. Now he believed he might have an unusual gift which could apprehend the killer. He co-operated fully with the police.

Steven was called in for a second round of in-depth interrogation. The questions were put to him as if he were actually in Phillips' apartment. He would volunteer what he had done and said. It dawned on Steven that he might be a suspect, but detectives soon put him at rest. He was told that in order to be used as a witness, he had to be ruled out as a suspect. That's why they required samples of his saliva, blood and hair.

After these items were tested, police dropped any pretence that Steven was not a suspect. The Bible student was devastated. He had led an exemplary life and had never been in trouble with the law. But now, because he had come forward to assist in a murder investigation, he found himself the chief suspect. It seemed to Steven that many of the ex-cons at the mission were far likelier suspects than himself. They were never questioned.

Six weeks after being told he was a major suspect, Steven was arrested and charged with the first-degree murder of Karen Ann Phillips.

No one who knew Steven could believe that this soft-spoken religious man was capable of a vicious rape murder. His background held no mysteries. His upbringing was without incident. Steven was born in Maine, where he attended high school. He joined the Navy and served for four years before receiving an honorable discharge. He then continued his education and was active in good works, such as his supervisory position at the mission.

The Linscotts were not experiencing any marital problems. Their two children, Katherine, 2, and 9-month-old Paul, were the young couple's pride and joy. At Steven's murder trial, Lois swore that she had awakened between 1 a.m. and 3 a.m., when the killing had taken place, to feed Paul. She testified that Steven had been lying asleep in their bed during that crucial time span. In fact, there never has been any physical evidence to link Steven with the victim.

The prosecution's case was based on the premise that Steven's story revealed facts that only the killer could know. Detective Robert Scianna told me, "It's been a long time and I have difficulty remembering details, but at the time Linscott's knowledge of the interior of the Phillips' apartment could only have been known by the killer."

Although fingerprints from the Phillips' apartment were not Steven's, a semen sample could have been his. It could also be matched with 60% of the male population of the U.S. Two strands of hair found at the scene could have been from the heads of thousands of other individuals, as well as from Steven's head. The prosecution's case was porous. Even the details in Steven's story and the actual facts about the apartment contained many discrepancies.

251

The victim was not black and the blows seen by Steven in his dream didn't match the wounds on Karen's head. She had been stabbed and strangled as well as having been clubbed with a tire iron. The one point the prosecution homed in on was the fact that when Phillips was found, the thumb and forefinger of each of her hands met in an "O." To practitioners of yoga, this signifies the peaceful acceptance of death. Phillips had practised yoga and Steven had said in his dream that the victim had seemed resigned to her death.

Steven Linscott was found guilty of murder and sentenced to 40 years imprisonment. Lois and the children moved so that they could be closer to Steven. Lois immediately hired a lawyer and began appealing her husband's conviction.

In 1985, the Illinois Court of Appeal ruled that the evidence against Steven was insufficient to sustain a conviction. They overruled the original jury's decision. Steven was released from prison.

The state took the case to the supreme court, which ruled that at the original trial the jury could reasonably have concluded that Steven was guilty. Another appeal has been launched and the supreme court is presently considering having a new trial or dismissing the case altogether.

Meanwhile, Steven remains out of prison on bail as he has for the last seven years. He is presently pursuing a doctorate degree in philosophy.

I spoke to the Registrar of Emmaus Bible College, Gordon Haresign, who was the principal individual behind the funding of many of Steven's legal manoeuvres. He says, "They really didn't have much to go on — just a dream."

The state feels differently. Authorities are still attempting to bring Linscott to trial for the second time.

LITTLE TOMMY TUCKER

You know how people will talk, especially in a tiny community where little else but the rumor mill is available to break the tedium of everyday life. That's the way it was in Riverside, Mass., back in 1904 when Tommy Tucker's wife accidentally drowned. At least, that's what the official inquest ruled. Others said, "Drowning my foot! The poor dear was murdered." There was absolutely nothing of a concrete nature to implicate Tommy and nothing ever came of the gossip.

Poor Tommy Tucker, a widower at age 24. For a while he worked as a clerk in Boston, but in the spring of 1904 he was unemployed and living with his parents in Auburndale, Mass.

A few miles down the road from Auburndale dwelt the Page family, in the small community of Weston. The topography of the area has changed dramatically in the 80-odd years since 1904. Paved highways now crisscross the countryside. To travel from town to town now takes a matter of minutes. In horse and buggy days, the same distances took much longer to traverse.

Edward Page was a 78-year-old retired businessman. His son Harold worked in Boston with the Boston and Albany Railroad. Edward's only daughter, Mabel, 41, lived at home with her father. The only other occupant of the house was Amy Roberts, the housekeeper.

On March 31, Harold left at 8 a.m. for his job in Boston. Around 9 a.m., Mr. Page went for a long walk, as was his custom. A few minutes later, Amy Roberts left the house for Boston to conduct personal business and run some errands for Mr. Page. Before Amy left, Mabel gave her some money to pick up purchases in Boston. The housekeeper noted that Mabel returned a few bills to her purse.

Mabel Page was now alone in her home. A little after 11 a.m., Harold Maynard, a laundry delivery man, dropped off laundry at the Pages'. Mabel paid him and he continued on his route.

At 2 p.m., about three hours after Maynard saw Mabel alive and well, her father returned home. The elderly gentleman was immediately struck by the overwhelming silence. He made his way upstairs, wondering if Mabel could be asleep. The door to her bedroom was closed, which was unusual. He opened the door to a sight no father should witness. His daughter was lying on the floor. Her eyes, open in death, seemed to stare at him.

Mr. Page recoiled in horror as he noticed a small puddle of blood around Mabel's throat. She had been stabbed in the neck, back and heart. Her skirt had been pulled away and left beside the body. Later, the skirt would be found to have bits of straw adhering to it. This straw originated from a downstairs carpet, indicating that Mabel had been murdered downstairs and dragged across the carpet to her bedroom upstairs. She was dressed in a hat and boots, as if she had been preparing to go outdoors when she was attacked. Her empty purse lay nearby.

A scrap of paper was found near the body. On it were written the words, "J.L.Morton, Charlestown, Mass." Downstairs, on a table, police found a rather strange note written in Mabel's handwriting: "Have just heard that Harold is hurt and at the Massachusetts Hospital. Have gone in 12 o'clock. Will leave key in front side door with barn key. Will telephone Mrs. Bennett."

Detectives analysed the notes. The Morton clue was considered to be false, no doubt planted by the killer. The names Morton and Charlestown had no connection with the murder. The second note alluding to Harold's illness was another matter. Police felt that the bogus information about Harold being ill was the method the killer had used to gain entrance to the house. Mabel was taken in by the ruse, wrote out a note for her father and started putting on outer clothing for the trip to the hospital. It was then she was stabbed to death.

Who knows, maybe her killer used the story in an attempt to get her out of the house so he could rob it later. It was possible that Mabel had come downstairs to find the stranger rifling through drawers. The killer had taken the murder weapon with him when he left the Page residence.

Detectives went about questioning anyone who was known to be in the vicinity of the Page's home around the time of the murder. It was in this way they came to question Tommy Tucker four days after the killing.

Tommy told police he had mowed his parents' lawn in the morning. He had then changed his clothing and had gone for a walk. Around 1 p.m., he had ventured up South Ave. where the Pages lived, but had turned around and walked home well before coming to their house.

While returning to his home, Tommy Tucker had quite an adventure. He and an acquaintance named Bourne got a lift with a 16-year-old boy, Arthur Woodward, who was driving a fish wagon. Tommy wasn't interested in the fish or Arthur, but he was very interested in Arthur's cousin, Mabel Walker.

And how did Mabel happen to be on a fish wagon on that day at that time? It was an experience she would never forget. Mabel, who hailed from Damariscotta, Maine, was visiting her uncle, Jeremiah Walker, who just happened to be a fish merchant. His grandson Arthur was about to take the fish wagon on deliveries when Mabel suggested she go along for the ride.

Arthur was glad to have the company. After they made

their last delivery of fish, the cousins were hailed by two men along the side of the road. They wanted a lift. The man named Bourne jumped in the back of the wagon. Tommy Tucker took a seat up front, wedged between the two cousins. He flirted with Mabel Walker, who didn't seem to mind that much.

The occupants of the wagon drove along for about four minutes. Bourne, Tommy and Mabel got off. Bourne separated from the group. Arthur looked back as he drove away and noticed Tommy and Mabel strolling arm in arm down the road. That afternoon, Tommy used all his guile, all his charm and all his romantic persuasiveness to seduce Mabel Walker within an hour of meeting her.

One can only imagine this Mabel's surprise to learn that her lover that afternoon was the major suspect in the murder of another Mabel only hours before their frolic in the woods. Mabel Walker took off before police could question her. Her name was soon to appear on the front pages of all New England newspapers. Police and private detectives sought her to testify to her adventure on that fateful afternoon but Mabel Walker was never found. We can only assume she went to her grave with her secret intact.

Police didn't believe Tommy's story of passing the time of day so near the Page home. Laborers who were digging a ditch along South Ave. told police they had noticed Tommy closer to the Page house that he had admitted.

When Tommy's picture appeared in newspapers, Arthur Woodward remembered something that had totally slipped his mind. After Tommy left his wagon, he had found a sheath on the front seat of the wagon. He had shoved it in his pocket and never thought much about it. Arthur turned the sheath over to police. Tommy admitted it was his. A search of Tommy's house uncovered the broken blade of a hunting knife in the pocket of one of his coats. The blade bore bloodstains and fit exactly the cuts in Mabel Page's corset and the wounds to her body. It also fit the sheath found by Arthur Woodward.

The New England jury deliberated seven hours before finding Tommy Tucker guilty of murder in the first degree. Protesting his innocence to the last, he was executed on June 11, 1906.

HENRY LED
TWO LIVES

Henry Wainwright led two lives.

In life number one, Henry had a large comfortable home, complete with loving wife, four children and servants. A big, jolly man, Henry was beloved by all.

In 1875, Henry and his brother William were brush manufacturers, whose business was located on Whitechapel Rd. in London, England. The brothers had inherited some money, enabling them to set up their own business and, for a while, partake of a rather pleasant lifestyle.

A lover of the arts, Henry often invited actors and actresses to his home for dinner with his family. Sometimes, in the style of the era, the performers would sing and recite for the Wainwrights.

As luck would have it, Henry's business was located beside the Pavilion Theatre, which was chock-full of winsome young actresses. Henry made the acquaintance of several sweet young things he didn't take home to entertain Mrs. Wainwright and the kiddies.

Harriet Lane, a cute little blonde of 20, met Henry quite by chance. The chance meeting led to a casual drink in a nearby pub. A few more meetings and Harriet was madly in love with the obviously successful, fun-loving businessman.

Harriet had her standards. She insisted on marriage. Well, not exactly marriage, but at least the pretence of marriage. She and Henry lived under the rather stylish name of Mr. and Mrs. Percy King. For three years, Henry ran his business and flirted with the showgirls as brush manufacturer Henry Wainwright. The other half of the time he led life number two, as Percy King. Mr. and Mrs. King had two healthy babies. Harriet never had it so good. Henry generously supported her and the two children.

Then things took a turn for the worse. Henry's business declined, forcing him to assume a large mortgage on his warehouse in order to satisfy his creditors. His brother William withdrew from the business.

Harriet, of course, immediately felt the strain. Her allowance gradually decreased. She confided her secret to only one person, a Miss Wilmore. Miss Wilmore often babysat for Harriet and was privy to the information that Percy King was really Henry Wainwright.

With funds rapidly drying up, Harriet soon got into the habit of drowning her sorrows down at the local. She even had the gall to occasionally show up at the brush factory. She became cranky, argumentative and downright annoying.

Henry had a bright idea. He purchased a box of chloride of lime. Then he invited Harriet to take a trip on some pretence or other. We know this for a fact, because Harriet told her friend Miss Wilmore that she and Henry would be away overnight. That same afternoon, three workmen who were employed near Henry's warehouse thought they heard three shots.

A few days later, Miss Wilmore dropped down to the brush factory to inquire about her friend Harriet, whom she hadn't seen for days. Henry didn't blink an eye. He told Miss Wilmore that he had sent Harriet to Brighton for a rest. Two more days passed. Henry had some sad news. Harriet had deserted him. She had met a lover in Brighton. Evidently he was an old flame, one Teddy

Frieake. Henry believed they had taken off for the continent and might even marry.

Miss Wilmore smelled a rat. She knew Teddy and decided to inquire if he was still in town. Sure enough, Teddy was in London and had not seen Harriet for years. To add to Miss Wilmore's consternation, she received a letter, signed E. Frieake, describing his elopement with Harriet.

When Miss Wilmore told Teddy about the letter, he was furious. He looked up Henry, who once again didn't blink an eye. Henry laughingly told Teddy that a coincidence had taken place. He was referring to another Teddy Frieake. The real Teddy was understandably dubious. After all, there were not that many Frieakes around.

Time heals all wounds. Miss Wilmore took care of Harriet's two babies. Henry provided financial assistance. Harriet's father made a few inquiries, but since he had nine daughters, he found it quite difficult to keep track of them all.

Months passed. Henry's business did not improve. He received some financial help from another brother, Thomas, who ran an ironmonger business on the south side of the Thames, but nothing could save the brush business.

As the anniversary of Harriet's disappearance, or elopement if you wish, drew near, the brush business went bankrupt. Creditors prepared to take possession.

On September 11, 1875, Henry asked a former employee named Stokes to help him carry some parcels. Stokes agreed to help and the two men went to the warehouse, where Henry produced two large parcels wrapped in oilcloth. Henry and Stokes were attempting to hail a carriage when Stokes, out of curiosity, opened a corner of the large parcel he was carrying. He observed a human hand. Just then, a carriage pulled up. Stokes, white with fear, assisted Henry in getting the two awkward parcels into the carriage.

Stokes watched as the carriage went down the road and stopped. Henry had recognized a chorus girl, Alice Day.

He asked her if she would like to drive over London Bridge. Alice accepted and so started on a ride she would never forget. Meanwhile, Stokes swung into action and raced after the carriage. He implored passers-by and police to help him.

Finally, two police officers paid attention and caught up to the carriage in time to see Henry enter his brother's building carrying one of the large parcels. The police talked to the startled Alice Day as Henry reappeared from the building. He was annoyed, "Why do you interfere with me? I'm only going in to see an old friend of mine."

The police would have none of it. They herded Henry inside. In desperation, he said, "Look here, say nothing about this, ask no questions and here is £50 for each of you." The police officers rejected the bribe. Instead, they told Henry to open the parcel. He refused, begging the officers, "Don't open it! Pray don't look at it, whatever you do, don't touch it!"

The officers opened the parcel. They recoiled at the sight of the year-old parts of Harriet Lane's body.

Henry and Alice were hauled down to the police station. Poor Alice, who didn't know what in the world was going on, spent an uncomfortable week in jail before she was completely exonerated of any implication in the murder. It had been quite a carriage ride.

Henry stood trial for Harriet's murder. He didn't have much of a chance after the principals in the case told their stories. His brother Thomas confessed to writing the letter signed E. Frieake. Thomas had also purchased a chopping block, a spade and the oilcloth used to wrap the body.

Thomas Wainwright was convicted as an accessory after the fact of murder and was sentenced to seven years imprisonment. Henry was found guilty of murder and sentenced to death. He claimed to be innocent until the end. Immediately before he was hanged, he confessed and even agreed that the sentence was just.

Young Stokes received a reward of £30 and set himself up in business. Alice Day became something of a celebrity and was promoted to lead dancer in the chorus line at the Pavilion Theatre. After her rather unpleasant experience with Henry and his two macabre parcels, Alice developed a distinct aversion to carriage rides.

GREY OWL

The little boy liked to play cowboys and Indians. Unlike other little boys, he always wanted to be an Indian.

Much later, he would tell his story to tens of thousands of fascinated listeners. He claimed he was born in Hermosillo, Mexico in 1888, the son of Katherine Cochise, an Apache. His father was a Scotsman, George MacNeil, a buddy of Buffalo Bill Cody. He related how, at the age of 15, he left his parents and made his way to Ontario, where he was adopted by the Ojibways. It was the Ojibways who gave him the name Grey Owl.

It was a great story. Unfortunately, it was a pack of lies. But let's not divest Grey Owl of all his laurels. He did become an accomplished lecturer, successful author and conservationist. One of his books, Tales of an Empty Cabin, went through seven printings. Another, Adventures of Sajo and her Beaver People, ran to 14 printings.

Archie Belaney was born in Hastings, England on September 18, 1888. Shortly after his birth, his father deserted the family. Little Archie was brought up by two maiden aunts, Ada and Carrie. The young boy, always a bit of a loner, loved to read about the life of Indians in the northwoods of Canada. He kept animals in the attic and amused school chums by bringing them to school.

Archie spent a lot of time outdoors in Hastings and developed a swarthy complexion. He attempted to emulate Canadian Indians at every opportunity and dreamed of travelling to Canada to live in the woods. In 1906, at the age of 18, he persuaded his aunts to pay his way to Toronto.

While other young boys only dreamed of life in the wild, here was a young man determined to make his dreams come true. For a year, Archie worked as a clerk in a dry goods store. He then made his way to Cobalt, Ont., where he obtained a job with a tourist camp operator. The Ojibways taught him how to handle a canoe.

While working at the tourist camp, Archie met a young Indian girl, Angel Aquena. Angel was a religious girl who didn't believe in sexual activity outside the sacrament of marriage. The couple went together for two years before Archie asked Angel to marry him. She agreed. Rev. D.A. Schaefer conducted the marriage ceremony on August 23, 1910. Angel was 20, Archie 22.

Initially, the marriage seemed to be made in heaven. Archie and Angel took long canoe trips into the bush. They hunted and fished and made love. Slowly, Archie took on the mannerisms of his wife and her people. The pair settled in Temagami. To support himself and his wife, Archie would often be away hunting for three or four months. Patient Angel would always be there waiting for her man. When she received a message that Archie had joined the army, Angel waited. It wasn't that different from the usual hunting trip.

Archie served overseas and was shot in the foot, a wound which enabled him to receive a $75 a month pension for the rest of his life. He was sent to England, where he bigamously married an old childhood sweetheart. Archie tried to talk her into accompanying him to Canada, but the proper English girl would have none of it. After he returned to Canada, wife number two divorced him.

In 1919, Archie returned to his Angel, but stayed with

her only a short while. He left to steep himself in the Ojibway culture and way of life. The tall, hawk-nosed Englishman mastered the crafts of the Indian and took on the personality of the Indian. The Ojibways adopted him into their tribe. Grey Owl was born. Now an Indian in every practical way, he returned to Angel and their three children for the last time in 1925. Then he left her for good.

In May 1925, Grey Owl met a beautiful Iroquois maiden, Anahareo, and was immediately smitten. Within two years they were married in an Indian ceremony. If you are keeping track, Grey Owl has now taken his third bride. The happy couple settled in Coudet, Quebec. A daughter, Shirley Dawn, blessed the union in 1932.

It was while living in a cabin he had built for his wife and daughter that Grey Owl began submitting articles to newspapers and magazines. His writing emphasized conservation of our natural resources, particularly our wild life. They were touching and sincere. Grey Owl had long since given up hunting.

Slowly, the saga of the Indian who could write well and champion the cause of our natural heritage caught the imagination of the public. The federal government, intrigued with Grey Owl, gave him a position in Prince Albert National Park, where he and Anahareo cared for a colony of beavers, as well as other animals, in their natural habitat.

Grey Owl's popularity and fame spread. He was invited to England to go on a lecture tour, extolling the virtues of conservation. Accompanied by Anahareo, he was an instant hit. Here was this tall, lean Indian, the very epitome of a man who pitted his brawn and brain against the harshness of the Canadian north and came away victorious. Despite their close relationship, Anahareo and Grey Owl amicably separated and did not see each other after November 1936.

When summoned to Ottawa in connection with his post at the park, Grey Owl met Yvonne Perrier. She and Grey Owl married in St. James United Church in Montreal —

number four if you're still counting.

Once again, Grey Owl was invited to lecture in England. This time, Yvonne accompanied him. Today, Grey Owl's popularity is hard to fathom. He spoke to standing-room-only audiences. Always, he spoke of his respect for the animals. He also had a dry wit, which the English loved.

At the conclusion of the tour, Grey Owl was invited to Buckingham Palace to be presented to King George and Queen Elizabeth. Also present were Princesses Elizabeth and Margaret. At the conclusion of his lecture, Grey Owl bade goodbye to his host. He lightly slapped King George on the shoulder and said, "Goodbye, brother, I'll be seeing you." The royal entourage ate it up.

Grey Owl was an international celebrity. Photos of him, erect and proud in his buckskins, adorned the front pages of newspapers all over the world. What wasn't printed was that, to alleviate the pressure of his hectic schedule, Grey Owl had become a heavy drinker. Only his close associates knew of his moods and bad temper. To the public he was the tall Indian who pleaded for the conservation of wild animals.

Throughout all the glory years, a woman named Angel waited in Temagami for her man. He never returned. Once, Angel heard of Grey Owl giving a lecture in Toronto's Massey Hall, but that was the only news of her husband until she learned that he had died of pneumonia in April 1938.

That's when the beavers hit the dams. Grey Owl's false history was exposed by the North Bay *Nugget* the day after his death. The newspaper had learned the truth of Grey Owl's identity some time earlier, but had chosen to suppress the story. Now, newspapers throughout the world carried the story of the Englishman who had posed as an Indian. Why, he had even fooled the King of England.

Grey Owl had drawn up a will over a year before his death. His estate amounted to about $15,000, not a great deal of money now, but a sizable amount in 1938. He bequeathed one half of his estate and future royalties from his books to his daughter, Shirley Dawn. The balance was left to his last wife, Yvonne Perrier. He didn't leave a cent to Angel.

Angel applied for a share of the estate under the Widows' Relief Act of 1930. This act allowed a widow to apply for a share of her husband's estate if she is left less than she would have received had her husband died without a will. Angel had a good case. Her application claimed that she was Archie Belaney's only legal wife. She claimed one third of the estate and appeared to deserve every penny.

However, there was one catch. Another section of the same act stated that the widow would not share in the will if her behavior was such that if her husband were alive, she would not have the right to receive alimony payments. A young lawyer named John Diefenbaker acted for Yvonne Perrier. Diefenbaker attempted to prove that Angel had committed adultery and was therefore not entitled to her claim.

From the time of his last visit to Angel after the First World War, Grey Owl had contributed nothing towards the support of his wife and three children. She had brought up the children herself and had waited for her man to return. It was true that, during Grey Owl's absence, she had given birth to a boy who had died at the age of three months. Angel claimed that the pregnancy was the result of being raped by one Charlie Potts. Charlie stated that Angel had consented and had thus committed adultery.

The judge hearing the case chose to believe Angel. After legal fees, she received one third of Grey Owl's estate. Incidentally, the young lawyer named John Diefenbaker went on to make somewhat of a name for himself in Canadian politics.

THE GREATEST COUNTERFEITER

Charles Becker was the most successful counterfeiter who ever passed a phony ten spot. Charlie, who learned his trade as an assistant engraver in his home town of Württemberg, Germany, was a fine cut of a lad. The Beckers were poor and Charlie was forced to quit school to help support his family. Because he had a natural flair for drawing, he became an apprentice engraver at the age of 12.

Eight years later, in 1866, 20-year-old Charlie was a master engraver and had outgrown Württemberg. When his parents died, he had no further reason to stay at home. In order to get away, he took a job as a stoker on a New York-bound freighter.

Charlie had made up his mind that he would not go through life as a poor man like his father. He decided that the easiest way to get ahead in the land of milk and honey was to become a criminal.

Charles Becker was a strange criminal in many ways. He loved the opera, haunted art museums and relished rare wines. He approached the crime business much as an artist approaches his profession. First would come the learning process. Charlie made friends with an elderly house burglar and became his lookout. For three years he plied this dubious trade, but he knew in his heart that the route to real money lay in manufacturing it.

For starters, he had one leg up on the boys who were currently pushing phony bills. After all, he was a master engraver. He also had the patience of Job.

Charlie checked out the queer paper being bandied about by other counterfeiters. He found it amateurish. The paper was of poor quality and the ink had a tendency to run and fade. It was imperative that he learn more about paper and ink. To this end, he secured a job working in the laboratory of a chemical company. Gradually, he stole small quantities of materials out of the lab and set up his own operation in a rented room. Here, night after night, Charlie performed experiments with ink on paper. He came up with an original idea which was clever in its conception and brilliant in its execution. He would bleach U.S. one dollar bills and use them as his source of paper.

With the paper problem solved, our boy engraved a copy of a 10-dollar bill. A small printing press was purchased and Charlie was in business. It took over a year before the master engraver was satisfied with his product. To test the authenticity of the tenner, Charlie went to a bank and explained to a teller that he thought he had been passed a phony $10 bill. The teller examined it carefully and assured Charlie that it was the real thing. At last the master engraver was ready to distribute his unique product.

Each week Charlie produced a few 10s at night in his rented room. He took them to different banks and cashed them in for 10 $1 bills.

Like any worthwhile entrepreneurial endeavor, the counterfeiting game is competitive. Charlie's competitors got wind that a newcomer who worked at a chemical plant was turning out $10 bills every bit as good as Uncle Sam's genuine article. When Charlie realized that any one of a number of underworld characters could turn him in, he decided that accomplices weren't such a bad idea. If he wanted to spread his wings, he had to have a distribution set up.

Charlie recruited Joe Elliott, a blueblood who couldn't resist the thrill which a life of crime provided. Joe attended all the big society bashes in and around New York. He charmed the ladies, conversed with the gentlemen, and stole their jewels and wallets.

The next man to be asked to join the consortium was Joe Chapman. Joe had once worked in a Chicago bank, where he had developed the unacceptable habit of taking home samples. He had been forced to vacation at Joliet prison for some months, but was now out and itching for action.

The third man approached to join the exclusive club was a middle-aged, suave gentleman named Carlo Siscovitch. Carlo could talk the birds out of the trees.

Charlie explained to the three men that they would open up operations in Europe. Once there, they would enter the brokerage business and use the business to distribute phony cash. To finance the operation, they would first rob a Baltimore bank, which Charlie had already cased with his usual thoroughness. The bank's vault was only a reinforced room which backed on to a vacant store. Charlie was sure that the rear of the vault consisted of only a brick wall backing on to the brick wall of the vacant store.

Charlie was explicit about two hard and fast rules. Firstly, there would be no splitting of the loot. His three assistants would receive $1,000 a month each whether they worked or not. Secondly, Charlie was boss. His word would be law. All three men drooled at the opportunity to earn $12,000 a year, over twice as much as the salary of the bank manager of the Baltimore joint they were going to rob.

The first order given by Charlie to the three new employees was to grow beards. Siscovitch travelled to Baltimore and rented the vacant store behind the bank. He claimed to be an executive of Stabler and Co. of Milwaukee, a well-known grain and feed company.

Ten days later, the gang moved in. There was a great deal of hustle and bustle. Bags of grain and feed were moved into the store. Then, on one quiet weekend, the boys dug through the bricks and scooped up $415,000. When the Third National Bank of Baltimore opened on Monday morning, there was a surprisingly inadequate amount of cash available to them. Instead, there was a big hole in the rear of their vault. The gang shaved and individually took off for Europe.

Charlie set up a brokerage firm in London. He hired clerks and commenced to do a legitimate business in bonds and stocks. Surprisingly, the business made money after only a few months operation. At night, Charlie produced £5 notes out of £1 notes. It took him nine months to manufacture samples which passed his inspection. A second brokerage company, Williamson and Larkin Ltd., was opened by Chapman and Siscovitch. The scam was simple. Charlie bought legitimate stocks and bonds with his phony money. Williamson and Larkin sold the stocks and bonds for authentic coin of the realm. The money poured in so quickly that Charlie had a hard time producing enough of the queer to keep the scam going. Sometimes he worked all night. He solved the lack of product by upgrading to £100 and £500 pound notes. The loot poured in at the rate of a half million dollars a year. Not bad for a 30-year-old in 1876.

Charlie travelled the continent, ate at the better restaurants, stayed at the best hotels and wasn't averse to bedding down with a sweet young thing when he wasn't busy churning out his phony paper. Each of his confederates were now receiving $2,000 per month.

In his fifth year in business, Charlie expanded. He opened brokerage offices in Paris, Rome and Berlin. To keep up with demand, he also manufactured bogus securities.

All good things come to an end. Charlie's organization was simply producing so much phony paper that the French government noted discrepancies in its fiscal accounts. They brought in the Surete to investigate. That efficient organization discovered that there were more securities of certain issues on the market than had been

271

printed. When the news became public, holders of securities had no way of knowing whether their paper was phony or authentic. Security prices fell in Paris. The news spread to Germany, Italy and England.

It was time to fade. Charlie paid each of his key men two years salary, some $48,000 each, and proceeded to close his European offices. On his arrival back in New York with Joe Elliott, Charlie had a cool $2.5 million. At age 40, he looked around for a legitimate business to purchase, finally settling on a saloon in Brooklyn. He refurbished the place and named it Becker's. It proved to be a fabulous success. No one knew that the owner, dishing out suds behind the bar, had hoodwinked the police forces of four countries and was a bona fide multi-millionaire.

The most successful counterfeiter of all time couldn't stand the life of a successful businessman. As the years passed, he longed for the old thrills. Eventually, he went back into the brokerage business in San Francisco, turning out perfect $10 bills. For reasons known only to himself, one day he doctored a small cheque, raising it from under $100 to $20,000.

Charlie, who had never been caught as the greatest counterfeiter in the world, was quickly apprehended for raising the cheque. He was incarcerated in San Quentin Prison. In 1903 he was paroled at age 57 and effectively disappeared from public view forever.

ALL IN THE FAMILY

In 1952, Sir Jack Drummond, his wife Lady Drummond and their only daughter, 10-year-old Elizabeth, were vacationing in France near the village of Lurs. Sir Jack, 61, a former professor of biochemistry at London University, had been knighted for his outstanding work in the field of nutrition during World War II.

Having recently recovered from a serious illness, he was touring France with his family and visiting friends from England who maintained villas on the continent.

On the night of August 4, the Drummonds decided to camp out. They chose a picturesque location near Digne, close to a modest farm with the grandiose name of La Grande Terre. As darkness fell, the Drummonds prepared to retire for the night in their sleeping bags. Within hours, all three would be murdered.

Around 6 a.m. the next day, Gustave Dominici, the son of elderly Gaston Dominici, who owned La Grande Terre, hailed down a passing cyclist, Jean-Marie Olivier. Gustave excitedly told Olivier, "I have just found a body!" He implored the startled cyclist to summon the gendarmes.

In a matter of an hour, police were at the farm. Gustave led them to the body of Elizabeth Drummond. The little girl was lying near a river. She had been beaten on the head. Lady Drummond's body was found at the

273

Drummonds' campsite, which was across a road from the river. Sir Jack's body lay nearby. Both adults had been shot to death.

Initially, the motive for the triple murder was thought to be robbery. After all, the Drummonds were strangers and there could be no other reason for their cold-blooded slaughter. However, upon examination of the scene of the crime, there was no sign of anything being missing. Money and clothing were found intact.

The killer had left spent, as well as unused, cartridges at the scene. The broken stock of a rifle was found floating in the river. When officials scanned the bottom of the river, they found an American army carbine. Unused bullets fit the weapon and the stock matched the rest of the carbine. Later tests proved that this was the murder weapon.

Members of the Dominici family were questioned. Gustave revealed that he had found Elizabeth's body while looking at the damage done by a small landslide beside a nearby railroad track. He also told police that he had seen the Drummonds the night before and was somewhat surprised that they had picked a spot so close to the road.

At 1 a.m., he had heard shots. At the same time, his wife Evette had awoken and fed the baby. At 5:30 a.m. he had arisen as usual and had found the girl's body. He waved down Olivier, who had fetched the police.

Gustave's father, Gaston, corroborated his son's story. He had noticed the Drummonds the night before while he was tending his goats and he, too, had heard the shots. He thought poachers were hunting for game. He had only learned of the murders later that morning.

Gaston explained to his interrogators that only his wife, Marie, his son Gustave and Gustave's wife and baby lived on the farm. In all, he had nine children, but the other eight, all adults, lived away from the farm.

The French detectives were stymied. Although the Dominicis appeared to be in the clear, there was something about their pat stories that led investigators to believe they knew more than they were revealing.

The first concrete hint that their suspicions were well-founded occurred weeks after the murders. Paul Maillet told police that Gustave had said, in front of other members of the Dominici family, "The little girl's left arm moved as I looked at her. She was still groaning and there was a rattle in her throat."

Police re-enacted the discovery of Elizabeth's body. Gustave positioned himself in such a way that it would have been impossible for him not to have seen the Drummonds' bodies. Yet, in his initial statements to police, he claimed to have only seen Elizabeth's body. Gustave was faced with Paul Maillet's evidence that he had said that Elizabeth was alive when he came upon the scene. At first, he denied having made the statement, but eventually admitted it was true. As a result of his confession, Gustave was charged with "having failed to give aid to a person in peril of death."

In court, Gustave admitted that when he had come upon the scene, Elizabeth had been alive. Before finding him guilty of the charge and sentencing him to two months imprisonment, the presiding judge castigated him for not calling a doctor. Gustave could only meekly respond that he had hailed a passing cyclist and had him notify police.

Nearly a year passed before old Gaston's nephew, Roger Perrin, came forward, informing police that the night before the murder he had seen Lady Drummond and Elizabeth call at the farm with a bucket, requesting water. This was considered a real break in the case, because the Dominicis had sworn that they had had no physical contact or conversation with the Drummonds at any time.

Gustave was questioned again. This time he stated that he had heard cries for help at the time of the murder. He had arisen and twice visited the scene of the crime. In relating his story, Gustave broke down and blurted out, "It was my father who did it! He told me so at 4 o'clock in the morning." Another son, Clovis, also told police that his father had admitted to him that he had killed the

Drummonds.

Faced with the statements of his two sons, Gaston broke down and confessed. On the night of the murders, he had noticed Lady Drummond undressing. He had approached her and made an improper advance. Sir Jack interceded. Gaston claimed to have killed both the Drummonds in a moment of extreme emotional excitement.

As soon as he had shot the couple, their daughter Elizabeth had screamed and had run toward the river. Gaston went on to tell the police that he had dropped bullets on the ground, but had no more in the rifle. He had taken off after the horror-stricken child on foot. When he had caught up with her, he had clubbed her with the butt end of the rifle.

The stock of the rifle had been broken previously and repaired. It broke free. He threw both parts in the river, not realizing that the stock would float. Gaston had then returned to the farmhouse, where he met Gustave. He told his son, "I have killed the English. Keep quiet and no one will know." It was then that Gustave went to the scene of the crime and realized that Elizabeth was still alive.

Later, Gustave, Clovis and Evette agreed to tell police a concocted story that corroborated their father's version of the events preceding the murders.

Gaston Dominici was arrested and charged with the murder of the Drummond family. He retracted his confession and pleaded not guilty. Gustave withdrew his statement, maintaining that he had involved his father because he had been beaten by police. Only Clovis stuck with his original statement that his father had admitted the killings to him. Old Gaston swore at Clovis from the witness box.

Gaston Dominici was found guilty and sentenced to die by the guillotine. However, this sentence was commuted to life imprisonment. After spending six years in prison, Gaston, now 84 years old, was paroled, still swearing that he had initially confessed to the murders to protect other members of his family.

TRUE
CRIME
STORIES

*Forty-eight tales of murder and mayhem
from the popular syndicated columnist
and television personality.*

*What is the true story behind the
Amityville Horror? What really happened
to the high-flying D.B. Cooper?
Why is "The Tramp" a highly appropriate
sobriquet for the late Charlie Chaplin?*

*Max Haines investigates these cases and
other crimes, cons and murders in this
collection drawn from his well-known
Crime Flashback column.*

ISBN 0-451-16452-0

TRUE CRIME STORIES BOOK II

Join syndicated columnist Max Haines,
Canada's Master of the Macabre, as he
traces the devious deeds of felons undone
by sloppy schemes and suspicious threads.
Relive the Yorkshire Ripper's six-year reign
of terror, the shocking Zebra Murders of San
Francisco and the puzzling Australian dingo
case in Max's ninth book of murder most foul.

"I enjoyed True Crime Stories, Book II *and
hope you enjoy it as much as I did."*
—Don Cassidy, Executive Director of the
Canadian Association of Chiefs of Police.

ISBN 0-451-16453-9